THE CRIME WRITER'S CASEBOOK

REVISED EDITION

A Reference Guide to Police Procedure and Investigation Then and Now

Stuart Gibbon and Stephen Wade

Straightforward Publishing
www.straightforwardbooks.co.uk

Straightforward Guides

Revised edition
Copyright © Stuart Gibbon and Stephen Wade 2023

ISBN 978-1-80236-148-3

Printed by 4edge www.4edge.co.uk
Typeset by Frabjous Books

Reviews for the Crime Writer's Casebook

"A superb guide that I keep by my laptop at all times. I highly recommend you read it before putting pen to paper"

Carol E. Wyer – bestselling crime fiction author

"An excellent, up-to-date resource for anyone who writes crime fiction or has a keen interest in British police procedures and legal processes"

Jackie Kabler – TV presenter and crime writer

"I'm thrilled that Stuart Gibbon and Stephen Wade have written such a wonderful book – I think this is going to become a must-have for many authors. The Crime Writer's Casebook is an intriguing, fascinating, illuminating source of information. I love it!"

Ronnie Turner – Book blogger and author of psychological thriller 'Lies Between Us'

"The Crime Writer's Casebook is a brilliant easy-to-read guide to police procedure, whether you're writing crime fiction or just have an interest in the topic. It is a fascinating, well-written and well-planned book with so much packed into its 250 or so pages"

Victoria Goldman – Journalist, editor, proofreader and author

"A detailed and entertaining resource for writers of contemporary and historical fiction. I highly recommend it"

Tracey Emerson – author of psychological thrillers

"This is a comprehensive and well-written guide for anyone wanting to write a realistic crime novel or a non-fiction work involving police operations"

Police History Magazine

"That's me set up for my new writing project. Thank you for my invaluable crime reference writing tool ... I think it will be my writing bible."

Sheryl Browne – author of psychological thrillers

"A fantastic addition to any crime writer's bookshelf!"

Caroline Mitchell – author of psychological thrillers

"It's a must for all aspiring UK crime writers."

Stephen Booth – author of the Cooper and Fry crime fiction series

"What a massive compilation of facts this book is – a must for anyone writing crime. Everything that you need to know, expertly indexed for ease of reference. When I was writing my first book, which had a small part of it concerned with the abduction of a child, I would have loved to have had this book by my side".

Pam Fish – National Association of Writers' Groups

"A must buy for all crime authors..."

CL Taylor – author of psychological thrillers

* * *

Contents

Note: This book contains details of true crime cases which some people may find upsetting. These details are included for clarity and explanation.

Introduction

(revised 2023)

The Crime Writer's Casebook was first published in December 2017 and has since received much positive feedback from the crime writing and reading community. Six years on, an awful lot has happened in our society, and we felt it was time to bring the *'Casebook'* up to date and to include some of the key pieces of legislation and guidance affecting the police and criminal justice system in the last few years.

The Coronavirus pandemic presented huge challenges for everyone and policing was no exception. For a police service which relies on the support and consent of the community, maintaining a social distance and the wearing of face masks, although totally justified and necessary, did little to strengthen those relationships. Guidance was issued to police officers and staff in relation to keeping themselves and others safe, cleaning their personal equipment, vehicles and workspaces. Decisions on whether to arrest, in some cases, also needed to include the consideration of whether it was safe to do so, from a public health perspective. Staff shortages, due to those impacted by and those having the virus, increased the pressure on all emergency services across the UK.

The onset of COVID also presented some people with the opportunity to use the virus or the threat of the virus as a weapon, with regular reports of police and other emergency workers being bitten, spat at, coughed at, or otherwise threatened with deliberate transmission of the virus. Additional measures were required to protect those workers and to ensure that the gravity of such behaviour was highlighted and reflected in appropriate sentencing, wherever possible. Here are just two of many such examples -

CASE STUDIES

1) A man who spat at a police officer while claiming to have COVID-19 during one of the worst periods of the pandemic has been jailed for 12 weeks. Daniel Rodgers, targeted two policemen in York, spitting at one and hurling racist abuse at the other. The district judge hearing the case commented 'This was a serious attack on public officials. The officers were seriously affected. Officers doing their job should not be subjected to abuse like this.' Rodgers was sentenced to 12 weeks in prison for the assault and the judge outlined that he had tripled the sentence for the public order offence to 12 weeks due to the racial aggravation. Both sentences were ordered to be served concurrently. Rodgers was also ordered to pay £150 compensation to the officer he racially abused and £100 to the officer whom he spat at.

2) A man who coughed on a police officer and claimed to have coronavirus has been jailed for six months. Adam Lewis told the officer 'I am Covid and I'm going to cough in your face and you will get it'. The Metropolitan Police officer had been flagged down by a member of the public in Westminster and told that a man had been seen trying car door handles in the area. Lewis resisted the officer's attempt to search him and smashed a bottle of wine he was holding onto the floor. As well as coughing on the officer, Lewis also tried to cough up phlegm and threatened to bite the officer. Lewis was sent to prison by Westminster magistrates after being convicted of assaulting an emergency worker.

The police custody environment was also assessed during the Covid pandemic and was adapted to cater for detainees and staff. One of the main concerns related to the provision of legal advice, where requested, for those who had been arrested and were detained at a police station. The usual practice of a personal visit by a solicitor was temporarily suspended with consultations taking place remotely, either by telephone or video conferencing facility. This situation was far from ideal but clearly necessary, given the public health emergency during those critical months of the pandemic.

The criminal justice system was also badly affected by COVID, with criminal courts being closed, trials suspended and the introduction of temporary courts (known as Nightingale courts) in response to the fact that about half of all existing courts being unable to provide services in 'lockdown' conditions. In July 2020, it was announced that ten temporary courts were to be opened in venues across England and Wales, including a medieval chamber and the headquarters of the Ministry of Justice, with the aim of reducing delays and delivering speedier justice for victims. Other 'Nightingale' venues followed and were located in buildings such as theatres, town halls, sports arenas and hotels. In March 2022, it was announced that around half of the Nightingale courts were to close, although it was also acknowledged that there was still a significant backlog of cases. This situation had been the case prior to COVID but was exacerbated throughout the pandemic. The remaining 30 Nightingale courts have been extended and will remain open until March 2023 when the position will be reviewed. In the meantime, additional support measures have been put in place including the increase of maximum sentences at magistrate's court from 6 months to 12 months, the creation of two 'super court rooms' which can accommodate up to 12 defendants at one time and the opening of more than 3,000 Cloud Video Platform virtual court rooms capable of holding over 13,000 hearings every week using audio and/or video facilities.

Assaults on emergency service workers have increased throughout the years and it's reassuring to see that legislation has now been put in place to recognise these offences in their own right and hopefully resultant sentences that reflect the serious nature of such actions. Following the tragic killing of PC Andrew Harper in 2019, his wife, Lissie, has campaigned tirelessly to request harsher sentences for those convicted of killing emergency service workers whilst committing a crime. In June 2022, following the introduction of the Police, Crime, Sentencing and Courts Act (PCSCA), those who kill emergency service workers, including prison officers and frontline health workers in the course of their duties, will receive a mandatory life sentence on conviction. This particular section of the Act is often now referred to as 'Harper's Law'.

The new PCSCA doubles the maximum penalty for those who assault police or other emergency workers from 12 months to 2 years, recommends whole-life orders as the starting point for the pre-meditated murder of a child and puts an end to the automatic early release of offenders deemed to be a danger to the public. The Act is wide-ranging and covers a number of different areas which impact modern-day policing.

Changes to the law can take some considerable time to reach the point where they receive Royal Assent and are written into statute. Most Acts will start as a Bill and will be subjected to five separate readings/stages in both the House of Commons and the House of Lords before finally becoming law. As you can imagine, the process can be halted at any time and not all recommendations are eventually agreed.

In this revised edition, our intention is to make you aware of some of the key pieces of legislation which have become law since the original publication of the 'Casebook' and to highlight some parts of this legislation which we feel are the most relevant to crime writers and readers. We've also included website links where applicable so that you can look at the legislation in more detail at your leisure. However, the main parts of the legislation are laid out in Appendix 1 and detail the following important Acts:

The Offensive Weapons Act 2019
The Coronavirus Act 2020
Covert Human Intelligence Sources (Criminal Conduct) Act 2021
Domestic Abuse Act 2021
Police, Crime, Sentencing and Courts Act 2022
Crown Court (Recording and Broadcasting) Order 2020

We hope that this revised edition of the Crime Writers Casebook provides an interesting and informative read.

The Authors and the Scope of the Book

Stuart Gibbon

Stuart Gibbon joined the Metropolitan Police as a Constable in 1982 and served for nearly 20 years, a large part of this period as a Detective. He was responsible for the investigation of many crimes including rape, serious assault and robbery. He was also involved in the investigation of Murder cases. In 2000 Stuart transferred to Lincolnshire Police where his career continued to develop. He served as a Detective at every rank from Constable to Chief Inspector, during which time he qualified to become a Senior Investigating Officer (SIO) leading Murder cases. As a DCI he was seconded to the newly formed East Midlands Special Operations Unit (EMSOU) and was then one of a small number of SIO's responsible for the investigation of Murder throughout the five East Midlands police forces.

Stuart retired from the police service in 2012 and is now a writing consultant, advising authors on police actions and procedures to ensure accuracy. He also talks at writing conferences on the subject of 'Murder Investigation' and the challenges facing a Senior Detective in such cases.

BECOMING A MURDER DETECTIVE

As long as I can remember, all I ever wanted to do was become a Detective. In 1980 that journey began when I was invited to London to take part in the Metropolitan Police selection process. As a naïve 16-year-old from a working-class part of north-east England I was completely out of my comfort zone. After a tough but enjoyable 18 months spent learning law, marching and enjoying the delights of central London, I successfully passed out (not literally, although some poor individual did) from the Hendon Training school and was posted to Wembley as Police Constable 727. I looked about 12 and my police helmet felt (and looked) massive.

Those early years were, at times, just like being an extra on the set of 'Life on Mars' except it was real. I dreaded going upstairs to the CID office as, more often than not, the welcome wasn't particularly friendly. Those Detectives not already on the phone or busy with something would make sure they were by the time I reached their desk. I swore that if I ever managed to get into CID, I'd adopt a more positive approach with my uniformed colleagues. Little did I know then that I would eventually end up as a Senior Detective leading Murder cases and in charge of a large team of CID staff. True to my word, I never forgot those early experiences and made sure, where possible, that CID went out of their way to help their uniformed colleagues.

One of my first 'quality' crime arrests was more luck than judgement. As a uniformed bobby working a late shift, I was keen to finish at the scheduled time of 10pm so decided to take a quiet stroll around the streets opposite the police station, looking to keep my head down (which wasn't easy with the size of my police helmet!). I had an appointment in front of the TV to watch 'Match of the Day' at 10.30pm. As I did so I became aware of the sound of breaking glass and soon realised that I was on the pavement outside a house which was in the process of being burgled. Alerting colleagues via my radio I began to approach the house then saw two rather large men run down the side of the house and out into the street away from me. I gave chase and updated as I did so. I can only assume that these two characters (who were hardened criminals from The East End of London) hadn't 'cased the joint' very well because they proceeded to run along the street, turned left at the end and headed straight towards the police station. They were met by a number of my colleagues running out of the police station who safely apprehended them. Two arrests for burglary and I was certainly the flavour of the month, even with CID. I call it dedication to duty; others would probably call it differently. Incidentally, I didn't finish duty until about 3.00am and missed the 'footie' anyway.

Following a tough 'apprenticeship' I became a Metropolitan Police Detective and was posted to Kilburn police station in north-west London as a Detective Constable (DC). Within a matter of days, I was to become Acting Detective Sergeant following a surreal conversation with my new boss. He advised me that he was being temporarily promoted to Detective Inspector and wanted me to be in charge of his team of six DC's. Talk about a baptism of fire. The next few years were spent investigating fatal fires, rapes, serious assaults and other crimes in a particularly busy part of the capital.

In 2000 I transferred to the East Midlands and spent another enjoyable period in the rural county of Lincolnshire. Most of that time was spent as a Detective, at various ranks, investigating crimes which proved equally as challenging as those in London. Due to the size and geography of the county, offenders often proved harder to identify as they were 'travelling criminals' originating from other parts of the country and returning there after commission of the crime. When I became a Senior Detective, reaching the dizzy heights of DI, I was chosen to apply to become one of the few Senior Investigating Officer's (SIO) in the Force. SIO's are the lead Detective in charge of Murder and the most serious of cases. I had to attend a particularly rigorous training course, followed by a period of Continuous Professional Development and the requirement to maintain a portfolio evidencing my work. I now began to investigate Murder and unexplained deaths. There is no greater responsibility than investigating the Murder of another person and no greater reward than identifying and bringing those responsible to justice.

The world of the victim's loved ones has been turned upside down but you have the opportunity to provide just a little comfort at such an awful time.

Being on-call is a unique experience with your mobile phone switched on 24 hours a day and the requirement that you need to be in a position to respond at short notice. You could be eating your evening meal one minute then on the way to a Murder scene some considerable distance away the next. Inevitably it's 3.00am or some other unsociable hour when your ringtone sounds, waking up the family and causing you to jump out of bed with that feeling of dread. I would then be inundated with lots of information by the Force Control Room and asked for my instructions. I think they sometimes may have forgotten that, although they had been on duty throughout the night, I had just been woken from a fitful sleep and was sitting on the edge of my bed in my nightwear. The pen and paper at the side of the bed was a necessity on such occasions. I always had my 'Murder Bag' packed and ready to go. This included items such as protective forensic clothing, maps, torch, police radio and an overnight bag just in case. The bag was an important part of the on-call Murder Detective kit.

Throughout my career I've had some unpleasant experiences, attending Murder scenes and Post-mortems. Some images will stay with me forever. A deceased baby or child is particularly difficult to comprehend. You must develop 'coping' strategies and rely on the support of family and friends to get through these challenges. Whilst carrying out your role in a professional way is important, we're all human and can relate events to our own loved ones.

During my police career I have experienced first-hand a

number of changes which have had a major impact on policing during the last few decades. From the introduction of the Police and Criminal Evidence Act (PACE) 1984 to the advances in forensic science, particularly in areas such as DNA, the world of Murder investigation is a very different one now to past times. From the initial crime scene examination to the drama in the courtroom, Stephen and I will discuss and debate Murder cases past and present.

I hope that you enjoy reading 'The Crime writers Casebook' whether you are a writer or reader. For anyone interested in crime, whether historical or modern day, I think it's an essential companion, providing useful reference material together with a number of fascinating true crime case studies.

Stephen Wade

MY LIFE IN PAST MURDERS

The readers I have in mind – and hopefully you are such a reader – will most likely be writers aspiring to write crime, fact or fiction, along with crime writers who are in need of more substantial reference material. My historical contributions here cover most periods in British history, as generally understood. Naturally, the cases will range across these dates, in no chronological order, so the reader needs to use the index to find specific topics.

I had been researching murder stories from the past for a few years, relying mostly on old books, archives and photos. The whole business seemed to be a heady mix of scholarly research and a need to winkle out the truth from events clouded by the passing years. Then one day, an entirely new perspective came along. It was when I saw the so-called 'execution suite' at HMP Hull where, back in the 1930s they were still stretching the necks of killers- the women along with the men.

I looked at the tiny cell where Ethel Major had spent her last night on earth, the 18th of December 1934. In the early morning of the next day, with a crowd of locals outside making some noise, as their petition to save her life had failed, she would be grabbed, pinioned, walked swiftly across a landing and into the room with the 'drop.' It would be a matter of one minute between taking her inside and slipping on the hood and pulling the lever to send her into eternity.

This would all be done with the muttering of a prayer from the chaplain behind, who had held her tiny hand and tried to offer comfort. She was 42 years old, built like Edith Piaf, who was called the 'Sparrow' and indeed Ethel, pictured for posterity mainly with a ridiculous hat, thin-framed glasses and a flowery pinny, was the Lincolnshire Sparrow – a wife from Kirby on Bain, near Horncastle. The jury had found her guilty of poisoning her husband, Arthur, and so hanging her in Lincoln would have been problematical, giving the police a great deal more work to do than they would have in Hull.

When I went back to my books and my study, as I was in the middle of writing a casebook of criminal cases from Liverpool, I couldn't avoid more dramas from the death cell, and for a while it all became too much. I had to pause and think, take some time out. What was I doing? Why was there such a solid readership for murder stories? Even more unsettling was the realisation that readers are there for the more gruesome side of killings, whether they happened when two Saxon farmers fell out back in 1000 A.D., or whether some poor weekend drinker was attacked and strangled in London last week.

I had to rethink my business. For myself, I had to make it clear that I was writing these books because I enjoyed the challenge of delving into the distant past and testing out the legal process, especially before the days of the British professional detective force (which was created in London in 1842). In the centuries between the first assizes in the thirteenth century and the important legislation of 1861 when capital offences were reduced to only four, there had been enough bloodthirsty history to slake the thirst of the most rabid 'bloody murder story' *aficionado*. To put it brutally simply: countless poor folk from the underclass had been wheeled away to the gallows in those years for trifling offences, and proper professional defence work from barristers on their case were impossible. Wealth gets you off in most cases, as in the case of Jane Austen's Aunt Jane, who had been charged with shoplifting in the 1790s and had spent some time in a jail. But she was married to a millionaire and was allowed to live with the jailer's family instead of rotting in a cell and contracting typhus with the plebs.

After this space of time, looking into myself as a writer, I came out determined to become more of an investigator than a straightforward historian. So many of the classic murder cases in the chronicles of evil were arguably really manslaughter or even accidental deaths. Then there is the whole question of diminished responsibility: time and time again, in the Victorian years particularly, defence barrister tried to show that the accused was very drunk when he slaughtered his poor victim and therefore should not be hanged or imprisoned for his life; generally the arguments were futile, but sometimes cases came along – such as the killing of a village constable in 1857 – which fortunately caught the eye of a famous medical man, and the convicted and condemned man was saved by expert testimony: he had epilepsy at the time he killed.

I remember reading around to find the kind of murder investigations I wanted to write, searching for a template. I found this in the work of a man who is generally reckoned to be the doyen of true crime writers: a professional Writer to the Signet in Edinburgh, William Roughead (pronounced *rock-heed*). He coined the word 'criminous' for the kind of study-bound murder investigation I was doing. It is a word which explains the almost universal interest in whodunits and it explains also why the works of Agatha Christie remain so popular. Yes, it is a game, in one sense, but also, for writers such as Roughead and me, it is detective work without the footslogging and interview-room procedure. In my study I can gather all the available facts and evidence from say, 1820, and put together an argument, an interpretation. My contribution to this book will be of that nature.

Of course, I have ventured outside the study at times. For my book Unsolved Yorkshire Murders, I walked around Hull, Leeds and Bradford on the trail of crime-scenes. I have contemplated a few square feet of flagstones where once a corpse lay, knifed and lifeless. You never forget these; the location is tainted forever afterwards.

Of course, this kind of investigation is still about people. Some years ago, I researched and wrote a book on crime in Dublin history, and I walked one day to the part of that city which is where the Newgate jail once stood – now a child's playground – and I wanted to visit the court in Green Street which I knew was historically important. When I arrived, there was a police cordon around the whole block and I was about to be turned away when I told the *Garda* officer why I was there. It emerged that I had arrived on the day of a major trial which involved a gangland element, and trouble was expected. A sergeant appeared on the scene; he was told who I was and he took pity on me. The result was a guided tour of the old courtroom and the horrendous cells beneath. I walked through where such men as Robert Emmet and William Kirwan had stood and received their death sentences. The place was all shiny polished mahogany above and all sawdust and spitoons below.

That activity is part of the job. I never wrote in the same way again after that. It is this back-story which explains why Stuart and I have written this casebook. We thought that it was time a book was on the shelves which put alongside some murder stories which came from both the police at work today and the historian at work on yesterday. Where Stuart can speak of interviews, family liaison or modern forensics, I can explain the sheer chaos of a murder scene, let's say in the years when Britain was at war with France and paranoia ran through the streets like some black stream of hatred and fear.

Stuart, a professional detective, can take the reader into the backrooms and planning meetings, the enquiries and arrests; I can lead you back through time, to step into the shoes of a constable who stumbles across yet another Ripper victim or onto the London to Leeds train from which master criminal Charlie Peace jumped to escape his police escort on his way to trial.

My world is one of dusty archives, and it might even be as dry as sawdust at times, but past crimes are full of surprises, and all knowledge links to more knowledge as crime investigation becomes more sophisticated. DNA has been a revolution in murder investigation, but even that had teething troubles in the courts for many years before the experts streamlined their work and had more savvy approaches to the use of their new science in front of juries. Stuart is well accustomed to working with DNA and all the other modern aspects of crime detection. But for me, the excitement is in the bungling of the past as well as in the lives of the extraordinary killer-trackers who gradually turned sleuthing into something between a science and an art.

Chapter 1

The Murder Victim and Crime Scene

Present

From a crime investigation perspective, the murder victim will often 'hold the key' to the solving of that case. There are a number of important lines of enquiry relating to a murder victim which, if pursued successfully, will improve the chances of bringing the person(s) responsible to justice.

Identifying the victim

The speed and method by which a murder victim is identified varies considerably according to the circumstances, but it's fair to say that the investigation will progress more effectively once the victim has been positively identified. This process may be very straightforward if, for example, the victim has been killed in their own home or there is a person who can identify them. Alternatively they may have personal possessions or other items which indicate who they are. If the victim is known to the police it may be possible to identify them by fingerprints, DNA or perhaps even dental records. Some people who commit murder will go to great lengths to conceal the identity of the victim in the hope that this will hinder the police investigation. They may set fire to the body or dismember it in some way.

Following the murders of Holly Wells and Jessica Chapman (Soham 2002) the person responsible, Ian Huntley, set fire to the bodies and clothing of the two young girls in an effort to cover his tracks. Serial killer Dennis Nilsen (London 1978–1983) murdered at least 12 young men, dismembered their bodies and tried to dispose of them by cooking some body parts, flushing others down the toilet and burning some on bonfires in his garden.

If a person is found dead, in suspicious circumstances, naked and outdoors, it can be very difficult to identify them, particularly if they are not known to police, have no marks, scars or tattoos which may assist and are not known in that area. Identification of the victim is crucial and the sooner this is established the better for all concerned.

Victimology

Victimology is a branch of criminology that scientifically studies the relationship between a victim and an offender. In crime investigation, particularly murder cases, it is very important to gather as much information about the victim as possible including lifestyle, relationships, routines and movements amongst others. It's unfortunate that the police have to trawl through the victim's personal life but this often provides information to assist the investigation.

In the majority of murder cases there has been some prior association between the victim and the offender. For this reason it is entirely possible that the answer to the question of "Who did it?" lies within the victimology. There is a maxim used by SIO's, 'find out how the victim lived and you'll find out how they died' which is often true and emphasises the importance of detailed research into the background of the victim.

Motive

Working out why a crime has been committed, whether murder or other crime type, is a main line of enquiry for the criminal investigation. Establishing a motive could very well provide information in relation to the identity of the offender(s) as there is likely to have been some prior association between the victim and offender in many cases (see victimology).

There are many different reasons why a person may commit a crime, some more obvious than others. For example a victim whose wallet, mobile phone and other valuables have been taken may suggest that the offender(s) seeks financial gain. A victim whose clothing has been removed or disturbed may indicate a sexual motive. Other types of motive include jealousy, revenge, gang-related, hatred (racism, homophobia), power/ control or political/terrorism. This list isn't exhaustive but gives an idea of the variety of motive types.

As in the case of 'identifying the victim', early confirmation of a possible motive is likely to improve the chances of finding those responsible. Sometimes, despite lengthy and thorough investigation, the motive isn't clear. The SIO must keep an open mind and take care not to make assumptions about the reason why a crime has taken place.

Family Liaison Officer

The role of Family Liaison Officer (FLO) is one of the most challenging roles carried out by police. FLO's will be deployed to a family who have suffered bereavement, whether the victim of a murder, a Road Traffic Collision (RTC) or other circumstances where the family need support and a police investigation is required. FLO's will generally be deployed in pairs for a murder investigation and solo for an RTC. Their role is to provide support for the family and to gather information to assist an investigation. FLO's are specially-trained to enable them to effectively carry out an emotionally demanding role. They will have regular contact with the family of the deceased and will support them throughout any criminal justice proceedings, whether that is a criminal trial or an inquest. An FLO is likely to be of Constable rank and may be required to carry out the role on more than one case at a time, depending on resources and commitments. In murder cases it's very important that the FLO's work closely with the Senior Investigating Officer (SIO) to make sure that information is passed to and from the family in the most appropriate way. The FLO will be key to obtaining background details of the victim (see victimology).

Past

AN ARSENIC CASE

In the past, the murder victim was often someone whose demise could be 'logged' because often homicides were lengthy affairs – deaths by poison for instance, or as a result of a vicious attack. A typical instance of this is the case of a woman in 1794. This was Anna Scalberd, and it took her six days to die. She had been bed-ridden and had suffered horrific agonies on each of those days, insisting all the time that her daughter-in-law, Ann, had poisoned her. Was this true? The only way to find out was to bring in the best medical men available. She had been attended in her dying by George Swinton, a Dewsbury surgeon, and he was the one who heard the woman making the accusations. No detail in this report hints at why this might have happened. How it was done is no mystery: arsenic was used around the home at the time for all kinds of purposes, mainly as a pesticide, and most homes had a problem with vermin. It was easily available, as anyone could buy a quantity from a druggist, and these retailers were not to be regulated until after the 1851 Arsenic Act.

Arsenic does not make for an easy death; when the most typical form, white oxide, was used, it caused a burning sensation in the victim's throat, and then violent vomiting followed. The skin becomes bluish in hue before the final collapse. The experienced doctors who attended Mrs Scalberd would have seen this familiar pattern of symptoms. Before there was an inquest, because of the suspicions aroused in

Swinton's' mind, a well-respected doctor named Benjamin Sykes was called in to help. He was a graduate of the highly-regarded Guy's Hospital (founded in 1724). Sykes, who was near at hand in Gomersal, joined Swinton at the post-mortem. Sure enough, they both agreed that Mrs Scalberd had died of arsenical poisoning.

The long and painful dying was now explained fully, and Ann was the one who had been responsible. Anna Scalberd's death had been caused by a steady administering of arsenic, and medical expertise had pinpointed the cause, and so the finger pointed at Ann, who was tried and convicted. She was hanged on 12 August, 1794.

Past

THE MURDER SCENE WAS CLEANED UP!

They never found out who killed James Smith at the toll-house in Hebden Bridge back in 1850. There were many reasons for this, the main one being that the locals moved in to clean up the mess caused by the bloody murder. The dead man was found with his throat cut, but when Constable Dugdale arrived to investigate, all he had to go on was the description of what the scene had looked like before it was washed and cleaned.

He had been found dead and apparently there had been blood on the walls, furniture thrown around the room and curtains had been ripped. But this was all hear-say and anecdotal testimony. Poor Dugdale only knew that the body had been found by a little boy who had screamed out in terror that 'Jimmy' was dead, and then the local moved in with cloths and mops.

At that time and long before, who gave a thought to the inviolability of a crime-scene? Very few did. After all, the neighbours would have thought, we don't want the shame and bother of having a corpse lying around, in this respectable locality. For centuries, the crime scene was flattened, disrupted and dirtied; folk trudged across it and crowds gathered to steal chattels or gawp at the deceased.

It was only when, after the new training approaches of the 1930s in the police, and with the gradual professionalisation of the forensic personnel, that things changed. Stuart's description of the current situation took a long time to emerge. As for Dugdale, we can be sure that he gave up in frustration and went back to his office for a cuppa.

In the training manuals for the police after the foundation of the Hendon Police College, there is much attention paid to the importance of the crime scene, but even then, detective work was still in an early stage of development (Lincolnshire had no detective force as a separate special unit until 1931) and such skills as interviewing and communications systems were in their infancy.

Chapter 2

The Investigation Process

Present

There are a number of ways in which a murder can be solved. There may be witnesses, forensic evidence or some other lead which helps to identify those responsible. Murder investigation is about keeping an open mind and following the ABC principle (**A**ssume nothing, **B**elieve nobody, **C**heck everything) in other words make sure any information you are given is accurate. The investigation process has evolved considerably throughout the years as technology and police methods have advanced and developed. The following true murder case led by me as the Senior Investigating Officer (SIO) demonstrates how technical methods of detection can be used effectively to track down and convict the killers.

Circumstances

On the evening of 29th October 2011, three men went to a residential house in the city of Lincoln where they confronted the occupier, a man of poor health in his seventies. They ransacked the interior and subjected the man to a merciless and brutal ordeal. He was beaten, throttled and scalded with boiling water from a kettle. The motive for the attack, which lasted about half an hour, was believed to be financial with the 'torture' carried out in an attempt to persuade the man to reveal where his valuables were located. Once the men left his house, he was able to stagger outside and alert nearby residents. Emergency services were called and the victim was taken to hospital by ambulance. A police investigation commenced.

The victim had received serious burns to his hands and body, significant bruising and was clearly and understandably in shock. Despite the best efforts of medical staff, his condition deteriorated over the course of the following days. On 31st October, some two days after the attack, the victim tragically died as a result of the injuries sustained. He was found to have a total of 46 separate injuries. A murder investigation was launched.

Lines of enquiry

A murder investigation will often focus on a number of actions or lines of enquiry which need to be carried out in order to provide the best opportunity of identifying those responsible and ultimately bringing them to justice. These enquiries will include a forensic examination of the scene, a detailed search of the area and house to house enquiries, to name but a few. Having been appointed as the SIO and, as such, the lead detective for the investigation, it was my responsibility to ensure that all reasonable lines of enquiry were explored.

Initial enquiries in the immediate area consisted of visits to each address by police officers with the intention of establishing whether anyone had seen the three men, whether they had or were aware of any closed circuit television (CCTV) in the area and whether they were able to provide any information about the victim which may assist the investigation. During these enquiries one of the residents explained how three men had simply walked into their house through an insecure back door on the night in question, apparently thinking it belonged to the victim. The men were given directions to the victim's address nearby. This information was very important as, not only did it provide witnesses who had seen the three men, albeit briefly, but it also suggested that the men may not be local as they were clearly uncertain of where the victim lived. As such, I was able to hypothesise that the men may have travelled to the address in a vehicle and, due to the geography of the area, may have used a main arterial road to get to and from the location.

Passive data generators

'Passive data generators' is the term used to describe automated systems that gather information for purposes unconnected to criminal investigations, but which can be accessed by investigators. Examples of passive data include CCTV, ANPR and telephone billing systems. All three were utilised during this murder investigation and played their part in providing evidence to support the case.

ANPR

Automatic Number Plate Recognition (ANPR) systems are a rapidly developing source of investigative opportunity for SIO's and can be pivotal in a murder enquiry. ANPR consists of a series of cameras on roads throughout the country. The index number of every vehicle which passes through the camera is noted and the system can provide other evidence which could be vital in a criminal investigation. In this particular case, officers were tasked with interrogating the ANPR system to see whether any vehicles reported stolen or otherwise of interest to police were using the main roads during the material times on the day in question. Although this research took some time and resulted in a significant amount of data, trained intelligence officers were able to identify a particular vehicle which had not only used the road in both directions at times which were consistent with before and after the attack, but had also used the same road earlier that day. This first journey was later confirmed as a reconnaissance visit to the area prior to the attack. It was noted that the index number of the vehicle, a VW 4-wheel drive, had been noted on ANPR as slightly different on the first journey. This was established by the intelligence officers and later explained by the fact that the offenders had carried out the recce but had then disguised the identity of the vehicle to commit the offence by changing the index number using masking tape. This was clear evidence of pre-planning and criminal activity. The vehicle was eventually located and seized. It was subjected to a thorough forensic examination and yielded some evidence which assisted the investigation.

CCTV

Closed-circuit television (CCTV) footage is another investigative tool which can be a very important line of enquiry in a murder investigation. This proved to be the case once again during this particular enquiry. The challenge with CCTV evidence is not only to identify that it exists but also to access and be able to view the relevant footage. Part of the initial action in the area surrounding a murder scene is to physically check the vicinity for the presence of CCTV cameras. During the house visits it was established that a residential property nearby had their own private CCTV cameras facing onto the street. When checked they showed footage, although grainy and dark, of three people walking past the front of the house in the general direction of the victim's address then running past in the opposite direction some thirty minutes or so later. Although the footage was not of sufficient quality for identification purposes, it confirmed the times, number of people involved and gave an idea of the type of clothing worn.

During the following months, dedicated officers viewed thousands of hours of CCTV footage, based upon intelligence relating to the VW vehicle, trying to locate the vehicle and it's occupants on the day of the attack. The officers were able to show that the vehicle had travelled to the area on the day from many miles away, the route it had taken and the journey away from the scene after the attack. About four months after the murder, a key piece of evidence was found which would help to convict those responsible. CCTV footage seized from a petrol station some distance from the scene was viewed and showed the VW vehicle entering the station shortly after the time of the attack. Three men were seen to get out of the vehicle, enter the garage to buy items, then get back into the vehicle and drive off. Unlike the first CCTV footage, the garage system was in colour and of excellent quality. As a result it was possible for all three men to be positively identified. Technical experts were used to confirm that the three men were those near the scene based upon their clothing and appearance. The same methods were used in relation to the vehicle and it's route, based upon specifications which were unique to that vehicle.

Communications data

Another important line of enquiry in murder investigation is the analysis of communications data. Different types of such data include internet/e-mail, sat nav and telephone.

Most people these days have a mobile phone, sometimes more than one, and it is used not only to make and receive calls/texts but often to access the internet. During this investigation, mobile and landline analysis was carried out with a view to evidencing that the suspects were in contact with each other and that they were in the area of the attack during the material times. Although this analysis didn't produce what is referred to as the 'smoking gun' (evidence unlikely to be disproved) it did provide supporting evidence which could be used as part of the prosecution case.

The result

Over a period of several months a large amount of evidence was gathered and prepared in a format capable of being presented to a criminal court. A charge of Murder was authorised by the Crown Prosecution Service (CPS) and the case was prepared for trial. In March 2013 two men were found guilty of Murder and sentenced to life imprisonment with a recommendation that they serve a minimum of 28 and 26 years.

There is no doubt that the 'passive data', in particular the CCTV and ANPR evidence played a significant role in helping to secure convictions for a brutally violent attack which resulted in the loss of life. The trial Judge described as "remarkable" the work of a dedicated CCTV officer who had spent 14 months compiling footage of the killers' getaway vehicle.

Technical methods of detection and a determination to find the truth combined to solve this case of Murder.

Past

AMATEURS LET LOOSE

In cases from history, the modern reader will see almost every potential error made in investigative process. In the years before c.1900 in particular, a study of murder cases will throw up such bungling as cleaning the crime scene, handling important evidence, allowing witnesses to disappear from the scene without questions, movement of the body, and even in some instances, the lack of communication between officers.

In the Georgian period, before the first professional police force, almost anyone could try their hand at being a detective. In fact, such examples from crime fiction as Dorothy L. Sayers' detective, Lord Peter Wimsey having lots of time to study a body in a bath before the police come anywhere near (which happens in one of her novels) is something that has happened on several occasions.

There were no professional detectives in Britain until 1842, except for the members of the Bow Street Runners who were called to use their expertise on cases both in and out of London. There are examples of magistrates playing detective and being successful in some examples, but essentially, until quite recent times, legal professionals were happy to accept circumstantial evidence, waving away counter arguments. The great judge Lord Bramwell wrote in his memoirs that circumstantial evidence was always the most important basis for legal process!

Criminal history is packed with examples of crime scenes breached, interfered with or sometimes absolutely cleaned up, with all evidence thrown away, and the same goes for the investigation process. The first professional detective unit appeared in the London policing structure in 1842, and before that, the Bow Street Runners would occasionally be sent out to the shire to investigate, but that would be in extraordinary circumstances. This was also the case with a special body of men known as the King's/Queen's Messengers, but they were more concerned with escorting important prisoners or assisting in difficult arrests.

The investigation process, prior to the landmark date of 1830 when the London police were finally at work as a professional body, had been random and haphazard, depending largely on what we would call today the 'snouts' or grasses' and who were in earlier times known as 'thief-catchers' Sometimes individuals such as magistrates would take on the kind of work we associate with detectives, but until late Victorian years the very word was something which created fear and suspicion in the minds of the general public. By the early twentieth century, with the advent of MI5 and related outfits engaged in home security during wartime, investigative measures widened and became more sophisticated. But until the post-1945 years simple things we take for granted – such as identikits – did not exist. There had been, since the eighteenth century Bow Street magistrates' days, the publications listing wanted persons, deserters and brief accounts of crimes committed, but by the side of modern investigation, this all looks so basic.

Chapter 3

The Murder Investigation

Present

The investigation of murder is a particularly complex area of policing, regardless of the circumstances. There is no greater challenge than trying to identify the person(s) who have unlawfully taken the life of another and successfully bringing those responsible to justice. You have a duty to the victim's loved ones which you must never lose sight of.

There are many different strands to a murder investigation and even those cases which appear simple, from an investigation point of view, are likely to present difficulties at some stage. I liken the role of an SIO, the detective in charge of murder cases, to the conductor of an orchestra. Although you're in charge, you're very much reliant on the other members of the team to make sure that 'the music' is in tune and comes to a satisfactory conclusion. As an SIO you must keep an open mind during the investigation and remember to stick with the ABC approach, Assume nothing, Believe nobody, Check everything. You must also be prepared to listen to other people's views and ideas, delegate responsibility for certain tasks and be led by the evidence.

Initial response

The first police response is likely to be a uniformed police constable (PC) or perhaps a police community support officer (PCSO). The latter are members of police staff who wear uniform but have limited powers. They may well have responded to a 999 emergency call from a member of the public to find a scene of devastation. The actions of the first officer(s) on scene are vital to the success of the subsequent murder investigation. A major crime scene, particularly a murder, is perhaps the most important an officer will ever be required to attend. They will become the initial investigating officer in control and responsible for making crucial decisions until further assistance and supervision arrive. This will involve an initial assessment being relayed back to the force control room supervisors (by police radio or mobile phone if more appropriate) upon which the level, nature and type of response are likely to be determined.

The first attending officer must use their practical and investigative skills to gain as much information from the scene as possible. Often aspects which seem irrelevant in the early stages of an investigation can become significant later. The officer should note as much detail as possible whilst at the same time trying to preserve evidence. The preservation of life is always the first priority but if a doctor/paramedic has already confirmed that the person has died then the focus turns to finding out what happened, identifying who is responsible and taking steps to locate/arrest them.

One of the most important early aims is to identify, secure and protect any crime scenes. This will include the deceased, the area where the murder took place and any weapon or other evidence which may have been discarded. It's important that all areas relating to the scene are cordoned off using police tape and that an officer carries out the role of 'scene guard', preventing unauthorised access to the scene. This officer should record details of people attending the scene in a book known as a 'crime scene log' if available. The role of scene guard is very important and isn't just about protecting the scene. Sometimes witnesses and even suspects return to the scene and, as such, an observant and inquisitive scene guard could gather vital evidence.

At some stage it's likely that a supervisor will attend the scene to take command and CID will also attend. If the incident takes place between 8am and 10pm the initial CID attendance may be from the local police station but if it occurs during the night then an on-call Detective is likely to respond. The rank of on-call Detectives varies from force to force. Sometimes it's a Detective Sergeant (DS) or a Detective Inspector (DI). They will arrange for other Detectives to respond. Once it has been established that it is a case of Murder, a Senior Investigating Officer (SIO) will be informed and assume responsibility for the investigation.

The 'Golden Hour' principle

The term 'Golden Hour' is used in photography and medicine as well as policing circles. In medicine it refers to a period of time, up to an hour or less, following traumatic injury or medical emergency, during which there is the highest likelihood that prompt medical treatment will prevent death. In policing terms, it relates to a period of time, which could be anything from a few minutes to an hour (or even longer) when effective action by those responding to an incident could help to secure a successful outcome. This could be anything from saving a person's life to preserving important evidence. Sometimes the person who has committed a murder is still at the scene or nearby, for whatever reason, and the prompt action of attending officers to identify and detain this person is likely to have a positive impact on the subsequent investigation. A killer may stay at or return to the scene and claim to be a witness to events. In murder cases, the person responsible will sometimes want to get involved and be the centre of attention. Forensic psychologists explain this behaviour as the actions of a person

31

who wants to have power and control over others as they are often the only person who knows exactly what has happened.

Following the murder of Holly Wells and Jessica Chapman (Soham 2002) the killer, Ian Huntley, not only heavily involved himself in the searches for the two young girls but also provided a live TV interview for Sky News. He claimed that the two girls had walked past his house and spoke briefly with him on the day that they went missing. He was referred to by the reporter as 'probably the last person to see the girls', which chillingly proved to be the case as he had killed them both in his house before hiding their bodies in a ditch several miles away.

Another high-profile case which demonstrates that a killer can act in such a way is the disappearance of Tia Sharp (see Missing Persons) where, once again, the person responsible (Stuart Hazell) was involved in searches and media interviews, as well as being the last person to see Tia before she went missing.

Some offenders will return to the scene of the crime at some point. This can often happen in cases of arson where a fire has been started. It's not uncommon for the person responsible to hide nearby or stand with a crowd of onlookers to watch the Fire and Rescue Service tackle the blaze. This is another reason why the role of a 'scene guard' can be so important.

The 'Golden Hour' also applies to the identification of witnesses. It's rare for a person to witness the murder taking place but people sometimes see or hear the events immediately before or after the incident. They may be just passing through the area on their way to another location and may not actually realise the significance of what they have seen. Identifying witnesses and obtaining some form of account from them at an early stage is another important part of the 'Golden Hour' principle.

Forensic evidence may be left at the scene of a murder but may not remain there if steps aren't taken to identify, secure and protect it. The evidence could be anything from a murder weapon to small bloodstains, invisible to the naked eye. The evidence could be destroyed by a change in the weather conditions (sudden rain/snow) or could be removed from the scene, inadvertently or otherwise, by another person. Early effective action, in such circumstances, will prevent that evidence from being lost or destroyed. This could be something as simple as placing a dustbin lid or upturned box over small stains on the ground to prevent any evidence being lost. If an officer takes any such action which changes the appearance of a murder scene, in any way, they must make sure that details of their actions are passed on to investigating and forensic officers to prevent misunderstanding and unnecessary delay to the investigation. Officers are taught to touch nothing but if you may be about to lose evidence, you may feel that you have no choice.

In addition to the offender(s), witnesses and potential forensic evidence, 'Golden Hour' actions (sometimes referred to as 'fast-track' actions) could also include the identification of CCTV in the area. The 'Golden Hour' is a time when forensic evidence is most fresh and easiest to detect (blood may still be wet), memories are still sharp and lies/alibis are at their most vulnerable.

* * *

The crime scene
The term 'crime scene' often refers to where the actual crime took place but in murder cases it's not uncommon for there to be several scenes. For example, if I murdered a person in the kitchen of my house by stabbing them with a knife, then put the body into the boot of my car and disposed of it in a wooded area some distance away, the following would be designated as

scenes for the purpose of the subsequent murder investigation. The kitchen would be a primary scene as this is where the murder took place. Other scenes would include the rest of my house, the route taken to my car, the route taken in my car and the place where I put the body (known as the deposition site). If I happened to get rid of the knife somewhere else, then if/ when found, that location would also become a scene. Two of the most important scenes in a murder case are the victim and the offender as important evidence can be obtained from both. As you can see from my brief scenario, I have identified eight scenes which will require searches and forensic examination to a greater or lesser degree. Each scene will be given a number from 1 onwards and will be prioritised by the SIO and forensic team. The places where the murder took place and the body was left would usually be referred to as primary scenes, the remainder secondary scenes.

Crime scene examination

The examination of a crime scene can take some considerable time. In murder cases this could be days, weeks or even months of painstaking forensic examination and searching.

There is only one opportunity to examine a murder scene when it is under your control so it's imperative that it's done correctly. Once the SIO has made the decision to release the crime scene (remove the scene guard(s), tape and open to the public) it is thereafter 'contaminated' and anything found subsequently would be challenged vehemently by defence solicitors who would be likely to claim that the evidence must have appeared after the scene was released.

The key rule is that the crime scene should be retained as long as is necessary for all possible examinations to take place. The SIO must ensure that the scene isn't released too early as this could have an adverse impact on the investigation.

There are two main types of crime scene, indoors and outdoors. Indoor scenes, such as inside a house are generally easier to manage as they are out of public view and can usually be contained with the posting of a scene guard at the front (and sometimes the back as well). Outdoor scenes, such as in a park or open field present additional challenges such as the weather, the press and the public. These days you will often see a forensic tent being used outdoors to protect the evidence and prevent unwanted attention.

Any person who enters a murder scene should be wearing protective clothing. This comprises of a forensic suit with a hood, facemask, latex gloves and overshoes. The only exception to this could be the first attending officer(s) who may not have the time/opportunity to put them on due to the circumstances. If they have entered the scene, their footwear (and possibly their police uniform) will be seized when they return to the police station. The reason for this action is to eliminate them if any footwear marks or fibres are recovered from the scene. A lot of TV crime dramas are accurate in their portrayal of a crime scene examination but you still see some where the SIO or some other individual, normally a police officer, is trampling all over the scene in their civilian clothing with no gloves or overshoes in sight.

In a murder case, once the primary scene has been secured and preserved, the first action which will normally take place is a recording of that scene with an audio commentary. This will normally be a DVD recording made by the Crime Scene Manager (CSM) or another member of the forensic team. If the scene is inside a house or other building, this recording will start with a confirmation of the date, time and location and will then contain full video footage of the exterior and interior of the property with audio commentary throughout. The same principle would apply to an outdoor scene. This recording is important as it can be used as an effective briefing tool for the investigation team and reduces the need for officers/staff to attend the scene as they can view the scene clearly from the recording back at the police station. This recording (or relevant sections of it) is often played to the jury at any subsequent court trial. Once the recording has been viewed, decisions will be made as to how the scene examination will be progressed.

The SIO, CSM, Pathologist (if in attendance) and any other experts who may have been requested will discuss priorities and methods which will include fingerprinting, swabbing for DNA and tapings of the body and clothing of the deceased. The use of tapings is similar to the application and removal of sellotape to an area which may capture forensic evidence of value such as fibres or hair. The CSM will co-ordinate the forensic examination and will generally use forensic officers from their own team/area. For many years these officers have been known as Scenes of Crime Officers (SOCO's) and in some areas of the country they still are, but they are also often now referred to as Crime Scene Investigators (CSI's). Prior to the forensic examination it's likely that a brief search of the area would have been carried out by specially-trained police officers, co-ordinated by a Police Search Advisor (POLSA) to look for any evidence which may have been discarded. The officers would be wearing protective clothing, gloves etc so as not to contaminate the scene. Once the forensic examination has been completed, the area would be searched thoroughly.

Depending on the size and geography of the area, this search could take several days.

The crime scene examination is one of the most important strands of a murder investigation. It could very well provide evidence which helps to bring those responsible to justice and must be carried out in a thorough and detailed manner.

Staffing

Murder investigation is very demanding and resource-intensive. Back in the 1980's the investigation team would be made up of a number of detectives from the local police station supplemented by additional officers from other parts of the Force area. As a Detective Constable in the Metropolitan Police I remember being taken from my current duties and told to report to another area where I would remain, as part of that investigation, until I was no longer required. This wasn't an ideal situation, for all concerned, and eventually led to the formation of countrywide Murder Investigation Teams (MIT). These teams consist of detectives, uniformed officers and civilian police staff who deal with all murder cases committed within their geographical boundaries. The numbers and make-up of each MIT will depend on the resources available to that particular Force. The Metropolitan Police have many MIT's across the London area whereas a more rural force may only have one. A number of forces have decided to amalgamate their MIT resources on a regional basis. A good example of this practice can be found in the East Midlands Special Operations Unit (EMSOU) which has it's own Major Crime capability for a number of forces in that region.

As a Detective Chief Inspector (DCI) based in Lincolnshire but seconded to EMSOU, I was the first SIO in the force to lead a murder investigation as part of the EMSOU arrangement. This meant that I was able to call on specialist resources from other forces in the region to supplement local staff. Everyone plays their part in a murder investigation from the detectives carrying out enquiries to the staff who input information into computer systems. It would be very difficult to discuss every role so I'm going to briefly mention a few key members of the team.

Senior Investigating Officer

The Senior Investigating Officer (SIO) is in overall charge of a Murder investigation. They will be responsible for all key management decisions and will keep a written record of their decisions in a Policy File. The SIO in a murder case will be either a Detective Superintendent (D/Supt) or a Detective Chief Inspector (DCI). If the case is particularly high profile (several victims, intense media interest) then it's likely that the investigation will be led by a Detective Superintendent.

Having said that, a large number of murder cases are led by DCI's. The SIO will be specially-trained and may be expected to lead more than one case at the same time.

Deputy SIO

The Deputy SIO (DSIO) will, as the title suggests, deputise in the absence of the SIO. They will also be expected to lead certain aspects of the investigation such as the intelligence strategy or the house to house enquiries.

The rank of the DSIO will depend on the rank of the SIO. If the SIO is a Detective Superintendent then the DSIO is likely to be a DCI, if the SIO is a DCI then the DSIO will probably be a Detective Inspector (DI).

Crime Scene Manager

The Crime Scene Manager (CSM) co-ordinates all forensic activity throughout the investigation, from initial scene examination through to submission of items for analysis. They assist in developing the forensic strategy, deciding how things will be done and in what order. The CSM will be a civilian member of police staff with considerable experience in the field of forensics. Every murder investigation will have a Forensic Management Team (FMT) which should meet regularly to discuss all forensic aspects of the investigation.

This team should include the SIO (and/or their deputy), CSM and the exhibits officer. If there are any other experts involved in the investigation such as fingerprint or forensic scientists, they should also be part of the FMT. The CSM appointed to a murder investigation should be the SIO's first port of call for any deployment of Crime Scene Investigator (CSI) staff.

Exhibits Officer

The exhibits officer (EO) has a pivotal role to play in any investigation, particularly a murder investigation. They will normally be an experienced detective or member of police staff who is trained in all aspects of exhibit management including packaging, storage and documentation. In a murder case there are likely to be thousands of individual exhibits which may or may not be used in evidence at a later court hearing. These will include clothing, forensic samples and items recovered from the scene to name but a few. Every exhibit needs to be correctly packaged, sealed and signed for with the person responsible for the exhibit giving it a unique reference number before passing it to the exhibits officer. The reference will be the exhibitor's initials followed by a number in chronological order. For example, if my name was David William Smith then my first exhibit would be DWS/01, my second DWS/02 and so on.

The exhibits officer is responsible for logging all exhibits onto a computer database and then accounting for any movement of exhibits throughout the investigation, whether to a laboratory for analysis or to a police officer for enquiries. When a case goes to court the exhibits officer is responsible for making sure that all required exhibits are available and held in a secure area for production as evidence if required. Attention to detail is vital in this role as the strongest prosecution case can fail if there is a breakdown in the continuity or integrity of a key exhibit.

Police Search Advisor

The role of a Police Search Advisor (POLSA) is to advise the SIO on all aspects of searching. If the investigation is particularly complex there may be more than one POLSA deployed. The POLSA is specially-trained in search techniques and will play a vital part in helping the SIO to develop a search strategy. POLSA's are normally police officers of Constable or Sergeant rank who will form an integral part of the investigation team.

HOLMES

In 1986, UK police forces started to use the original Home Office Large Major Enquiry System (HOLMES) in all major incidents including serial murders, multi-million pound fraud cases and major disasters. Whilst HOLMES was a very effective administrative support system for investigating major crimes, the progress of technology revealed some fundamental weaknesses, particularly in the areas of investigation support and linking separate incidents. Police forces needed to have the capability to exchange information more easily. In 1994, the police service launched a plan to replace the existing HOLMES systems with one new system. During the next few years HOLMES 2 was introduced and is now available to all UK police forces.

In essence, HOLMES 2 is a computer-based system where all information is typed, given a unique reference number and indexed to allow for searches to be made within the system. Details of people, addresses, vehicles, exhibits and other documents are entered and cross-referenced where appropriate. The contents of witness statements, police interviews and other documents are typed onto the system where they can then be viewed by members of the investigation team. The HOLMES team will generate enquiries, known as Actions, which will be given to appropriate members of the investigation team to complete. These may be requests such as taking a statement from a witness, obtaining CCTV footage or researching an individual who may be of interest to the investigation. HOLMES 2 is used in the vast majority of murder investigations. It allows for the retention of a large amount of data which is capable of being retrieved and searched. It is also particularly useful in cases involving more than one police force as the systems can be linked together and accessed remotely.

Identifying the offender

There are many ways in which a killer can be identified. They may be seen by a witness, recorded on CCTV or identified through forensic evidence. If the person(s) responsible is 'on the run' and knows that police are looking for them, what sort of enquiries could the SIO consider which may help to track them down?

The following are just a few examples of 'suspect enquiries' which may be considered.

Mobile phone

Most people these days have a mobile phone, some people have more than one. If a suspect is trying to 'lie low' they are likely to be in contact with other people to arrange for transport to another area or accommodation when they get there. If there is intelligence to suggest that the suspect uses or has access to a particular mobile phone(s) then the SIO will want to know as much information about the use of that phone during material times. This will include calls/texts made and received, voicemail messages and internet history/activity. It may also be possible to identify whether the phone is still in use and, if so, it's current location (within geographical parameters). These enquiries will have to be justified and authorised by a senior officer but in a murder case this should not present too much of a problem. The investigation team are also likely to want to look at mobile phone data for phones belonging to associates and family of the suspect to establish whether there may have been contact with the suspect since the murder.

Financial enquiries

The suspect is likely to need money at some point whilst trying to evade capture. This may be to pay for transport, food or perhaps clothing. If the suspect has a bank account then the police will be monitoring the account for deposits, withdrawals and any other activity which may help to locate them. This could include the use of credit/debit cards, cashpoint machines or bank transfers. As with mobile phones, the police will need to justify their actions and obtain authority, which in some cases may result in an application to a Judge at a Crown Court. During the course of these enquiries the police may also need to investigate the bank accounts of associates/family of the suspect who may be looking to support them financially. If they do so, knowing or believing that the person is guilty of the offence and with the intention of impeding apprehension then they would also have committed a criminal offence known as 'assisting an offender'.

Vehicle

If the suspect has access to a vehicle there are a number of investigative tools which may help the police to locate them. The Police National Computer (PNC) holds details of all vehicles registered in the UK. From the PNC it is possible to establish if the vehicle is currently taxed and insured. The police can register interest in a vehicle by placing what is known as an 'information report' on the record so that if anyone checks on that particular vehicle on PNC, they will be advised to contact the originating force. An example of such a report may read 'occupant of vehicle believed to be John Smith who was seen leaving the scene of a murder in Wembley 12/6/17. If seen, do not stop but contact SIO DCI GIBBON Operation Wayward immediately'. This type of report will ensure that appropriate action can be taken even if the vehicle is seen elsewhere in the UK. The PNC can also be checked to see if that vehicle has come to notice prior to the murder and, if so, in what circumstances. If the suspect was previously stopped driving the vehicle, that may suggest that they still have access to it.

Another useful resource is the Automatic Number Plate Recognition system (ANPR). A lot of police vehicles these days are fitted with ANPR capability which means that if they pass or are in the vicinity of a vehicle which has an information marker such as no tax or involved in crime, the occupants of the police vehicle will be alerted to that vehicle and provided with the reason for interest. In addition to the police vehicles, ANPR is located in a series of cameras on roads throughout the UK. There are in excess of 8,000 cameras at various locations which record details of every vehicle which passes through the camera. As with the police vehicle ANPR, if a vehicle has a report on it and passes through an ANPR camera then it will alert operators who can take appropriate action. If the police have a vehicle registration number they are interested in, they can check to see whether that vehicle has passed through one or more ANPR cameras. This could give investigating officers crucial evidence including direction of travel and even current location. The cameras can provide other evidence which would support criminal investigations.

The recovery of a vehicle involved in a murder can provide forensic opportunities. If a person has committed a murder then got into a vehicle and made off, there is a strong likelihood that they will have left evidence somewhere in or on the vehicle (see DNA – Locard's Exchange Principle). This could include fingerprints, blood, fibres, hair or some other type of forensic evidence. Once the vehicle is found, it should be subjected to a thorough forensic examination. The vehicle will be transported on a low-loader to a secure, covered police garage where this examination can take place. The vehicle will be retained by police for evidential purposes until it is no longer required.

* * *

Social media and the Internet

Both social media and the internet play a key role in crime investigation these days. It's not unusual for an incident to be recorded on a mobile phone and almost instantly downloaded onto social media for the world to see. This can prove problematic for police investigators, as not only do they have to try to locate the footage, they also have to identify the person who downloaded it who could well be a key witness. Footage is often available before the crime has even been reported to police. Comments made on social media can help but also hinder a police investigation. In 2011, I was the SIO leading a Murder investigation in the East Midlands where a man had been stabbed to death and the suspect was 'on the run'.

Inaccurate information on social media about the circumstances and the subsequent police investigation didn't help. At one stage, I had to hold a press conference, making it clear that any false information about the case may result in those responsible being prosecuted. On the positive side, social media can prove really useful when used correctly to trace witnesses, circulate details of a crime and reassure the community. The police are using it regularly with their own

Twitter and Facebook accounts. Like most things, provided it is used appropriately, it can be a valuable asset but when it is abused it can cause real difficulties.

Researching the internet is generally a line of enquiry in a criminal investigation, particularly a Murder case. A huge amount of information can be obtained from a few social media and internet searches. It forms part of the 'victimology' process and may help the police to locate a wanted suspect. It's not unheard of for a person who is wanted by the police to divulge information as to their whereabouts to other people or maybe post a photo with a current location.

Some people still think that, once the 'delete' button is pressed on their computer, all traces of their search history will be erased. Even if the user cannot find any trace which may incriminate them, there's a good chance that computer experts will be able to recover data. Computers and mobile phones are always seized from murder suspects and, believe it or not, it's quite common for incriminating evidence to be found on them. In one particular murder case which I lead, an examination of a computer revealed searches on 'how can I disguise tablets in food' and 'what is the thing that kills you that doesn't show on a post mortem'. This information was given as evidence and supported the prosecution case which resulted in a conviction for Murder.

Every single keystroke on a computer leaves a 'footprint' and any internet activity does the same. Social media and the internet are now integral to any Murder investigation.

CASE STUDY – MURDER INVESTIGATION

A ten-year old schoolgirl had been playing with some friends during a warm summer evening near to her home. She failed to return and was reported missing. A search of the local area began involving family, members of the public and the police. Unfortunately her grandfather found the girl in the early hours of the following morning in nearby dense woodland. She had been beaten to death and concealed in undergrowth, beneath a pile of leaves.

The scene was cordoned off and a murder investigation commenced involving over 400 police staff. A detailed forensic examination of the crime scene, which covered a large rural area including trees, bushes and shrubs, was carried out. Within a few feet of the body recovery site, forensic scientists found minute airborne droplets of the victim's blood on surrounding leaves and vegetation at various height levels. This was consistent with the actual site and nature of the attack which had caused the death of the young girl.

During the early hours of the investigation a 17-year old youth was identified as being one of the last people to see the victim alive. He was seen by police and, as part of the elimination process, his clothing and footwear were seized for blood and fibre screening. On initial visual examination of his training shoes, small spots of what appeared to be blood could be seen.

The youth was arrested and taken into custody for questioning. Whilst in custody his training shoes were sent off for fast-track forensic examination. Within three days, with the youth remaining in police custody being questioned, the tests were completed. They revealed blood on the training shoes which had originated from the victim and was of the exact shape and size as the airborne blood distribution found at the attack site. This result linked the youth to the victim at the time of her death. He was subsequently charged and later convicted of the murder based on the evidence from the blood found on his training shoes.

Past

A BODY UNDER THE BED

This case is a classic example of a pursuit – a detective from the city trailing a man across the North Sea to Antwerp and then having to hold the man until there was extradition; the killer he was after may well have slipped away. It is a tense and exciting tale, though at its heart is a morbid and everyday killing. In May, 1921 Mary Pannell advertised a room to let in her large Victorian property at number fourteen, Brownlow Street. It was common practice then to let out rooms, and Liverpool was a busy commercial city with thousands of travelling men coming and going on commercial transactions. She soon had a response and a man with a foreign accent, wearing a bushy moustache, came to call. He was middle-aged, and strangely brought no luggage with him. But he was quiet, well-mannered and smartly turned-out. He gave his name as John Brown and explained that he was in the sales business, concerned with textiles. He accepted the rent of ten shillings a week and was given a key.

Brown came and went at all hours and was usually out for most of the evenings. Sometimes he was away from the flat for several days and he explained this by saying that his sister, a woman who needed him to nurse her, had nobody else. All this added to the generally good opinion formed of the quiet man of mystery at number fourteen. In July he turned up with a woman whom he announced as being the sister he had spoken of previously: she was a thick-set, middle-aged woman who talked of her heart problems. The story was that she had had to retire from any regular work due to the deteriorating state of her health. The couple were seen around the area by several people and so everything about them seemed normal. But on 16 July, when she went to do the housework in Brown's room, the door was locked, and was still locked five days later when she tried again. Had the man left without paying his rent? Miss Pannell naturally thought that because his rent was due on the day she went again to clean for him.

When a lodger called Grant was asked to go around and enter the room by the outside window, a shock was coming to the residents of number fourteen Brownlow Street: the man at the window saw a woman's legs on the floor – he felt certain that there was a body under the bed. The lodger, Grant, rammed the window open and it was then that he experienced a rank smell; the body had been there for some time. He wasted no time in calling for the police.

The first detective on the scene noted that the body was cut to pieces and that there was only one garment on the corpse – a chemise. She was lying in a pool of blood, and the most repulsive detail on the scene of horror was a little heap of flesh by the body. 'I thought it was rats' urine, as it dries like a little hill...' he said. But it turned out to be the genitals organs, neatly taken out. Her throat had been cut. But there were several other cuts on jaw, chin and neck. A forensic report of the time notes that 'The wounds were putrefying and were covered with mould... On the left side of the wound and upon the left thigh were some abrasions as if scraped by a sharp instrument.'

Miss Pannell identified the body as that of the person introduced to her as Brown's sister. It was a strong and vicious attack, but the wounds were mostly done after death, and with a clean instrument. The person the police were looking for was some kind of obsessed or perverted fetishist, it seemed. A clean instrument had been used to take out the genitals. It was a macabre business cleaning up the room: the mattress was soaked in blood and there were clothes littered around, mostly bloodied.

Some little objects found in some of the clothes provided some leads, though. One of the most interesting, bearing in mind Brown's foreign accent, was the name 'E. Braem' with the Liverpool address. There was also a false lead, to a seaman called Nicholson, but the turning-point in the first enquiries came when the identity of the dead woman was confirmed. She was Mary Sarah McKenzie Clarke; she was apparently not on the game, but she was a known heavy drinker, and objects found in her lodgings made it certain that she was living by doing thefts from motor vehicles. Then, from markings on collars in the room at Brownlow Street, details of another place used by Brown were found. This was at 40 Guelph Street. The man of mystery was indeed a puzzle for the law. But the lead that led to Brown being traced was found, courtesy of the paperwork required by the Aliens Act of 1905. 'Brown' had had to fill in a form; this revealed that he was really Mr Braem of Courtrai in Belgium. He had given his date of birth, an Antwerp address and a note that he had served in the Belgian army as a lancer. Not only did the form lead to useful information; there was a central register of aliens in London. The Home Office then stated that Braem had a record: in Sheffield he had been arrested for living by false pretences. Then the police even had a photograph of him, held at the Criminal Records Office; he had served a short gaol sentence.

The chase was on in earnest now: a detective went to the Antwerp address and he was tracked down; in his possession were press cuttings about the Liverpool murder. Of course, on arrest, he told a story; the story was that a man called Fisher from Manchester had done the murder. With the Belgian authorities insisting on a proper extradition order, D C S McCoy was desperate for his superiors in Liverpool to have a warrant and extradition papers from home; finally these came, and were signed by the Prosecuting Solicitor back home.

The hunt for the supposed 'Fisher' went on and at first there was no result, even after a methodical search for all people named Fisher in Manchester. Eventually, by sheer persistence, officers came across a sailor called Harry Fisher, and a thorough questioning made it clear that this man had indeed been a drinking acquaintance of Braem; but there it ended. There was no more to it. Braem had said that Fisher was Australian, and this sailor worked for a steamship company operating between Liverpool and Australia. It was soon obvious that Braem had fabricated a personality from the actual Harry Fisher, the genial drinker and talker. In fact, in Antwerp, Braem could not identify Fisher from a picture shown him in a sequence of images. Detective McCoy had earned his pay with all his hard work on the case. After more testing at the scene of crime, and with Belgian officers present, it was found that any noise in the killing would not have been heard, as the next room was lived in by a man who was deaf and very ill. It was all over for Braem. It was in 1922 that he was finally sentenced, but he escaped the noose, despite the verdict of guilty of wilful murder.

Medical circumstances saved his neck and he was given penal servitude for life.

Past

In a case known as the Broughty Ferry Mystery of 1863, there is one of the clearest examples of what difficulties face the police in matters of identification. A wealthy woman was murdered in her own home, and a man was seen coming out of the house. Several witnesses gave descriptions of the man, and when the account of the affair was read by officials down in Kent, there was a sure feeling that the wanted man was in Maidstone gaol for a theft. He was a Canadian, and he was leading an adventurous life. The group of witnesses was taken down from Scotland to Kent and they were shown an identity parade. As the suspect was the only man with the essential descriptors of the right height, moustache, build and hair colour, they picked him out. It looked as if the case was solved. But then the suspect provided a convincing alibi. He was released and the case remains unsolved to this day.

The great crime writer, William Roughead, summed up the issue of identification by discussing the nature of suggestion, and how people give in to suggestion; he quoted *Hamlet*:

Hamlet: Do you see yonder cloud that's almost in the shape of a camel?

Polonius: By the mass, and 'tis like a camel indeed.

Hamlet: Methinks it is like a weasel.

Polonius: It is backed like a weasel.

Hamlet: Or like a whale?

Polonius: Very like a whale.

Chapter 4

Murder – Or Manslaughter?

Present

Both murder and manslaughter result in the tragic loss of life and have devastating consequences for loved ones and those affected. There are clear differences between the two offences which I'll briefly explain.

Murder

Murder is a criminal offence contrary to Common Law. In order to prove an offence of murder, there must be the death of another person and the person(s) responsible must have the intention to kill or to cause serious injury. Attempted murder differs from Murder in that there must be an intention to kill, the intent to cause serious injury does not apply.

Murder is triable on indictment only (at Crown Court) and, on conviction, carries a sentence of life imprisonment. The Judge will set a minimum time that must be spent in prison before the offender can be considered for parole. A person sentenced to life imprisonment spends an average of 14 years in prison. Cases which include aggravating factors such as rape or robbery are likely to result in sentences of 20 or more years. The man who murdered two 10 year old girls in Soham, Cambridgeshire, Ian Huntley, received a minimum term of 40 years. An estimated twenty prisoners in Britain have been recommended for lifelong imprisonment, these include Dennis Nilsen, Jeremy Bamber and Steve Wright.

A person who is found not guilty of murder may be found

guilty of certain other offences including manslaughter, causing grievous bodily harm (GBH) with intent to do so or infanticide (the killing of a newborn within 24 hours of birth).

Manslaughter

Manslaughter is considered a less serious offence than murder. It carries a maximum sentence of life imprisonment but will often result in a fixed term sentence at the Judge's discretion. The difference between murder and manslaughter rests with the presence or otherwise of premeditation. In England and Wales, the usual practice is to prefer a charge of murder, with the Judge or defence able to introduce manslaughter as an option. The jury then decides whether the defendant is guilty or not guilty of either murder or manslaughter. There are two types of manslaughter, voluntary or involuntary.

Voluntary Manslaughter

Voluntary manslaughter requires the intent to kill or cause serious bodily harm. A conviction for this offence can only occur if the defendant puts forward either of the two partial defences against murder, loss of self-control or abnormality of mental function ('diminished responsibility') which can be proved by the defence and is accepted by the court/jury.

Involuntary Manslaughter

For involuntary manslaughter, it has to be proved that the person(s) involved were responsible for the death but had no motive (reason) that can be established. Types of involuntary manslaughter include:

Gross negligence manslaughter – where there is a duty of care which has been breached by an individual through gross negligence resulting in death;

Unlawful act manslaughter – where there is an intentional and unlawful act which results in death which was neither foreseen nor intended;

Corporate manslaughter – the organisation of activities by senior management which involves a gross breach of the duty of care that results in death.

As you can see, this area of law is complex and often subject to change. If you want to use a reference to this type of crime in your writing, particularly manslaughter, it is well worth researching at the time to make sure that your approach is accurate and current.

CASE STUDY – 'STALKER' CONVICTED OF MANSLAUGHTER

A man whose campaign of threats and harassment caused his former partner to kill herself has been jailed for manslaughter. In what is believed to be a legal first, Nicholas Allen, was initially charged with coercive behaviour and stalking but Crown Prosecution Service lawyers later brought a charge of unlawful killing against him after an enquiry into the death of Justine Reece. The 46 year old was found hanged at her home in February 2017 after leaving a note saying that she had 'run out of fight' following six months of threats from Allen.

The pair met in 2015, but within months Allen became increasingly obsessive and controlling. In 2016 Justine left Allen to live at a women's shelter, prompting him to begin stalking other people in an attempt to track her down. After they split up, Allen made in the region of 3,500 attempts to contact her, via phone, Facebook and WhatsApp. The behaviour included visiting home addresses, contacting employers and posting offensive photographs.

Allen had numerous previous convictions for offences against women including threats and assaults. After learning that Justine had killed herself, Allen carried out an internet search in an attempt to establish whether he could be held legally responsible for her death.

Having admitted manslaughter, coercive behaviour and stalking at Stafford Crown Court, Allen was sentenced to a 15 year extended sentence with 10 years in prison and 5 years on licence, the Judge commented "You clearly caused her to lose her life and before that to experience, over a protracted period of time, what must have been a living nightmare. It is not suggested that you intended at any time that she should die but clearly you intended that she should suffer serious psychological harm. She committed suicide as a direct result of your sustained and determined criminal actions, actions which you clearly knew were having a profound effect upon her."

This is believed to be the first time that a stalker has been held liable for the suicide of their victim and could set a precedent for future prosecutions.

Past

Often, people settling in another country take their divisions and conflicts with them, and one of the clearest instances of this is the case of Irish immigration into the north of England in the early decades of the nineteenth century. On many occasions, crime resulting from such conflicts happened in the open air and in the streets, and in Bradford in 1844, there was a typical case. In the heart of a series of terrible outrages against ordinary people in Ireland, the year 1792 saw the foundation of the Orange Order. The loyal Protestants of the north of Ireland split the nationalist phalanx.

That organisation would prove to be the focus for a horrendous killing in Bradford in the early Victorian period: the death and public fight had nothing to do with the Order as such: it was simply part of an ongoing antagonism in general, and Bradford happened to be a place where many Irish had settled. This confrontation led to five people being charged with manslaughter.

Behind this unpleasant and vicious attack was a contentious area of social history: the nature of the Irish communities in the fast-growing Northern towns. There were very large numbers of immigrants, of course, coming across to Lancashire and Yorkshire to work in the textile industries. Social segregation naturally meant a process of ghetto-creation, such as the area of Manchester known as 'Little Ireland' near the river Medlock. There were thirty-four thousand Irish in the city in 1841. In fact Bradford had a much larger Irish population than Leeds, for instance, and that cultural presence was marked in the mid-Victorian period.

The cultural and political dissensions and divisions of course came with the immigrants. The general population knew that the Irish worked hard and had built most of the roads and railways, but the image was unkindly and harshly insulting, as in the appearance of Irish people in *Punch* sketches and satires. The events of 1844 would do little to counteract this negative image: an everyday march turned into something quite savage in the streets of Bradford. It began with the members of the Calverley and Greengates Brass Band holding the Orange Day parade and moving in procession through High Street, dressed in all the regalia of that order. As with all the garlanded parades of that era, happening every week, they carried flags and banners as they walked. Their repertoire for the most part was quite general and innocuous, but towards the end of the set they began to play the melodies of *The Boyne Water* and *Croppies Lie Down*. Now, the very word 'croppy' is almost always going to be potentially something to incite trouble. The song was always linked to the Orange yeomanry in the year of terrible repression in Ireland, 1798, referring to the vogue of cropping the hair short, in a mimicking of the French Republicans.

The words of the song include a direct affront to these people:

Oh Croppies ye'd better be quiet and still
Ye shan't have your liberty, do what ye will,
As long as salt water is found in the deep,
Our foot on the neck of the croppy we'll keep.

The Irish watching the march began to make a row and hoot at the marchers, in derision. But the band went on and eventually arrived at their lodge rooms. But the matter was far from finished. A band of thugs had waited for the right time to get some satisfaction after this provocation (as they saw it) and they had hung around until some band members dispersed and set off home. At about eight that night the bandsmen were followed home, and in Eccleshall Road, near Airedale College, they were attacked. The drum was ruined, and then the musicians were set about and severely beaten up. The assault happened quickly and took place ruthlessly, the villains running into the night leaving a band member lying on the roadside, bleeding and mortally injured. He was badly cut and his head was bleeding profusely.

This unfortunate was one Benjamin Gott, and he died the next day, his skull fractured. It emerged later that the poor man had been hit by a cobblestone. It had been a relentless and furious attack by a rabid gang, on unarmed and defenceless people. Five men were tried for the attack initially, and later four more men from Keighley. The first group were found guilty of manslaughter and transported. In such an affray, it is hard to prove an intent to kill, and of course, there were assaults, but in that time, and in that social context, manslaughter was seen as a fitting offence, as it would open up the option of transportation. In legal terms, it would have been impossible to prove a *mens rea* – the malice behind and intent to take a life.

Prison sentences were given to the second group, and the whole affair was assessed and understood as what we might now call an 'isolated incident' but with hindsight and some more historical reference, it is not difficult to see this as indicative of a deeper malaise, and one that has never really gone away. The general image of fear and mistrust in this period regarding Irish activities was never really eased, and such things as Arthur O'Connor's sensational act of confronting Queen Victoria with an unloaded pistol as she stepped down from a carriage near Buckingham Palace did not help to remove this bad press.

Chapter 5

Forensic Pathology

FORENSIC PATHOLOGY

When investigating unexplained, unnatural or suspicious deaths and murders, the Senior Investigating Officer (SIO) relies upon a significant contribution from a Forensic Pathologist. Whilst a deceased person cannot explain how they met their death, their physical body can still provide a wealth of information and forensic evidence. They become an important crime scene for the collection of forensic samples and pathological evidence which is likely to help any subsequent criminal investigation.

Forensic pathologist

Amongst all professionals who assist in the investigation of a suspicious death, the Forensic Pathologist plays a pivotal role in determining the cause and manner of death. As such, it is crucial that the Forensic Pathologist is contacted at an early stage and fully appraised of the circumstances. They will sometimes, but not always, attend the scene so that they can make an assessment with the body *in situ*, particularly if there are unusual circumstances or some other reason which may benefit their expert opinion, such as the position of the body or extreme blood loss/spatter. They will also advise on the most effective way to recover the body to minimise evidence contamination/loss. In a number of murder cases, once life has been pronounced extinct, it's not unusual for the body to remain *in situ* until such time as a full assessment of the immediate area and body can be carried out. A forensic tent may be erected around the body to protect evidence, preserve dignity and prevent unwanted attention.

Post Mortem

At some appropriate stage the body will be removed to a local mortuary where it will remain. As soon as practicable a Post Mortem (PM) will be carried out in an attempt to establish the cause and manner of death. This medical examination will be conducted by the Forensic Pathologist who will fully examine the body, noting the size, physique and condition of the deceased including any injuries, before carrying out the full head to toe examination. A number of samples from vital organs will be taken and submitted for analysis to check for disease or other factors which may have contributed to the death.

Other than the pathologist and an assistant, the PM will be attended by the SIO (or their deputy), a Crime Scene Manager (CSM), a Crime Scene Investigator (CSI), an exhibits officer and the Coroners Officer. Only HM Coroner can authorise the removal of a body and subsequent PM and, as such, the Coroners Officer working on their behalf is a very important part of the process who must be kept regularly updated throughout the investigation.

Sometimes the cause of death cannot be established or isn't clear which can provide a challenge for any criminal investigation.

Even when it may appear obvious, such as a person who has a number of puncture/stab wounds to the torso area, the SIO must keep an open mind as subsequent examinations may reveal that the person was actually asphyxiated and the puncture wounds may have been caused post-mortem (after death).

Time of death

Estimating the time of death can be a contentious area of pathology so it's preferable to rely upon factual evidence such as witness testimony or closed circuit television (CCTV) if available. Nonetheless, it's still an extremely valuable piece of information and, if confirmed, is likely to provide some focus for the criminal investigation. There may be complicating factors for the pathologist, such as the environment the body has been kept in.

Inclement weather, indoor heating, air conditioning and the amount of time taken to discover the body are all aggravating features which could hinder an accurate prediction based upon body temperature. Post-mortem changes such as hypostasis, rigor mortis and putrefaction can be additional factors which the pathologist may need to consider. Good observations at the scene may also help such as changing weather conditions post-mortem, for example rain, where underneath the body is dry. Estimating the time of death isn't an exact science and the TV drama pathologist who states that "this person died at 12 minutes past eleven yesterday" based purely on medical findings cannot be relied upon with any certainty.

CASE STUDY – MURDER OR SUICIDE?

The badly burnt body of a man was found fastened to a tree by strong, thick metal wire secured with the ends twisted firmly together. A petrol can was found nearby and the body, due to the injuries caused by the fire, was very difficult to identify. An initial hypothesis was that a brutal gangland-style torture and execution had taken place. A full-scale investigation began, with a pathologist and Fire Service examination team being requested by the SIO to examine the body *in situ.* The examination revealed that the deceased had a malignant tumour in his abdomen. A pair of pliers were eventually found in the undergrowth near to the body, far enough away to prevent his release.

Police enquiries showed that the deceased had bought the wire and pliers from a local DIY store and had been captured on CCTV buying a container and fuel from a local petrol station. It was proved to the satisfaction of the Coroner that the man had voluntarily made his own way to the secluded location, tied himself in such a manner as to prevent escape, poured petrol over himself, and set himself alight. The main seat of the fire was found to be around the area on his body where his tumour was located, as if he was trying to burn it out. The evidence from both the pathologist and police enquiries supported a Coroner's verdict of Suicide.

Past

THE FIRST DABS CASE

Today, fingerprints are routine, and of course they have been dramatically overshadowed by DNA applications. But the thrill of tracing a culprit by means of these daubs is still one of the most exciting elements of police work as seen by the public in general. On a visit to Wood Street, at that time the police museum for the City of London force, I arrived to meet the curator only to find him surrounded by lively youngsters all firing questions at him. Before they left, they all gave their prints. Naturally, I had to join in, and my print is now on my key-ring.

One of the most celebrated detectives of the twentieth century, Fred Cherrill ('Cherrill of the Yard') explained his early fascination with fingerprints by telling the tale of his going to an old mill with his father in a storm. The miller was ill and someone was needed to grind the corn to meet demand. In the mill, flour was sprayed everywhere, putting a white film over every surface, and young Fred found himself grabbing an eel his father threw across the room at him, with orders to put it in a sack. His hands were caked in eel slime and then he writes, 'Startled, I put out a hand to steady myself. For just a moment my slime-covered fingers rested on the wooden chute, which had become highly polished by all the flour and meal which had passed over its surface...I was gazing at the chute in awed fascination... There, by the agency of nature alone, were my fingerprints!'

Cherrill's story accounts for the long history of the knowledge of fingerprints, long before they were used in forensics. There had been various academics who had done work on prints but nothing had come of it: a professor at the University of Breslau in 1823 had read a Latin thesis on fingerprints in a lecture, and the artist Thomas Bewick had done wood engravings of fingerprints, using them as identifying signatures on his works. In China, for many centuries, thumb-prints had been used in documents for identity purposes in ratification. Similarly, these impressions had been used in India with illiterate members of the population; when the scientist Francis Galton got to work on the subject, he wrote a book-length study, simply called *Fingerprints*, published in 1892. In some ways, the introduction of fingerprinting into police work is similar to the rivalry to reach the South Pole: while Sir Edward Henry was using fingerprints in India for crime investigation, the same work was being done in Argentina by Francesca Rojas. But after Henry had introduced fingerprinting into the repertoire of detection methods at the Yard, it was to effect a revolution in detective procedure.

The prototype scenario and first conviction by the use of prints came in 1902, when the Yard had around one hundred fingerprints in their first small volume of records. It was a murder case, and it took place at Chapman's Oil and Colour

Stores in Deptford. An old couple, Thomas and Ann Farrow, ran the shop and they had an assistant, young William Jones, who , along with Louis Kidman, found Thomas's corpse and later the still breathing Ann Farrow.

The old man had been brutally beaten, with a broken cheekbone and a fractured skull; the doctor said that the man had died around ninety minutes earlier. When Ann Farrow had been taken to hospital and the scene was ready for some inspection, Chief Inspector Fred Fox arrived to do his work, with two photographers. Crime scene investigation, in something close to the modern sense, was being born that day. No less a figure than Melville Macnaghten came to assist and then took charge. The killer had not forced an entry: that was the first important detail established. There had been a frenzied search of the whole shop and house, but after going upstairs and hitting Mrs Farrow, the scene suggested that they had come downstairs and then fought the old man again, as he had recovered from their first blow.

There were no witnesses; three masks were found abandoned in the shop so now Macnaghten knew he was looking for three killers, and that made the murder all the more savage and reprehensible. There was no indication as to what weapon had been used in the murderous attacks either. The question now on the detective's mind was whether Ann Farrow would recover and give descriptions. What was particularly unhelpful in the course of following the usual tracing procedure in pawn shops and similar outlets, was that the killers had only taken money. That created a dead end in the normal line of enquiry. It was looking desperate for the Chief; another shopkeeper had been killed in London the same day. Then, the final blow: Mrs Farrow died.

Macnaghten went back to the bloodbath that was the sitting room of the Farrow household. Casting his eye across the room and the pools of blood, he thought of the surface prints that had just been used in smaller scale arrests. Would the Farrow murder be the first opportunity to try this new device? He established that none of the police personnel at the shop had touched the cashbox, then he covered his fingers with a handkerchief and showed his team the print on the box. Collins, of the new Fingerprint Branch, was a sleuth with a scientific bent; he had been working on other types of basic forensics and was excited about this new technique. It was a matter of magnifying glasses and intense study at that time; he had a small collection of filed prints from known criminals and that was that. There had been a long-established method of filing basic records of habitual offenders, so there was some hope of a 'result.' But the print on the cash box had no match in Collins's shelves.

Basic police work, however, provided the lead that would eventually take the investigation back to the cash box. A milkman at work on the day of the killing had seen two men leaving the shop and he gave a description of them. The milkman saw that they had left the door open and told them so but they took no notice as they said there was someone behind them. To tally with this, three men had been seen in a local pub very early that day – and they answered the descriptions. It was when a certain Ellen Stanton came forward that things accelerated; she had seen two men running at the right time , and they had the same appearance as two suspects, and Ellen knew one of them. Macnaghten was now searching for one Alfred Stratton. The man was taken in Deptford. The identification parade failed, but Collins took the prints of Stratton and his brother. One print matched that of Alfred.

What happened then is a pattern for almost all succeeding scientific forensic advances when it came to actually implementing the knowledge and seeing it take part in a process of law in the courts. In other words, this new detective force, with its fingerprints and other types of records, was going to find it hard to convince judge and jury about the new methods of detection. But the Stratton brothers went to the gallows; hangman John Billington officiated at Wandsworth. The judge, Mr Justice Channell, had said in court that the men should not be convicted on fingerprint evidence alone and that was the case. But the first trial involving fingerprint evidence had happened; from that point on the concept would be a little more familiar, and the newspapers played their part in ensuring that.

As usual when some new kind of evidence appears – and there is science involved – there are problems in dealing with the new material with regard to the jury. That was as much a challenge as actually obtaining the prints in this case.

Chapter 6

DNA

Present

Forensic evidence is one of the most important strands in any criminal investigation. There are a number of different types of forensic evidence including fingerprints, footwear marks, fibres and instrument (tool) marks. Whenever a crime is committed it is likely that the person(s) responsible will leave some kind of forensic evidence at the scene. The challenge for the investigation team is to find and interpret that evidence. This is particularly relevant in a murder case where the victim and offender normally come into contact at some point.

Back in the early 1900's a French scientist called Edmond Locard identified that criminals would leave evidence at the scene and take away evidence from the scene with them. If there was any contact between the victim and the offender, there would be a cross-transference of evidence between the two. This could be something as minute as a fibre from clothing or a hair. This process became known as 'Locard's Exchange Principle' and can be summed up in the phrase 'every contact leaves a trace'. Locard's principle is something which police officers (particularly detectives) are taught and still applies to this day. It is one of the reasons why a forensic examination of the scene is so important.

Deoxyribonucleic acid (DNA) is the genetic code found in the cells of our body which we inherit from our parents. It is probably the one type of forensic evidence which has developed more than any other during the last thirty years or so. DNA can be extracted from blood, semen, saliva, hair roots and skin cells. During the early 1980's a British geneticist called Alec Jeffreys developed techniques for DNA fingerprinting (DNA profiling) which are now used across the globe to assist police detective work. In 1984 Jeffreys 'eureka moment' came in his laboratory in Leicester whilst looking at the x-ray image of a DNA experiment, which unexpectedly showed both similarities and differences between the DNA of different members of his technician's family. Jeffreys realised the possible scope of DNA fingerprinting which uses variations in the genetic code to identify individuals.

This DNA method was first used in 1985 when Jeffreys was asked to help in a disputed immigration case to confirm the identity of a British boy whose family originated from Ghana. The case was resolved when the DNA results proved that the boy was closely related to the other members of the family, a result which brought great relief to the boy's mother.

DNA fingerprinting was first used in a police forensic test to identify the killer of two teenagers who had been raped and murdered in the Leicestershire area in 1983 and 1986. Colin Pitchfork was identified and convicted of their murders after samples taken from him matched semen samples recovered from the crime scenes. Without this identification it's entirely possible that an innocent man would have been convicted of these crimes. Not only did Jeffrey's work prove who the real killer was, but it exonerated Richard Buckland, a 17 year old with learning difficulties, who had originally claimed to have murdered one of the girls. In 1988 Pitchfork pleaded guilty to the two rape/murders along with another sexual assault. He was sentenced to life imprisonment to serve a minimum of 30 years (reduced on appeal to 28 years) and has recently been moved to an undisclosed open prison.

Identical twins

Your fingerprints are unique to you and no-one, not even your closest relative, has the same fingerprints as you. This is not the case, however, in relation to DNA. Identical twins, triplets etc have the same DNA because they originate from the same egg, which divides into two embryos after it is fertilised. This can prove problematic for investigators trying to solve crimes, particularly if there is no other evidence to support the DNA findings.

There have been a number of cases highlighting these issues. Here are just two examples:

– In 2013 twin brothers were both charged with raping a woman in Berkshire as the police were unsure which one the DNA came from. Eventually one of the twins was convicted and charges were dropped against the other as mobile phone evidence placed him elsewhere at the time.
– In 2016 at Gloucester Crown Court prosecutors offered 'no evidence' against a man accused of dangerous driving and possession of a lock-knife after the man claimed that his twin brother was the actual offender and there was no evidence available to prove otherwise.

Scientists around the world continue to look at this anomaly. Tests have been carried out which involve melting the DNA in an attempt to establish differences between twins. This may be a huge step forward but currently seems to be reliant on identifying differences in the lifestyle, environment and diet of the twins concerned. The more similar these factors are, the more difficult this process would appear to be. I have no doubt, however, that the continuous advances in forensic science will overcome this challenge sooner rather than later.

* * *

CASE STUDY – THE MURDER OF MELANIE ROAD

In June 1984 a 17 year old girl, Melanie Road, was walking home from a nightclub in Bath when she was attacked and murdered. She was stabbed 26 times and subjected to a lengthy and brutal sexual assault. Forensic evidence was recovered from the crime scene but, despite a detailed police investigation, the killer remained unidentified.

In 1995 after DNA became a regular part of police work, a profile of the killer was created and entered onto the National DNA Database. In 2000 a more detailed DNA profile was obtained and police began to look for potential family matches but the killer remained at large. By 2010 hundreds of potential DNA matches had been traced and eliminated from the enquiry.

In 2014 police were called to a domestic incident involving a woman called Clare and her boyfriend. During an argument she had snapped his necklace and was arrested for criminal damage. As part of the routine arrest process, a sample of her DNA was taken by way of a mouth-swab. This would have been subsequently entered onto the national DNA database. She was later cautioned for the offence.

In 2015 cold case detectives ran a check of the database to include the 1 million people added during the previous five years. At this point the police received confirmation that the sample taken from 'Clare' was a familial match to the crime scene sample belonging to the killer of Melanie Road. This meant that, although the sample wasn't identical, there were enough similarities to suggest that the killer could be a member of her family. They then began to look at male family members, which included Clare's father, Christopher Hampton (aged 64). A voluntary DNA sample given by Hampton to police outside his workplace was subsequently confirmed as matching the DNA belonging to the killer. Hampton was arrested but refused to speak with police or his legal team.

Hampton pleaded 'not guilty' to murder but on 9th May 2016, on the first day of his trial, he changed his plea to 'guilty'. He was sentenced to life imprisonment, to serve a minimum term of 22 years. This was a senseless and brutal killing of an innocent 17 year old girl for sexual gratification. Some 32 years later the killer was identified and brought to justice with the use of familial DNA.

Past
THE FIRST MAJOR CASE IN BRITAIN
DNA has caused so many revolutions in criminology, police work, the criminal law and so many areas of life beyond crime that it is an everyday concept. But the truth is that it took a long time for it to be accepted in the courts. The chief reason for this is that the knowledge base is complex, and juries need clear information which can easily be absorbed. The first experts had to learn how to communicate with the layperson. Stuart has referred to the first major case, and I am amplifying the material in this section.

We know a great deal about this case because forensic profiler Paul Britton was involved in the work, and in his book, *The Jigsaw Man* (1997) he gives extensive details. Of course, Alec Jeffrey's work is central to this; in September, 1984 he had completed an experiment to find out if repeated sections of DNA could be used to track inherited diseases through families. He said in an interview in 2000: 'The last thing I was thinking about was paternity suits or forensics. But I would have had to have been a complete idiot not to spot the implications.' The rapes of Mann and Ashford around Narborough meant that he was invited to test the man who first confessed. The police asked Jeffreys to prove that the man, Richard Buckland, had murdered Lynda Mann. At first, the tests showed that the two women had been raped by the same man but that Buckland was not the man; the findings were not accepted by the police who told him that his technique was 'a dud.' But there was much more to come.

The police began the mass sampling of local men, taking blood and giving this to Jeffreys to analyse. There were 4,000 samples but Pitchfork had avoided taking the test and so his sample was not taken and no match was found at first, but he was soon found out and investigated.

Paul Britton was there to log the police investigation. He was a clinical psychologist at the time, working for Leicestershire health Authority and he worked sometimes at Carlton Hayes. While the more biologically based work was going on, Britton was thinking like a profiler: '... I knew that her killer was more than a caricature or comic-book villain. He also had a rich life which had shaped his personality and actions. What went through his mind, I wondered, when he saw Lynda? What did he see and why did he choose her?'

But then, on 2 January, 1987 The *Leicester Mercury* carried the headline, 'Blood Tests for 2,000 in Killer Hunt.' We have to recall that this was right at the very beginning of the arrival of DNA in England as a forensic tool. There was mystery and perplexity around the area. Paul Britton recalls that it was referred to at the time as 'The Bloodings' by the press.

As for Pitchfork, he was a baker, twenty-five, who had moved to Leicester not long after the Mann murder. When interviewed later he said that he had taken his wife to an evening class and then picked her up again later in the evening, on the day of the second murder. The couple had a baby, and of course, he was nursing the child, so that hardly fits with the profile of a serial killer or at least it was a major factor in the thinking at the time. As with the comments on the Yorkshire Ripper investigations, done with hindsight, it has to be said that at this time computers were not widely used by police. In fact, Pitchfork, in trouble before this on matters sexual(he was essentially a 'flasher' in his early phase) had been logged on three different lists: Also, he had been referred by magistrates to Carlton Hayes after a conviction for indecent exposure.

Pitchfork outwardly must have seemed so ordinary: he had been a baker, working initially at Hampshire Bakery in Leicester, then married young; he had been a volunteer worker for Dr Barnado's and become merely a suburban nine to five worker, as far as neighbours would be able to assess him. But his undercover life as rapist and killer was soon to become public. When the 'Bloodings' progressed, a man with his passport was tested and eliminated from the enquiry, but that man, Ian Kelly, loosened his tongue in a pub in Leicester while drinking with some friends, and he confessed what he had done. He said that Pitchfork had spun him a line and made it seem convincing that he had good reasons for avoiding the blood-test. But one of Kelly's listeners went to the police, and Kelly was arrested.

Kelly was charged with perverting the course of justice and the police wasted no time in going to visit Pitchfork at his home in Littlethorpe. He told the stories of the two killings and we now know the events leading to those repugnant rapes and murders. He is reported as giving his confession without remorse, and in a cold and detached manner. When he had gone looking for girls to 'flash' that night when he met Lynda, the baby was left in the car. He had met his victim and flashed, then she did something not at all typical of the usual reaction to such shocks: she ran into a dark place along the path. Pitchfork was clearly excited by this, so much so that he went to her and attacked: he raped her and claimed that he strangled her while she was penetrated.

In the case of Dawn Ashworth, he had seen her walk into a quiet lane off King Edward Avenue while he was on his motorbike, and he had stopped and gone after her. This time he moved in swiftly and raped her in a field. Lynda Mann then reacted in one of the ways that one has to respect for sheer courage and survival attempt – she said that she would tell no-one and asked to leave. But the killer strangled her from behind. He had raped and killed two 15-year-old schoolgirls, showing violence and, in the case of the latter victim, she was more than likely also buggered. The attacks were premeditated and no mercy was shown to the victims. When it came to Pitchfork's application for a term of sentence in August, 2008, heard at the Central Criminal Court by Mr Justice Grigson, these salient facts of his crimes were crucially important in the reconsideration of the situation. In 1994 he was sentenced to 30 years, which meant that he could be released on parole in 2017, but at the 2008 hearing, as is reported in the court proceedings, 'He should only be released when the Authorities are satisfied that he is no longer a danger to women. In any event, in view of the seriousness, callous and cunning conduct the actual length should not be less than twenty years.' In 1988 when he was sentenced, a judge was not obliged to set a minimum term; Mr Justice Otten at that time did not do so because of the heinousness of the crime, and so there was potential for a revision. The 2008 court had an option to increase the minimum term and did so: the judge said, 'I fix the minimum term at 30 years on each count of murder, less the four months and a day the applicant spent in custody on remand.'

Chapter 7

Custody Procedure

Present

After a person has been arrested they will be taken to a police station (unless they are ill/injured and require immediate hospital treatment). On arrival at the police station they will be presented before the Custody Officer (normally a police officer of the rank of Sergeant). The arresting officer will outline the facts of the arrest in the presence of the detained person (unless they are violent or too incapacitated through drink/drugs in which case they may be placed straight into a cell and given their rights when calm/sober). The Custody Officer, if satisfied that the grounds for arrest are justified, will authorise detention in order to secure and preserve evidence and/or to obtain evidence by questioning. These are the two grounds on which detention can be authorised. In most cases both grounds apply but if the detained person wasn't going to be interviewed, for some reason, then only the first ground would apply. The Custody Officer will then request personal details from the detained person including name, address, age and occupation. They will also be asked a number of questions as part of a risk assessment including health and medication issues. The answers are noted on a computerised custody record which is continually updated during their time in custody. The detained person will be searched and details of items in their possession recorded on their custody record. Anything which may be used to harm the detained person or others or is considered to be linked to an offence will be seized as evidence.

Your Rights

When a person is arrested and detained at a police station they have certain rights. They have the right to have someone informed that they have been arrested, the right to speak privately with a solicitor free of charge and the right to read a book called the 'Codes of Practice' which outlines how you should be treated whilst in custody. The detained person is given their rights shortly after their arrival at the police station and told that they can do any of them straight away or at any time whilst they remain in police detention.

In some cases the right to have someone informed and/or the right to legal advice can be delayed if the police can justify that to do so would lead to either interference/harm to evidence/ people, alert other people suspected of having committed an offence but not yet arrested or hinder the recovery of property obtained from an offence. To delay would also require the authority of a senior police officer. The rights can only be delayed for a maximum of 36 hours. Delaying these rights does happen, particularly in serious and appropriate cases, but it certainly isn't a regular occurrence.

In relation to your right to speak with a solicitor, you can request your own solicitor if you have one or you will be given the opportunity to speak with the Duty solicitor who is likely to be on-call and covering the police station area. The initial contact with a solicitor will probably be via telephone depending on when the police may wish to interview you. If the interview isn't going to be until the following morning, for example, then the solicitor would probably not attend until then. Any consultation with a solicitor, where the details of your case are discussed, must take place in private away from the presence/hearing of police.

The custody suite

The area where you will be detained following arrest is known as the custody suite. The custody officer(s) will be located behind a desk/counter which will probably be higher than you. Other than the computers and a whiteboard containing details of other detainees, the suite will have several cells, all individually numbered. There are likely to be other rooms within the suite including a doctor's examination room, interview room(s), fingerprint/photograph room and a kitchen-style room for preparation of hot drinks and meals for detained persons. The custody suite area, including the cells, will probably have CCTV for safety and evidential purposes.

Fingerprints, photograph and DNA sample

Following your arrest the police have the power to take your fingerprints, photograph and a DNA sample. This process will normally take place a short time after your arrival at the police station. The police don't need your consent to carry out these tasks. For many years police used to take fingerprints using ink, a rolling block and paper. Occasionally this method is still used if there is a particular requirement but most of the time these days the fingerprints are taken using a Live scan machine which allows for a set of fingerprints to be instantly compared with a national database. The majority of major custody suites in the UK are now equipped with Live scan which is quicker, more reliable and cleaner than the previous method. Even if you have been fingerprinted when detained on a previous occasion, your fingerprints will be taken again, indeed on every subsequent detention.

Your photograph will also be taken during this process. If you are wearing anything on your head or concealing your facial features, you'll be asked to remove it for the photograph. As with fingerprints, your photograph will be taken on every occasion that you are detained. This can assist police with identification, particularly where a number of photographs are available over a period of years which show changes in a person through age, hairstyle and other distinguishing features.

The DNA sample taken from you will normally be a mouth-swab type. The DNA kit which police use will consist of a large tamper-proof evidence bag containing a pair of disposable gloves, a smaller evidence bag, two small test tube-like containers and two sealed cotton bud style 'scrapers' (similar to small lollipop sticks with a cotton bud end shaped like a comb with a serrated edge). The final item in the bag is an A4 size card which should be completed by the person taking the sample. The card contains details of the person sampled, the offence and the date/time/location. The sample is taken by the 'scrapers' being gently and individually rubbed inside the mouth (one each side). By pressing the end of the 'lollipop stick' it detaches the 'comb' piece from the end into the test tube which is then closed shut. The result is that you end up with two samples in two separate tubes. Both tubes are then placed into the smaller evidence bag which is sealed. This bag along with the index card is then placed into the large evidence bag which is also sealed. The sample is then placed into a freezer until it can be transported from the police station. Unlike fingerprints and photographs, your DNA may not be taken every time you are detained as once the sample has been confirmed as belonging to you, there may be no requirement to take another one.

Forensic samples
Depending on the offence for which you are detained and the circumstances, the police may request forensic samples from you. Any such request has to be authorised by a senior police officer and justified by the officer requesting the sample.

These type of samples are split into two categories:

– Intimate samples such as blood, urine or pubic hair can only be taken with your consent. An intimate sample is likely to be taken by a doctor at the police station. A detained person can refuse to provide an intimate sample but if they do so, without good cause, it's possible that a Court/Jury could draw an adverse inference from this refusal at any future Court proceedings.

– A non-intimate sample such as a sample of hair (other than pubic hair), a sample taken from a nail (or under a nail) or a swab taken from a person's body, including the mouth, but not any other body orifice can be taken without the consent of that person. The request for the sample must be justified and authorised by a senior police officer. Some of these samples can be taken by a police officer/staff but may be taken by a doctor, depending on the seriousness of the case and the circumstances.

Searches
Depending on the offence for which you are detained and the circumstances, the police may wish to carry out searches. They may wish to search your home address, another address which you occupy/control, a business address or a motor vehicle. In serious cases it's likely that a number of searches may take place during your time in police detention. Each of these searches must be justified, lawful and authorised by a senior police officer not connected with the investigation.

Details of the authorisation and the address of the search will be recorded on the relevant custody record. If a search is required out of the force/station area it's possible that officers from that area will be requested to carry out the search on behalf of the station requesting. Any searches of property carried out lawfully whilst a person is detained don't require a search warrant.

Detention times

The legislation which governs police treatment of detained persons is the Police And Criminal Evidence Act 1984 (PACE). During this section I'll explain how long a person can be kept in custody without charge, how the detention process works and who is responsible for the decision-making along the way.

Apart from terrorism offences, (which afford the potential for longer detention periods) the maximum amount of time that a person can be kept in police custody without charge is 96 hours. It's only in the most serious of cases that detention will normally extend beyond 24 hours but the law does provide for longer if it can be justified. The period in custody is measured by the 'detention clock' which starts when a person's detention is authorised. During the first 24 hours of a detention there will be three reviews, carried out by a police Inspector (or above), the first review after a total of 6 hours and the second and third reviews no more than 9 hours after each other (around 15 hours and 24 hours after detention was first authorised). Regular reviews continue at intervals of no more than 9 hours prior to charge during the period of detention.

If the police want to keep a person in custody for longer than 24 hours they must, after the second review but before the third (between 15 and 24 hours detention) apply to a police Superintendent responsible for that area who will decide whether the request is justified. The Superintendent, if satisfied, can grant up to 12 hours additional time, making the total detention time 36 hours. They can't grant any more than 12 hours but they may grant less, for example 6 hours. If they are not satisfied that the application is justified, they may decline to authorise any additional time.

Any further detention time would have to be authorised by a Magistrates Court under what is known as a 'warrant of further detention'. The police, the detained person and their solicitor (if represented) would need to attend court and the police would have to apply for the additional time. The police may apply for up to a further 36 hours (making a total, if granted, of 72 hours). Once again, the Magistrate(s) may authorise the full 36 hours but they may authorise less, for example 12 hours. If the police feel that they require more than 72 hours total, then they would have to again apply to the Magistrates Court who may grant a further 24 hours, taking the total to 96 hours under what is known as an 'extension to a warrant of further detention'.

During my 30 years of policing experience, I've never been involved in a case where a person has been detained for 96 hours. The vast majority of criminal cases (with the exception of terrorism) are concluded, one way or another, well before the maximum time permitted.

Interviews

During your period in custody it's likely that you will be interviewed, possibly more than once. Interviews of detained persons used to be carried out contemporaneously with pen and paper. Audio tape machines were gradually introduced and these days, there's every possibility that your interview could be recorded onto a DVD or a computer hard-drive. Some interviews are also video-recorded.

Prior to an interview, if you are legally represented, your solicitor will have a private consultation with you. During this consultation they will give you advice. That may be to give an account of what happened or may be to answer 'No Comment' to all questions, depending on the circumstances. The solicitor will also speak with the police to go through a process known as 'disclosure', where they are provided with some information about the case and the reasons for the interview.

At the start of the interview, everyone present will be asked to introduce themselves, a script will be read out by the interviewing officer and you'll be reminded that you're under caution ("You don't have to say anything, but it may harm your defence if you don't mention when questioned, something you later rely on in court. Anything you do say may be given in evidence").

To put this caution in it's simplest terms, you have the right to say nothing but if you do remain silent during interview, then provide information at a later stage which has a bearing on your case, the court may wonder why you didn't provide this information when given the opportunity previously. This is often referred to as 'drawing an adverse inference' from your failure/refusal to provide information.

At the end of the interview you'll be asked to sign some paperwork and the interview tapes/DVD's will be sealed. You may remain in the interview room with your solicitor or be escorted back to the custody reception area. Some interviews can be fairly short but others, particularly for serious/complex cases, can last for many hours.

You are entitled to regular breaks and can ask for a private consultation with your solicitor at any time during the interview.

Case disposal

Following your time in custody there are three ways in which your case may be dealt with. If there is sufficient evidence to afford a realistic prospect of conviction then you may be charged with an offence(s). The Crown Prosecution Service (CPS) need to authorise charge in the vast majority of criminal cases. You will then be either released on police bail to attend court or remanded in custody to appear at the next available court. The bail decision will depend on a number of factors including your criminal history, the nature of the offence(s) and whether it is likely that you may abscond.

If the police need to carry out further enquiries into your case then you may be released on police bail. You will be given a future date/time to return to the police station. If you don't attend as requested you commit a further offence.

If the police have been able to eliminate you completely from any wrongdoing and have no further enquiries to carry out, then you will be released without charge (RWOC). This means that you don't have to go back to the police station and you won't face any charges. If the police identify fresh evidence which implicates you in that or another offence you may be arrested again in the future.

Chapter 8

The Experts

Present

In some criminal investigations, particularly murder and other serious crime, police will have to call upon the services of outside experts to assist in the forensic analysis of crime scenes (and perhaps other aspects of the investigation). Information supplied by these professionals can often provide crucial evidence to support a prosecution. There are many different types of experts, including the following.

Palynologist

Palynology is the study of pollen, spores and other microscopic organic compounds. A palynologist may be able to assist a case by identifying pollen or plant material on the clothing or body of a victim, unique to a particular outdoor location, which could indicate that the body had originally been elsewhere before being moved to the deposition site where it was found. Although palynology originated in the early 20th century, it's forensic use in solving crime is relatively new in the UK. Pollen evidence can link a person to a place, indicate if a victim was alive when they were left at a location, or help determine when they died.

During the investigation into the murders of Holly Wells and Jessica Chapman (Soham 2002) the person responsible, Ian Huntley, went to great lengths to try to conceal his involvement in the murders. This included him cleaning his car, having the tyres changed and throwing away items from the interior. Nonetheless, a thorough forensic examination of the vehicle still found evidence linking him to the girls. In the foot-well and the wheel arches, scientists found traces of a distinctive mix of chalk, brick dust and concrete used to cover the road leading to the ditch where the bodies of the girls were found. In addition, pollen from 64 types of plant at the site, some of them quite rare, was also matched to grains in the car and on Huntley's shoes.

Entomologist

The science of Forensic Entomology is the study of insects for medico-legal purposes. There are many ways in which insects can be used to solve a crime, but the primary purpose of forensic entomology is of estimating time since death.

Once a person dies, his or her body starts to decompose. The decomposition of a dead body starts with the action of micro-organisms such as fungi and bacteria, followed by the action of a series of insects (anthropods). Bodies decompose at different rates, depending on a number of factors including weather conditions, exposure to the elements and the presence of insects. The dead body goes through constant changes which allow investigators to estimate how long the person has been dead. The collection and study of insects which feed on a body enable the forensic entomologist to estimate when death occurred. Flies, beetles, maggots and pupae/empty pupal cases could provide crucial information to assist a criminal investigation.

In addition to the estimation of time of death, forensic entomology can also help with information about the lifestyle of the victim, whether a body has been moved from another area and potential wound sites on the body.

* * *

Ballistics

The use of firearms in crime, particularly murder cases, has increased significantly in recent years. Ballistics experts can provide compelling evidence in such cases following examination of guns and spent cartridges. Live rounds recovered from a crime scene can reveal DNA or fingerprint evidence. Whenever a weapon is found by police, an Authorised firearms officer (AFO) must attend the scene to make the weapon safe so that it is no longer capable of being fired. If the weapon has been used in crime, anyone handling it should wear forensic suit and gloves to prevent evidence contamination.

Whenever a gun is fired, a cloud of residue normally spreads from the barrel of the weapon for up to 2–3 metres. This is known as gunshot residue (GSR) or firearms discharge residue (FDR). The residues are from the primer and propellant enclosed in the cartridge along with the bullet. This explodes, forcing the bullet down the barrel at lightning speed. The barrelling effect spins the bullet for accuracy as it fires out.

GSR or FDR may be found on skin, hair, clothing, in a vehicle, or anywhere within close proximity when fired. It can also be transferred from fibre and spent cartridge cases. However, the chemical components of the residue can disperse quickly depending on the environment. It's essential that immediate swabbing of relevant areas and evidence recovery from a scene or suspect is given high priority in any case involving the suspected discharge of a firearm, particularly a murder.

CASE STUDY – FIREARMS RESIDUE EXAMINATION

Two young men, both linked to criminal gangs, were returning to their home on a local housing estate in a motor vehicle. As they pulled onto the driveway the vehicle came under gunfire from a group of 4–5 youths some 50 metres away across a grass verge. The two men managed to run to the house and avoid the bullets, although the vehicle and the side of the house were peppered by gunfire.

The police attended the scene and found the body of a youth who had been fatally shot through the head. Around his feet were 30 assorted spent cartridge cases. Subsequent ballistic tests found the cases to have originated from four separate weapons. It was initially thought that the youth had been shot by return fire and, due to this theory, the two young men were declared as suspects for his murder. Further forensic tests were carried out on the deceased, in particular the wound to his head.

The deceased had high volumes of GSR on his right hand and sleeve area consistent with GSR found on cartridge cases discharged at the vehicle. He also had large volumes of a different GSR on the back of his head at the point of impact. This shot was fired at close range (within 1 metre) and was consistent with other cartridge cases from another weapon, which were also discharged at the vehicle.

The conclusion of the tests was that the victim had been one of the group firing at the vehicle and had stood in front of an associate who had accidentally shot him in the back of the head.

Past

SAVED BY THE DOC 1876

This happened in my own county of Lincolnshire, where I have lived for 40 years. I had spent time around the place where the crime occurred, and after knowing what had happened there so long ago, the thought gave me a shiver. Somehow, crime scenes never really disappear for the historian: they cast a shadow over the imagination and their memory digs in like a batsman heeling his crease. When I first read about the case, I felt a sense of outrage that a man such as the accused could do such things without an initial response that he could not have been in full control of himself. But in times past, when we look at them through the distortions of time, criminal law and police investigation look disturbingly one-track, fixed on matters circumstantial and out for the straightest way to close the books.

The Lincolnshire police force was formed in January, 1857, with a man power of 207 officers led by Capt. Philip Bicknell. Before that time and indeed well after its formation the everyday police work in the remote villages of the county were supervised by parish constables. The small village of Hemingby, near Horncastle, has the dubious distinction of being the place where the last parish constable was murdered. This story of the killing of Constable Thomas Bett Gell is notable for two reasons: it took place in an area that had a unique local history of policing, and it involved a classic narrative of the Victorian criminal justice system when it came to understand insanity.

The victim was a parish constable, an office with a very long history. In the reign of Edward I a law was made placing two constables in each parish, though this was not eagerly enforced; then in 1285 the Statute of Westminster began the 'watch and ward' approach to crime patrolling: basically a night watchman who was to be alert late at night and in the early hours. But by the mid-Victorian period, rural areas still presented a tough problem for the local forces of law and order.

As research by historian B J Davey has shown, Horncastle had a most interesting policing structure in the years between 1838 and 1857. Because of an obscure Act of Parliament, the Lighting and Watching Act of 1833, the town in the Lincolnshire Wolds organised and paid its own constabulary. A young lawyer, Richard Clitherow, kept detailed records of the police functions and of crimes for almost twenty years, and we have a rich understanding of the nature of crime in the town.

Just before policing was revolutionised in 1857 Bicknell took up the post of Chief Constable; he was the one Chief Constable for the county, but the ultimate aim was to have one person in that office for each area. A fundamental problem – and it was one which was to have a bearing on this case – was the fact that Bicknell could not transfer a man to another area without the officer losing his pension rights. This was not remedied until 1865.

Difficulties like these were behind the cumbersome process of having a full-time officer close to the thousands of scattered villages across Lincolnshire, to help the amateurs when needed. Bicknell, who retired in 1902, was the man most responsible for improving the police administration in the county, but his efforts came too late for the constable of tiny Hemingby.

The constable featured in this story had been selected according to Bicknell's requirements. When he looked for a constable for the force he was anxious to recruit the right kind of man; his criteria were principally that the man should be clean, active, intelligent and 'of good height and well made.' Bicknell actually wrote an instruction book, Bicknell's Police manual, and in that, one of his directives was that each member of the force 'with his wife and children, is to attend service every Sunday, unless there be good reason to the contrary, and his children are to be sent to school.'

In Bicknell's long reign the Hemingby murder was one of the worst experiences he had – and that includes riots in Lincoln in 1862 and several high-profile murders. Thomas Bett Gell's death pinpointed the weaknesses of the attempts to police such a massive rural area. B J Davey, in his book *Lawless and Immoral* (see bibliography) which was concerned with the years shortly before the new county and borough police, makes it clear that the Horncastle force, covering Hemingby and other villages nearby, had a wide and demanding remit and a formidable range of crimes to deal with. The police notebooks Davey used for his study show that there was a very high incidence of violent crime. He says something very relevant to the Gell case that helps us understand how vulnerable and hard-pressed the constable was: *'The people of Horncastle were usually not very worried about serious crimes like robbery and they did not expect the likes of Ackrill and Gapp [constables previous to Gell] to be able to do much about things anyway. They wanted the policeman to deal with the lawless and immoral, to reduce drunkenness, vice and considerable disorder throughout the town...'*

Country towns always had their problems of social order and crime was often public and in the streets. While London was developing the status and workings of the first 'Peelers' after Sir Robert Peel's Police Act of 1829, and the Metropolitan Police were born, the provinces continued to cope for several decades with part-timers in the constabularies. The duties of a parish constable were onerous and included the supervision of prisoners, putting them in stocks or securing them in a lock-up, and taking them before a magistrate when the time came. He would not necessarily have a uniform and had only a wooden truncheon to symbolise his office or to instil fear. Nevertheless, the constables coped well. In 1876, when policing had been radically changed in many parts of the land, the villages clustered around Horncastle still relied on the local constable; in Hemingby the officer was a blacksmith when he was not on duty, and of course he was always on call in emergencies. In the 1871 census Gell was listed as a wheelwright master employing two men and two boys. One of his fellow tradesmen was to become his killer. What Gell was faced with when he was killed was nothing ordinary, and needed experts and a force of men to deal with it. This was not possible: Gell was alone.

On 15 October, 1876 the blacksmith William Drant, a man with a long history of violence and savage mood-swings, came home after a night of heavy drinking. His wife had left him some time before, and he was living with his mother at the time of this affair. He had brought home a family friend on the night in question. At first all was well but he began to change mood and to become loud and abusive. This happened after he had complained of feeling ill, and had been taken to the house of a Mrs Goddard for some sort of help, and then had been taken home again. At home he lay down and tried to sleep, but after half an hour he awoke and was dangerously aggressive.

Drant, thirty-seven years old and very sturdy and strong, started to rant about Mrs Goddard trying to poison him; she was extremely patient and tried her best to help him and quieten him, but he got to his feet and threatened her with his fists. From that time on his behaviour can only be called manic. *The Times* reported it in these terms: 'He then called for his mother, who, taking alarm, had run out to find assistance. He went out to fetch her and returned, dragging her by the neck into the kitchen of the house, where he flung her onto the floor, and kneeling on her, he took out a knife and threatened to murder her....'

The situation then escalated into an open confrontation as four neighbours arrived, two carrying wooden rails from a fence. They wrestled him away from his mother and took the knife. One managed to crack Drant on the head and this almost stopped him, yet he recovered and hit back, narrowly missing one of his assailants.

The next stage was an attack on another blacksmith of the village who obviously knew him. It is not clear whether this man, Leggit, tried to appease the rabid Drant or to tackle him, but he was threatened and ran off. There was so much noise in the street by this time that Constable Gell was roused and he arrived just as Drant ran out into the street, swinging a piece of rail. He struck Gell with considerable force. One witness reported: 'It felled him to the ground and repeated blows were heard, sounding as if striking an empty barrel.' The officer was dying, his brain severely damaged. A doctor attended him, but there was no hope and he died the next morning.

While the victim was battling for life, Drant had been caught and carried off to the Horncastle lock-up, the Roundhouse, after being arrested by PC Lawson from nearby Baumber (one and a half miles away), one of the 'new police.' Drant was charged with assault and attempted murder. His only reply was a deranged one: 'They have worked me up so much I couldn't stand it a minute longer, watching and peeping about my house, and I've given Gell one.' What emerged later was that Drant had once been employed by Gell, and had been sacked. There was bad blood between them and witnesses stated that Drant had spoken aggressively against Gell on several occasions. But now, in the lock-up, he began to change mood and eventually said, in a more sober tone, 'Oh dear Oh dear, I am sorry. I did not think I had killed him!' This was said as he was charged with murder at the inquest, held at the Coach and Horses pub at Hemingby, and the charge of wilful murder meant that he was on his way to the next Lincoln assizes.

The trial was on 29 December and Baron Huddleston presided. The prosecution was led by Barnard and Lumley, and the man charged with assembling some kind of defence was Horace Smith. Smith tried his best to approach the issue by way of the theory of insanity at the time, referring to the fits to which the accused was subject. Apart from that, his most relevant defence was that there was no real malice and intent to murder, so manslaughter would seem to be apposite. Smith had to rely, as every lawyer did then, on the McNaghten Rules, stating that if insanity is proven there is an absence of *mens rea*, an intent to kill, and so the jury should commit the prisoner to hospital and confinement for an indefinite period. For Smith, his only basis for argument was the instance of the 'fits.' The McNaghten Rules had been laid down as recently as 1844, and the crucially important words were, 'the accused... at the time of committing the act, must have been labouring under such defect of reason, from disease of the mind, as not to know the nature and quality of the act.' The formative event here was the murder of Sir Robert Peel's private secretary in 1843; the proceedings were halted over a plea of insanity.

In the middle years of the nineteenth century there was a steady realisation that the new science of psychology would play a part in the forensics of crime. The issue of who was bad and who was mad had become, by the 1850s, something demanding debate. A number of medical men working in asylums or in universities began to identify varieties of insanity and distinguish them from such behaviour as epileptic fits. None of this knowledge was likely to be applied in this murder case from remote Lincolnshire.

This was because Huddleston saw no problem at all with Drant's behaviour and general condition. His words were, 'The law presumed all killing to be murder and it rested upon the accused to show that the offence was manslaughter only.' Amazingly, he spoke directly to the jury in his summing-up and directed not to take 'a cowardly refuge' in either alternative [manslaughter or insanity] to avoid responsibility. To be fair, he instructed them with reference to the McNaghten Rules but then led the summary into a recounting of the accused's actions on the fateful day.

Drant, he reminded them, had been subject to no provocation from Gell in terms of an attempt to stop him injuring his mother. He did admit that Drant had had a violent blow to the back of his head, and that 'this had confused him' and rather unexpectedly opened up the possibility of an escape from the murder charge: 'The accused snatched up the first weapon near him and so caused the death of the deceased... the offence might be manslaughter...' The jury took twenty-five minutes to decide that Drant was guilty of murder.

On 7 December a major figure in the new psychology of

deviance wrote a letter to The Times about the case. This was Henry Maudsley, a man who was totally preoccupied with the debate on what was then called 'degeneration' – an off-shoot of Darwinian evolution – which was concerned with understanding criminality in terms of genetic and physiological traits. Maudsley was interested in the epilepsy alleged to be in Drant's medical profile. Maudsley drew attention to the condition of Drant before the onset of the violence: 'On the evening of the murder he had been taken ill in a neighbour's cottage; he was cold, trembled very much and was extremely pale in the face, crying out "Oh Lord save me!".' Maudsley had reflected on the progress of the outburst, read between the lines, and seen a familiar pattern of epileptic symptoms. Arguably, informed public opinion must have been affected by such a prominent medical man writing to the 'Thunderer' about the affair. His lengthy, detailed letter, expressed with care and precision, must have alarmed the legal professionals who had experienced such behaviour in previous cases. That such a respected doctor even noticed an obscure killing was also notably rare.

Maudsley then noted that the most useful information about the illness came from Drant's mother. She had said that her son had had fits since he was a child, and that he had had two such seizures on the Tuesday before the killing, and 'four or five' again on the Wednesday. She went on, 'He usually went violent after these fits. During the time he was in the house on the fateful night he was talking to himself. I washed him about seven o'clock when he was trembling violently and seemed to know nothing.' Quite rightly, Maudsley was acute enough to realise that the person closest to the killer, his mother, was well informed about the 'case history' and in fact expressed the symptoms and habits of the poor victim of the illness very ably and accurately. Once again, we have a Victorian murder trial in which the medical discourse available is very limited and mostly unheard.

Mrs Drant said that the local doctor, Boulton, had attended William several times recently, and that a few days before the incident she had slept with her bedroom door open for fear of her son's likely sudden fit of rage or distraction. All this was just what Maudsley needed to confirm an opinion that should have found a place in the trial: he wrote that such behaviour was 'epileptic mania... well known to have most furious and dangerous consequences.' His description of the condition certainly fits Drant's case: he was described as 'Sane enough, perhaps, and even amiable, industrious and well-behaved during the fits, then these unfortunate persons become immediately after them most violent and destructive beings for a time... and when they come to themselves they are utterly unconscious of what they have done in their state of alienation.' The doctor had seen the significance of the pattern of Drant's actions and suffering, and seen them as a template, a defining sequence of manifestations of the illness.

Perhaps Maudsley caught the real mood of the Hemingby people after the trial, because he put on his academic tone and said that if a lecturer were to be given a case study of Drant he would not be able to quote 'a more typical example than the painful case of William Drant who is now lying under sentence of death.' Drant's neighbours and fellow citizens petitioned the Home Office, asking for a reprieve, and it was granted. He was detained 'during Her Majesty's Pleasure.'

It was *The Times* reporter who had called this 'a painful case,' and it is a fitting description. As for the victim, Constable Gell, he was buried in the churchyard at Hemingby, surely respected and admired by his friends and clients.

Maudsley, who had played a part in helping the case to a satisfactory conclusion, went on to found a centre for research into mental illness, a happy departure from the normal practice of setting up yet another asylum. Ironically, only a short distance from Hemingby, the Lincoln Bracebridge asylum had by 1890 almost a thousand patients inside its dour walls. Sadly for Drant, there is no doubt that he faced a future in which his epileptic attacks would take place in very unpleasant circumstances, although there would be caring professionals caring for him.

There had been other deaths besides Gell's in the line of duty in the new police, and acts of heroism; only three years before this homicide PC Tidbury had received a medal for gallantry for jumping from a moving train to recapture a prisoner. Two years after the Hemingby drama PC Little had rescued a lady 'from a most perilous position' on a rooftop. The Albert medal was created in 1866, and preceded what was to become the King's Police medal in 1909. Unfortunately there was no such award for Gell; there will never be anything 'heroic' about running across town and meeting a crazed man in a homicidal fit, but somehow we have to feel that Gell deserves more than an honourable gravestone. Maybe this story, retelling those tragic events, will encourage us to think again about the more routine deaths in police history.

Chapter 9

Police and Criminal Evidence Act (1984)

The Police and Criminal Evidence Act 1984 is an Act of Parliament which instituted a legislative framework for the powers of police officers in England and Wales to combat crime, and provided Codes of Practice for the exercise of those powers. PACE came into force on 1st January 1986 with the aim of establishing a balance between the powers of the police in England and Wales and the rights and freedoms of the public. Equivalent provision is made with alternative legislation in Scotland and Northern Ireland.

Although PACE is a fairly wide ranging piece of legislation, it mainly deals with police powers to search an individual or premises, including their powers to gain entry to those premises, the handling of exhibits seized from those searches, and the treatment of suspects in custody, including interviews. Criminal liability may arise if the specific terms of the Act itself are not conformed to, whereas failure to conform to the Codes of Practice while searching, arresting, detaining or interviewing a suspect may lead to evidence obtained during the process becoming inadmissible in Court.

PACE was significantly modified by the Serious Organised Crime and Police Act 2005 which replaced nearly all existing powers of arrest, including the category of arrestable offences, with a new general power of arrest for all offences. PACE is applicable not only to police officers but to anyone conducting a Criminal investigation including Her Majesty's Revenue and Customs (HMRC) amongst others.

The 1981 Brixton riots and the subsequent Scarman report were key factors in the passage of PACE. It is probably the most important policing legislation for many years and has a profound impact on how police officers conduct their investigations. During this chapter I'm going to summarise a few of the key sections from the Act.

Stop and search

Section 1 of PACE gives police the power to stop and search any person or vehicle (including anything in or on a vehicle) in a public place for stolen or prohibited articles if the officer has reasonable grounds to suspect that they may find such articles. The police can detain a person or vehicle for the purpose of a search under this power. A prohibited article includes offensive weapons (knives, knuckledusters etc), any article made, adapted or intended for use in an offence of burglary, theft or taking a vehicle without consent (jemmy, keys etc), fraud (false ID etc), criminal damage (spray paint etc) or any prohibited firework. If such an article is found then the officer has the power to seize it and the person may be liable to arrest.

Search warrants

Police can apply to a Magistrate for a search warrant authorising them to search premises under a range of different legislative powers including the Theft Act 1968, the Misuse of Drugs Act 1971 and the Firearms Act 1968 to name but a few. PACE also contains a power under Section 8 for a Justice of the Peace (Magistrate) to authorise entry and search of premises for evidence. Providing that an indictable offence (triable in a Crown Court) has been committed, there is relevant material likely to be of substantial value to the investigation on the premises and entry would not be practicable without a warrant, a Magistrate (if satisfied that the application is lawful and necessary) may issue a warrant to enter and search the premises.

Sometimes, particularly in more serious cases, police will apply for a search warrant under Section 8 PACE before they attend an address seeking to arrest a person. There are other powers under PACE which entitle police to search premises without a warrant in certain circumstances following arrest, but if the suspect isn't present or the property is unoccupied, these powers cannot be used. A Section 8 PACE warrant would entitle the police to look for evidence such as a weapon, bloodstained clothing or other relevant items.

CASE STUDY – SECTION 8 PACE ACT

Police officers suspected that drugs were present at a residential address. A section 8 PACE Act warrant was obtained and enforced at the address. The warrant authorised officers to search the premises. The warrant was in relation to drugs but wasn't sworn out under the Misuse of Drugs Act 1971.

The householder, a member of the public, complained that she had been strip searched and was unhappy about the manner in which this was conducted and the officers who conducted the search. A complaint was made to the police. During the course of the complaint investigation it was found that the staff enforcing the warrant wrongly believed that the warrant authorised them to search anyone found on the premises in addition to the premises itself. Further enquiries revealed that this was a commonly held belief throughout the force, both for officers authorising Section 8 warrants and those enforcing them. The force Professional Standards Department (PSD) took immediate steps to correct this. A force-wide message was issued clarifying that a Section 8 PACE Act warrant allowed the attending officers to search the premises only, not the occupants.

The Police National Learning Database (PNLD) in respect of Section 8 PACE shows the following in the notes: 'Search persons – warrants issued under the provision of this section do not authorise a constable to search persons who are on those premises. Such persons may only be searched if arrested or if there is a specific power to search in the warrant (eg warrants issued under Section 23 Misuse of Drugs Act 1971 or Section 46 Firearms Act 1968.)

Entry for purpose of arrest

Section 17 PACE Act allows a police officer to enter and search any premises for the purpose of executing an arrest warrant, arresting a person for an indictable offence or arresting a person for one of a specified number of offences (including public order and driving under the influence of drink/drugs). Section 17 also applies to the recapture of a person who is unlawfully at large, having absconded from prison or a Young Offenders Institute (YOI) and the recapture of any person who is unlawfully at large and being pursued by the police. The final part of Section 17 relates to police being able to enter and search premises to save life or limb or prevent serious damage to property. This covers situations such as when a person has collapsed and police need to gain entry to provide medical assistance or in a house fire.

Entry and search after arrest

Section 18 PACE Act (amended by the Serious Organised Crime and Police Act 2005) refers to the entry and search of a premises occupied or controlled by a person who is under arrest for an indictable offence (triable at Crown Court) if the officer has reasonable grounds for suspecting that there is evidence on the premises which is related to that offence or some other indictable offence which is connected with or similar to that offence. The power may not be exercised unless a police officer of the rank of Inspector or above has authorised it in writing. Most of the Section 18 searches are carried out when a person is in police detention, having been arrested and taken there by police.

There are times, however, where this is not the case and which are catered for within Section 18 subsection (5) as follows. 'A police officer may conduct a search before the person is taken to a police station without obtaining the authority of an Inspector, if the presence of that person at a place (other than a police station) is necessary for the effective investigation of the offence'. If this happens the officer should inform an Inspector (or above) that they have made the search as soon as practicable after they have conducted it. An officer who authorises a search or is informed of a search under Section 18 (5) shall record in writing the grounds for the search and the nature of the evidence sought. If the person who occupies or controls the premises at the time of the search is in police detention when the record is to be made, the officer shall make the record as part of their custody record.

Around 75 per cent of all property searches in England and Wales are carried out under Section 18 PACE Act. This is an effective power, when used lawfully and appropriately, of searching premises occupied or controlled by arrested people and often results in the recovery of property relevant to the investigation.

Search upon arrest

Under Section 32 PACE Act a police officer may search an arrested person, at a place other than the police station, if the officer has reasonable grounds for believing that the arrested person may present a danger to themselves or others, possess anything they may use to assist in escaping from lawful custody or anything which may be evidence relating to an offence. If the offence for which a person is arrested is an indictable offence, Section 32 also allows entry and search of any premises where the person was when arrested or immediately before being arrested for evidence relating to the offence. The powers to search a person only allow a police officer to request the removal of an outer coat, jacket or gloves in public but they do authorise a search of a person's mouth. Any relevant items found can be seized and retained by police. Section 32 is used when police have arrested somebody and need to search that person or premises straight away for the reasons outlined.

Review of police detention

Section 40 PACE Act deals with reviews of people who are in police detention in connection with the investigation of an offence. If the person has been arrested and charged with an offence, the review will be carried out by the custody officer (usually a Sergeant). If the person has been arrested but not charged, the review will be carried out by an officer of at least the rank of Inspector who hasn't been directly involved in the investigation of the offence(s). The purpose of a review is to look at the circumstances and determine whether that person's continued detention is still necessary. There are timescales when the reviews should be carried out. The first review should be not later than six hours after the detention of the person was first authorised. The second review should be not later than nine hours after the first. Subsequent reviews should be at intervals of not more than nine hours. For example, if a person was arrested at 10.00am and their detention was authorised at 10.30am, their first review should be no later than 4.30pm. If they remained in police detention, their second review would be due no later than 01.30am the following morning. If a person is likely to be sleeping when the review is due, it's possible that the review may be brought forward so that the detained person isn't unduly disturbed.

So, in our example, the second review may be carried out at 11.30pm (rather than 01.30am). This would mean that the next review would be due no later than 8.30am (nine hours). Before determining whether to authorise a person's continued detention the review officer should give that person (unless asleep) or any solicitor representing that person who is available at the time of the review, an opportunity to make representations about the detention.

Limits on period of detention without charge

Subject to certain other sections of the PACE Act which I will cover shortly, a person should not be kept in police detention for more than 24 hours without being charged with an offence. The time from which the period of detention of a person is to be calculated (known as the 'relevant time') will be the time that person arrives at the relevant police station or the time 24 hours after the time of that person's arrest whichever is the earlier. In the case of a person who is arrested outside England and Wales the 'relevant time' will be either the time that person arrives at the first police station to which they are taken in the police area in England or Wales in which the offence for which they have been arrested is being investigated or the time 24 hours after the time of that person's entry into England and Wales whichever is the earlier. If you voluntarily attend a police station and are subsequently arrested at the station then the 'relevant time' will be the time of your arrest.

This is a particularly complex part of the PACE Act covered by Section 41 which really only requires closer inspection if a person is arrested outside England and Wales on behalf of another Force or is transported a long distance which may take longer than 24 hours.

Authorisation of continued detention

Where a police officer of the rank of Superintendent or above, responsible for the police station at which a person is detained, has reasonable grounds for believing that the detention of that person without charge is necessary to secure or preserve evidence relating to an offence for which they are under arrest or to obtain such evidence by questioning them, an offence for which they are under arrest is an indictable offence and the investigation is being conducted diligently and expeditiously, they may authorise the keeping of that person in police detention for a period expiring at or before 36 hours after the 'relevant time'.

A Superintendent (or above) cannot provide the authority for continued detention more than 24 hours after the 'relevant time' or before the second review has been carried out. In other words, the Superintendent, if satisfied that the conditions are met, must provide the authority after the 15th hour of detention but before the 24th hour. They can authorise up to an additional 12 hours detention, taking the total detention time to 36 hours, but they may authorise less than 12 hours.

* * *

To summarise, the decision to detain a person up to 24 hours without charge is made by an Inspector. If the investigating officer wishes to keep the person in detention for longer than 24 hours they must seek the authority of a Superintendent who can, if satisfied, authorise up to a further 12 hours detention, making a total of 36 hours.

Warrants of further detention

Section 43 PACE Act explains the procedure when police want to keep a person in detention for longer than the 36 hours outlined in the previous section. Any such application has to be made by a police officer to a Magistrates Court who can, if satisfied that the further detention of that person is justified, issue a warrant of further detention authorising the keeping of that person in police custody for an additional period of time which the Magistrates Court deems fit, having regard to the evidence before it. The period can be up to, but no longer than 36 hours, making a total of 72 hours detention. They may, of course, only authorise a further 6 or 12 hours but they can authorise 36 hours.

The same criteria apply as with the Superintendent's extension in that the warrant of further detention can only be justified if detention without charge is necessary to secure or preserve evidence relating to an offence for which under arrest, obtain such evidence by questioning, the offence is an indictable offence and the investigation is being conducted diligently and expeditiously. The officer making the application must attend Court together with the arrested person and their solicitor (if legally represented). Any application for a warrant of further detention must be made before the expiry of the first 36 hours in custody but if it isn't practicable for a Magistrates Court to sit at the time when the 36 hours expires, the Court will sit as soon as practicable within the following 6 hours.

During my police career I have applied for warrants of further detention personally and can say that they can be a particularly challenging and stressful experience for the investigating officer. On one particular occasion, I was rigorously cross-examined and accused of a lack of effort by three solicitors representing their clients who were in custody on suspicion of Murder. Unlike the cross-examination at a Crown Court where the Judge may interject if the line of questioning appears to be unfair, in my experience no such rules appear to apply in some detention cases.

Extension of warrant of further detention

Section 44 allows a Magistrates Court to extend a warrant of further detention up to a maximum of 96 hours from the time at which the person first arrived at the police station (the 'relevant time'). The same criteria and procedures apply as with the warrant of further detention. The Magistrates can authorise the full additional detention time or part of it but, in any event, once the 96 hour limit has been reached, the arrested person must be charged or released. There are separate rules for terrorism cases which allow for longer detention periods if justified.

Searches of detained persons

Section 54 relates to the searching of a person who has been arrested and taken to the police station. The custody officer (normally a uniformed Sergeant) has to establish everything a person has with him when arrested and make a note of the items on the custody record. Clothes and personal effects may only be seized by police if the custody officer believes that the person from whom they are seized may use them to cause physical injury to themselves or any other person, to damage property, to interfere with evidence, to assist escape or has reasonable grounds for believing that they may be evidence relating to an offence. Where anything is seized, the person from whom it is seized shall be told the reason for the seizure unless they are violent, likely to become violent or incapable of understanding what is said to them. The officer carrying out the search should be of the same sex as the person searched.

CASE LAW - SECTION 54 PACE ACT

The case of Lindley v Rutter (1981) relates to a case where there was an instruction given to Exeter police officers that the bras of all female prisoners should be removed and retained for safety reasons. This instruction was held to be unlawful as clothing should only be removed under Section 54 to prevent escape, injury or destruction of evidence. Each case should be taken on it's individual merits and what can never be justified is the adoption of any particular measures without regard to all the circumstances of a case.

Intimate searches

An intimate search is a physical examination of body orifices other than the mouth and could include the ear, nose, rectum or vagina. If a police officer of at least the rank of Inspector has reasonable grounds to believe that a person who has been arrested and is in police detention may have concealed on them anything which they could use to cause physical injury to themselves or others and may do so whilst in police detention, the officer may authorise an intimate search of that person. Any search should be carried out by a 'suitably qualified person' unless the Inspector considers this is not practicable, in which case it can be carried out by a police officer.

Alternatively, if there are reasonable grounds to believe that a detained person may have a Class A drug concealed on them and was in possession of it with the 'appropriate criminal intent' before arrest, the officer may authorise an intimate search. An intimate search relating to a drug offence only, should not be carried out at a police station and must be conducted by a 'suitably qualified person' (a registered medical practitioner or nurse) and not a police officer. The search should take place at a medical facility, ideally a hospital with resuscitation facilities. A search relating to a drug offence only cannot be carried out unless the detained person has given their consent in writing. Types of Class A drug include heroin, cocaine (including 'crack') and MDMA (ecstasy). The 'appropriate criminal intent' means either an intent to commit an offence of possession with intent to supply to another or exportation with intent to avoid a prohibition or restriction.

An officer can't authorise an intimate search of a person for anything unless they have reasonable grounds to believe that the item(s) cannot be found without the search being of an intimate nature. As with other searches, any police officer who carries out an intimate search must be the same sex as the person searched.

Right to have someone informed when arrested

One of the rights you are given upon arrival at a police station is to have someone informed of your arrest. This person would normally be a friend, relative or other person who is likely to take an interest in your welfare. Section 56 PACE Act states that this right can be delayed if you are in police detention for an indictable offence (triable at Crown Court) and a police officer of at least the rank of Inspector authorises such a delay (this is sometimes referred to as being held 'incommunicado'.) An officer can only authorise a delay where they have reasonable grounds to believe that informing the named person of the arrest will lead to interference with or harm to evidence connected with an indictable offence or interference with or physical injury to other people or, will lead to the alerting of other persons suspected of having committed such an offence but not yet arrested for it or, will hinder the recovery of any property obtained as a result of such an offence. Once the reason for authorising any delay ceases to exist, there may be no further delay in permitting the exercise of the right. In any event, the person in custody must be permitted to exercise the right within 36 hours from arrival at the police station ('relevant time') even if that right was initially delayed.

Access to legal advice

Another right you are entitled to is to consult a solicitor privately at any time (Section 58). This right can also be delayed for the same reasons as Section 56 (interference with evidence etc). Again, once the reasons for delay cease to exist, the person must be permitted to exercise the right and, in any event, within 36 hours of the 'relevant time'. A key difference between the delay of this right and Section 56 is that the authorising officer must be of at least the rank of Superintendent.

Intimate samples

Section 62 PACE Act covers the taking of intimate samples from a person in police detention. An intimate sample is a sample of blood, semen or other tissue fluid, urine, pubic hair, dental impression or a swab from a body orifice (excluding the mouth).

Such a sample can only be taken if a police officer of at least the rank of Inspector authorises it AND the person in detention consents to having it taken. It is sometimes portrayed that police can take blood from an arrested person without consent and using force. This is not the case as the above makes clear. An officer may only authorise the taking of an intimate sample if they have reasonable grounds to suspect the involvement of the person in a recordable offence (any offence where the police must keep records on the Police National Computer) and that the sample will tend to confirm or disprove their involvement in that offence. Most types of intimate samples will be taken only by a registered medical practitioner or a registered health care professional. On occasion, a police officer may take a urine sample depending on the circumstances. A dental impression will only be taken by a registered dentist. A detained person can refuse to provide an intimate sample but if they do so, without good cause, it's possible that a Court/Jury could draw an adverse inference from this refusal at any future Court case.

Despite the reference to semen samples, this is not something which the police can or do take. It relates to items which may be stained or parts of the body to be swabbed for the presence of semen.

Non-intimate samples

Section 63 PACE Act covers the taking of non-intimate samples from a person in police detention. A non-intimate sample is a sample of hair (other than pubic hair), a sample taken from a nail (or under a nail), a swab taken from a person's body, including the mouth, but not any other body orifice, saliva, a footprint or similar impression of part of the body. Such a sample can be taken from a person without their consent if they are in detention having been arrested for a recordable offence, and either they have not had a non-intimate sample of the same type and of the same part of the body taken in the course of the investigation of the offence by the police or they have had a sample taken but it has proved insufficient.

A non-intimate sample may be taken from a person without the appropriate consent unlike intimate samples where consent is always required. No adverse inference can be drawn by a person's failure or refusal to provide a non-intimate sample. In certain circumstances, such as when a person is being held in custody by police on the authority of a Court or where a person has been given a police caution or convicted for a recordable offence, a non-intimate sample may be taken without the appropriate consent on the authority of a police officer of at least the rank of Inspector. Non-intimate samples may be taken by a registered medical practitioner or a suitably trained police officer.

Confessions

If, in any proceedings the prosecution proposes to give in evidence a confession made by an accused person, it's represented to the Court that the confession was or may have been obtained by oppression of the person who made it or in consequence of anything said or done which was likely, in the circumstances existing at the time, to render any confession unreliable, the Court shall not allow the confession to be given in evidence unless the prosecution can show beyond reasonable doubt that it wasn't. In other words, if any confession appears to have been obtained through unfair means then the chances are that it will be rendered inadmissible and not used as evidence in the case. For the purposes of this Section (76) oppression includes torture, inhuman or degrading treatment and the use or threat of violence. Section 77 states that where the case against the accused depends wholly or substantially on a confession and the Court is satisfied that the person making the confession is 'mentally handicapped' and that the confession was not made in the presence of an' independent person', the Court should warn the Jury that there is special need for caution before convicting the accused in reliance on the confession due to the circumstances. An 'independent person' does not include a police officer or anyone employed or engaged on police purposes. The term 'mentally handicapped' relates to a person who is in a state of arrested or incomplete development of mind which includes significant impairment of intelligence and social functioning.

Section 78 deals with the exclusion of unfair evidence obtained as detailed in Sections 76 and 77. It states that, in any proceedings, the Court may refuse to allow evidence on which the prosecution proposes to rely if it appears that, having regard to all the circumstances, including the circumstances in which the evidence was obtained, the admission of the evidence would have such an adverse effect on the fairness of the proceedings that the Court ought not to admit it.

CASE LAW – R v Trussler (1988)

The confession of a drug addict was excluded because he had been in police custody for 18 hours without any rest whereas PACE required that he be given at least 8 hours rest in any 24 hour period. The confession was rendered unreliable.

R v Everett (1988)

The Court of Appeal quashed a conviction for indecent assault based upon the appellant's confession. He had a mental age of 8 and, had the police realised this fact, they should have ensured the presence of an independent person to look after his welfare.

R v Delaney (1989)

The Court of Appeal quashed a conviction for indecent assault based on the admissions of the accused who had an IQ of 80. The psychiatric evidence made clear that he was poorly equipped to cope with sustained interrogation and the longer this went on the greater the confusion felt by the accused. The requirements of PACE should have been observed and the conviction was held to be unsafe or unsatisfactory.

CASE STUDY – BREACH OF PACE ACT

Detective Superintendent Steve Fulcher was the SIO in charge of a case involving Christopher Halliwell, who initially managed to avoid a charge of Murder despite leading Detectives to the spot where Rebecca Godden was buried. Halliwell was jailed for life in October 2012 after admitting the Murder of Sian O'Callaghan as she made her way home from a night out in Swindon in March 2011. The taxi driver was arrested days later on suspicion of kidnapping Miss O'Callaghan and, during a three-hour period, Halliwell confessed to murdering Miss O'Callaghan and took the SIO to her shallow grave. He then made the startling admission that he had killed another woman and showed the SIO where Miss Godden was buried.

Under the rules of PACE, which govern the questioning of suspects, Halliwell should have been cautioned several times during the crucial three-hour period but wasn't.

The SIO admitted that, during the questioning of Halliwell, which lasted nine minutes, he asked Halliwell to confess to where Miss O'Callaghan was, dead or alive. During a Court hearing in 2012, the SIO stated that even after Halliwell had offered him "another one", meaning a second body, and taken him to the field where the remains of Miss Godden were later found, the taxi driver was still not cautioned. Later, at the police station, Halliwell declined to make any comment about what had happened earlier. Mrs Justice Cox ruled that Halliwell's confessions were inadmissible, as there had been "wholesale and irretrievable breaches of PACE and the Codes". With no other evidence tying Halliwell to the Murder of Miss Godden, the prosecution did not oppose an application by his defence team to dismiss the charge.

Some four years later on 19th September 2016, following a trial at Bristol Crown Court, Halliwell was convicted of the Murder of Rebecca Godden after Detectives uncovered other evidence linking him to the killing.

The original SIO, Detective Superintendent Fulcher, was found guilty of Gross Misconduct at a police disciplinary hearing in 2014 and was given a final written warning. He resigned from his force the following year. He maintained that the way he handled the questioning of Halliwell without giving him access to a solicitor was the "right and moral thing to do", adding "I felt that I correctly prioritised the human rights of the victims and their families, balanced against the rights of the perpetrator. It's perfectly clear that, had I not acted as I did, neither Sian nor Becky would ever have been found and Halliwell would be free to abduct and kill other girls". A relative of Miss Godden paid tribute to the actions of Mr Fulcher and stated that "I would like to thank him from the bottom of my heart for bringing my little girl home. I will always respect him and be indebted to him for making that moral decision as a police officer. He should never have suffered the consequences, the loss of reputation and career for doing such a thing".

This case demonstrates the type of dilemma faced by SIO's on a fairly regular basis. As a former SIO I can totally understand why Mr Fulcher acted in the way he did and we should not forget that his actions allowed two families to find out what had happened to their loved ones. The case also demonstrates the potential consequences which a breach of PACE can have on criminal proceedings.

Conclusion

I hope that you have found this section interesting and helpful. I have tried to provide an overview of some of the key elements of PACE which, as you can see, can be rather complex at times and open to interpretation. In addition to the Act itself, there are Codes of Practice (mentioned elsewhere in this book) which provide guidance. When a person is arrested and taken to the police station, one of their rights is to look at the Codes of Practice, a book governing police powers and procedures. It would make rather good 'bedtime reading' but is, nonetheless, part of what is probably the most important policing legislation for many years.

Chapter 10

The Criminal Courts

Present

Criminal cases will be heard in one of two Courts. The Magistrates Court tends to deal with the less serious cases including traffic offences, public order and assault/theft on the lower end of the scale. The Magistrates Court is limited in terms of sentencing to a maximum of 6 months imprisonment. On occasions, it may be necessary to refer the case to the Crown Court for sentencing if the defendant faces a lengthier term of imprisonment.

Alternatively, a number of cases are referred from the Magistrates Court directly to the Crown Court who have far greater powers in terms of sentencing. As the name suggests, the Magistrates Court consists of one or more Magistrates (known as 'the bench') who hear cases and decide how they should be progressed. These cases could be trials where all the evidence is heard from witnesses who attend (referred to as 'live' evidence) or their witness statements are read out to the Court.

A high percentage of cases now dealt with at the Magistrates Court are 'guilty' pleas for relatively minor offences. No witnesses are required in these cases, the facts of the case are read out and the Magistrates decide on the appropriate sentence.

At the Magistrates Court the prosecution (generally the police) are represented by a solicitor from the Crown Prosecution Service (CPS) and the defence, if represented, by a local firm of solicitors or a solicitor of the defendant's choice. Even though the Magistrates Court has limited powers, every case must pass through this Court to be formally sent to the Crown Court. This process is known as 'committal' and is often as simple as a brief appearance by a defendant so that the Magistrate(s) can agree that the case fits the criteria for the higher Court. Following 'committal' the Magistrates Court will have no further involvement with the case.

The Crown Court deals with all cases above the sentencing powers of the Magistrates Court, up to and including murder. They also deal with a number of 'guilty' pleas but a large proportion of Crown Court time is taken up with criminal trials. When a defendant pleads 'not guilty' to an offence, the case will be prepared for trial. Depending on the offence and the number of witnesses required, the trial could last from a few days to several weeks. When a case first appears at the Crown Court, there will be some discussion between the prosecution and defence as to how long it is likely to take before both parties are ready for a trial. A court appearance specifically for this purpose will normally take place well in advance of a trial. This is known as a Plea and Case Management Hearing (PCMH). The intention of this hearing is to discuss any difficulties with the case and confirm Court, barrister and witness availability so that a trial date can be set. If the court is particularly busy it's possible that a trial may not take place for several months. A single Judge will sit at a Crown Court to deal with all cases in that particular courtroom. Each court will have their own Judge. Also present in court will be the clerk who sits at the front directly below the Judge and a stenographer who records everything which is said in court during cases. The prosecution and defence will be represented by a barrister each. The prosecution barrister will have been instructed by the CPS. It's likely that a CPS lawyer will also be present to liase with the prosecution barrister and the police.

The Crown Court trial

At a Crown Court trial, once the jury have been selected and sworn in, the prosecution and defence barristers will deliver their opening speeches outlining their respective cases. In the majority of trials there will be one barrister for each team but in particularly serious cases, such as murder, there will be two sets of barristers on each team. The lead barrister will be a Queen's Counsel (Now King's Counsel), a mark of outstanding ability, appointed by the Queen and instructed to lead the prosecution in very serious or complex cases. The QC will be supported by a Junior Barrister who will present certain parts of the case.

The trial will begin with the prosecution case where evidence is provided by witnesses called by the prosecution (also known as the 'Crown'). These witnesses may be asked to give 'live' evidence in person or, if agreed by all parties in advance, the relevant contents of their witness statement will be read out in court. If the witness is called to give evidence they will be invited into the witness box and required to take the oath or affirm. The oath consists of the following words "I swear by Almighty God (or other religious belief) that the evidence I shall give shall be the truth, the whole truth and nothing but the truth". The affirmation as follows "I do solemnly, sincerely and truly declare and affirm that the evidence I shall give shall be the truth, the whole truth and nothing but the truth". The witness will then be introduced to the court and give their account (known as 'evidence-in-chief'). They will then be cross-examined by the defence and, if required, can be re-examined by the prosecution. This process will continue for each prosecution witness. Throughout the trial there may be evidence such as CCTV footage or police interviews played to the court. The Judge may ask questions of any witness throughout the trial. Once all prosecution evidence has been heard, the defence then call any witnesses they wish to. The process is then reversed with the defence leading their witnesses through 'evidence-in-chief' before cross-examination by the prosecution. The defence may call the person on trial (the defendant) to give evidence but there is no compulsion for them to do so. Once all evidence has been heard the prosecution and defence make their 'closing speeches' and the Judge carries out a 'summing up' before the Jury is invited to retire to consider their verdict.

The verdict
The burden of proof in a criminal case is one of 'beyond reasonable doubt', higher than in a civil case when it is the 'balance of probabilities'. The jury consists of 12 people, a mixture of men and women selected from the community, who will be asked to consider all of the evidence and try to reach a verdict on which they all agree (referred to as a unanimous verdict). After a period of time decided by the Judge, if the jury have been unable to reach a unanimous verdict, they will be called back into court and advised that they should continue to try to reach a unanimous verdict but if unable to do so, a majority verdict of 11 to 1 or 10 to 2 would be accepted. The two main verdicts in criminal cases are 'guilty' or 'not guilty'.

There is however a third conclusion which could be reached if the jury are unable to agree a majority verdict, no matter how much time they may be given. This situation is known as a 'hung jury' which would result in the jury being discharged from the case. If this happens, the prosecution have to decide, at some point, whether they will apply for a re-trial with a new jury or discontinue the case. Their decision will depend on a number of factors including the seriousness of the case, public interest and witness availability. If the verdict is 'not guilty' the defendant will be released from the dock (if on bail) or released from prison custody (if remanded) once the appropriate paperwork has been completed. If they are serving another custodial sentence already they will be returned to prison to continue that sentence. If the verdict is 'guilty' they may be sentenced straight away by the Judge or the case may be adjourned to another date for sentencing. A decision on bail will be made by the Judge who will take into consideration factors such as the seriousness of the offence, likelihood of absconding and the commission of further offences. The jury system is a part of our criminal justice system which has evolved over centuries and provides a fair and proper means by which to establish guilt or innocence.

Past
HABEAS CORPUS
After the fall of the Bastille and the first stages of the French Revolution in 1789, the next thirty years brought a series of repressive laws in Britain as paranoia, fear of a knock-on effect revolution and widespread treason grew. In the 1790s there were proclamations against seditious literature, and *habeas corpus* was suspended (meaning that people could be tried *in absentia*); in 1795 the notion of treason was extended to cover spoken and written words and the two Combination Acts of 1799 and 1800 prevented gatherings in public of any numbers above six people.

The writ of *habeas corpus* is a fundamental defence of the human right of being present at his or her trial. When that was suspended, in times of national emergency, it meant that the regulation of custody became an elastic concept. The treatment of the prisoner and the following trial could be exploited for quite nasty and cruel aims.

The criminal law followed suit; since the mid eighteenth century there had been a proliferation of capital crimes, but in the Regency years there were yet more statutes. There were also dozens of acts to prevent 'seditious assemblies' and this led to arrests, assaults and a swelling of the gaol population. At the most notorious of these gatherings was Peterloo, a meeting at St Peter's Fields in Manchester in 1819 which was intended as a peaceful meeting but the crowd numbered over 60,000 and the authorities reacted by sending in the local yeomanry to arrest the main speaker, Henry Hunt, and then anarchy was feared so the hussars went to help, swords drawn. The result was that eleven people were killed and over 400 injured.

One result of all this was that the gaols had a growing number of radical intellectuals in their cells. In addition to this, these revolutionary enemies of the state, as they were perceived, were complemented by another massive influx of prisoners: soldiers and sailors of Napoleon's army, and in 1812, American prisoners because for that year we were at war with the United States as well.

As far as local gaols were concerned, Sir Robert Peel's Gaol Act of 1823 at last put down rules for the management of these places, with inmates classified and separated according to sex, age and the nature of offences. But the government had to cater for the prisoners of war, so specific prisons were used, along with old decommissioned ship, known as 'hulks.'

This new category of prisoner was labelled either military or political, but the latter group only by the radicals themselves. In other words, such prisoners as Chartists (in the 1830s) or writers often considered themselves to be 'political' and therefore to be exempt from prison labour. One of the most important events in this period was the trouble caused by the Chartist prisoners, notably by William Martin. What has become known as the Sheffield Plot of 1840 involved Samuel Holberry, William Martin, Thomas Booker and others devising an attempted coup in Sheffield in which they planned to seize the town hall and the Fortune Inn, set fire to the magistrate's court, and then, linking with other Chartists, form an insurrection also in Nottingham and Rotherham. Their plot was betrayed by James Allen and Lord Howard the Lord Lieutenant, took immediate action. The result was that, at York Assizes on 22 March 1840, Holberry was sentenced to four years at Northallerton for seditious conspiracy: 'and at the expiration of that period to be bound himself in £50 and to find two sureties in ten shillings each, to keep the peace towards his Majesty's subjects.' He was leniently treated; under an Act of 1351 he could have had life imprisonment.

Chapter 11

Missing Persons

Present

In the year 2016 more than 300,000 calls were made to the police reporting a missing person. The majority of these people are found safe and well but some of them may have been the victim of a crime, including murder. There are a number of charities who help in the search for missing people but the key elements of a missing person investigation are the responsibility of the police.

Risk assessment

One of the most important features of a missing person investigation is the risk assessment which should be carried out by the first officer/staff to receive the report of a missing person, normally the force control room or police station front counter. The risk assessment should be continually reviewed and capable of change according to the circumstances. The police grade missing persons as either High, Medium or Low risk depending on a number of risk factors including their age, vulnerability (mental health or other issues), intoxication (drug and/or alcohol), any information which suggests that they may be subjected to crime, such as kidnapping, sexual exploitation or violence, and missing history amongst others. For example a 12 year old girl who hasn't gone missing before, is believed to have been contacted by a man in his 40's on social media and hasn't been seen or heard from in several hours will be graded as High risk whereas a 35 year old man who goes missing regularly, isn't vulnerable in any way and always returns after 2–3 hours is likely to be graded as Low risk. The risk grading determines the type of enquiries conducted and the urgency of those enquiries. Missing person investigations have to be reviewed by a senior officer at regular intervals.

Searches

An important line of enquiry in any missing person investigation are the searches carried out by police and other specialist teams, whether indoors or outdoors. The house where a missing person lives should always be thoroughly searched, not only for the person but also for signs of why they may have gone missing or where they may have gone. The police have a number of specially-trained officers, known as POLSA (Police Search Advisor) officers who should be consulted whenever searches are to be carried out. Outdoor searching is often resource intensive and particularly time-consuming, as such the use of POLSA provides a focus for the areas to be searched and the sequence of those searches. Searches of properties should include the loft, garage, vehicle(s) and any outbuildings.

There are a number of experts who assist police, particularly during searches of vast wooded and other challenging locations. They include search and rescue dogs, mountain rescue, Air Support Unit and the police Underwater Search Unit (UWSU).

Lines of enquiry

There are many lines of enquiry which are likely to be followed during a missing person investigation. The last person to see the missing person is often a very important witness who can provide information to assist police. This can include description, clothing, state of mind and intentions. Closed circuit television (CCTV) in any relevant areas should be checked as soon as possible to see whether it provides useful information.

If the missing person is believed to be in possession of a mobile phone then it's possible that the phone could be located and information relating to the recent use of the phone obtained by police. The use of bank cards may also help police to locate the missing person. All addresses connected to the person (friends, family, workplace, favourite places) should be checked.

Contact with the local press may be required to circulate details, a photograph of the person and appeal for information. A record should be kept of all enquiries carried out and the result of those enquiries.

CASE STUDY – THE DISAPPEARANCE OF TIA SHARP

In August 2012 a young girl called Tia Sharp (12 years old) was reported to have left her grandmother's house in South London to go shopping for some shoes. She didn't return and was subsequently reported missing. The last person to see her before she left was the grandmother's boyfriend, Stuart Hazell. A number of enquiries were carried out by police. Due to the circumstances and Tia's age, the case attracted significant media attention.

Members of the family, including Hazell, made televised appeals for information. Fifty-five sightings of Tia were reported by the public but none could be substantiated. CCTV was checked and searches conducted to no avail.

On 10th August during a further search, a body was discovered in the loft at the grandmother's house. The body was wrapped in a sheet and contained within a black bag. At this time, Hazell had disappeared from the house without explanation. Later that day he was located and arrested. The grandmother and a neighbour were also arrested during the investigation (the grandmother was later cleared of any involvement, the neighbour convicted of wasting police time).

On 12th August 2012 Stuart Hazell was charged with the

murder of Tia Sharp. He was remanded in custody and kept in isolation for his own safety. The body was confirmed to be that of Tia Sharp although the cause of death couldn't be established, probably due to the timescales and conditions. The absence of a definitive cause of death would be likely to make the prosecution case even more challenging than it already was.

Hazell pleaded not guilty to murder and on 7th May 2013 his trial began. Six days into the trial he changed his plea to guilty and was subsequently sentenced to life imprisonment with a minimum term of 38 years. The recovery of child pornography images linked to Hazell suggest a sexual motive but, to date, Hazell has refused to disclose why or how he murdered Tia Sharp.

Past

TEACHER DISAPPEARS

Israel Blum was Second Master at Bradford High School in the 1850s, and was said to live a regular, disciplined life, being a reliable and morally upright member of the school community. On the day he travelled out of town, never to be seen again alive by anyone who knew him, he had taught in the morning as usual, and then talked with another member of staff. We know that he bought a copy of Dickens's *David Copperfield* at Byles' bookshop and then went to the Midland Station.

On that occasion, he told lies to his colleague Anderson: he said he was planning to so some scientific work at home, whereas he was really dashing to catch a train. There has to be a reason for both the urgency and the need to evade telling not only the truth of his plans, but also to avoid mentioning his catching any train out of the city. So begins the first set of questions in this mystery.

The next questions concern the reasons why a man of this kind, with that social position, might leave for another city quite a long way from his home, with no clothes and no suitcase? That suggests a certain foreboding – that he knew this was his last journey in life. Yet there is an *unless*. Unless he was meeting someone with whom he was to have a business or personal meeting, settle something important, and then return to Bradford without delay. Such a meeting would have to be very urgent, and his haste suggests that.

Blum was not seen alive again; a body was found at Hoylake, close to the Mersey estuary. But as the Chief Constable of Bradford wrote to the paper, '... I immediately waited upon Mr Jacob Behrens, a Governor of the High School in which the late Mr Blum was master...His two sons were present at the interview; all were well acquainted with the deceased and had seen him but a few hours from his departure from Bradford. After reading the descriptions from Birkenhead, they came to the conclusion that it would be useless to send anyone to Hoylake as the description did not correspond in the most important particulars...' When it is realised that Blum was engaged to a young woman who was living in London, there is an invitation to indulge in some Holmesian thinking, particularly when this letter written to her by Blum is studied (written in April, a few weeks before he left Bradford):

'I had a strange letter from Leeds from a stranger who is staying here on business. He comes from Hamburg and wishes to see me. As it is impossible for me to go to Leeds until Saturday I must consider meanwhile what to do. A strange thing is it not?'

This letter was taken to Merseyside on Blum's person. The final part of the enigma is that Blum had a brother, and this man was hard up. Blum had met him once in Bradford, and had given him money. The brother had been staying in Hamburg but his aim was to emigrate eventually to Australia.

Marie Campbell tried to follow up records of the case, and to trace any further investigations. It appears that nothing came of this. She rightly points out interesting parallels between *David Copperfield* and the situation of Israel Blum: that his life and the plot have these things in common: a schoolmaster, and old school friend who dies in a storm at sea, a rich widow, and a close friend who goes to Australia. This puzzling parallel is probably the heart of the problem and we could speculate from this. It has to be said that shipwrecks and murder were also prominent in other very popular tales at exactly this time. Hannah Maria Jones's Penny Dreadful story, *The Shipwrecked Stranger* may also be relevant here. This was published in 1848, and includes the melodramatic narrative of a murderer and his being washed up after a shipwreck. But consider the possibilities of the story if it were to be a meeting with the mysterious man from Hamburg, about business, that went wrong; the 'business' may well have been related to debt – debts incurred by Blum's brother. The shipping links between Liverpool and Hamburg were strong then, as now. The man who wrote from Leeds was German, and so was Blum; Blum's brother had lived in Hamburg. Those two simple facts invite some thinking based on links that are more than coincidence. We know that Blum's brother was short of money and was desperate to go to Australia to start a new life. When I wrote about this tale in previous books, I had no knowledge of this letter from the Chief Constable, and I engaged in some fruitless speculations about a body which was not that of Mr Blum. But what is interesting for present purposes is that the police could only do a range of very limited things in their search: they could write descriptions and provide pictures of the missing person in the papers; they could ask questions around the neighbourhood, and of course they could circulate flyers and notices to display prominently around the town. But the Blum case goes on. A man disappeared, and his reason for doing so remains a mystery. In past cases there have been similarly odd and puzzling cases of missing persons, but there have also been horrendous cases, such as that in Flushing in 1863 in which, as the press reported, there were awful events: 'The inhabitants of Flushing... appear to have known perfectly well that the brother of a resident, a man named Porter, disappeared from among them twenty years ago. If they did not know, they more than suspected that the person missing was kept in confinement in some part of the unnatural relative's premises. For several years there were rumours in the place that the victim, who was of weak mind, was kept closely shut up in a room at the back of the brother's house...' Now there is a theme waiting for a novelist's treatment.

Chapter 12

Teenage Killers

Present

At present in England, Wales and Northern Ireland the age of criminal responsibility is 10 years of age which means that anyone under that age cannot be prosecuted. The reasoning behind this decision is that a person below 10 is deemed not to understand that they are doing something which is wrong. We have one of the lowest criminal responsibility ages in Europe and there have been attempts to increase the age, which no doubt will continue.

There have been a number of high-profile cases during the past few decades where young people have committed Murder and other serious crimes. One of the most well-known was the Murder of a 2-year old boy in Liverpool. Jamie Bulger was taken from a shopping centre, whilst his mother was distracted, in February 1993. His mutilated body was found on a railway line two days later.

Two 10-year old boys, Robert Thompson and Jon Venables were convicted of the Murder and became the youngest convicted murderers in modern English history the following year, aged just 11. There have been other cases in the UK where teenagers have committed the most serious of crimes.

The case I am about to discuss took place in April 2016 and resulted in the loss of two lives, taken away in the most brutal and callous manner. It happened in the market town of Spalding in Lincolnshire, a place with a relatively low crime rate and a strong sense of community spirit. Having served as a Senior

Detective in the area for several years, I know the impact that this crime will have had on everyone affected by the events. Had I not retired from the police service in 2012, I have no doubt that I would have been the Senior Investigating Officer (SIO) leading this particular Murder investigation. Instead, the unenviable task of unearthing the truth and bringing those responsible to justice, rested with my old deputy, Detective Inspector Martin Holvey, now a Detective Superintendent working as part of the East Midlands Special Operations Unit – Major Crime (EMSOU-MC).

Both during and after this case there have been many discussions, amongst the public and professionals, as to whether the two people responsible for these Murders were the victims of a troubled upbringing and a violent society or just plain evil. I'll let you decide.

CASE STUDY – SPALDING MURDERS

On 14th April 2016 two 14 year olds, a girl and a boy, were reported missing from Spalding in Lincolnshire. The usual police enquiries were carried out in an effort to trace them. The following day, police attended a residential address in the area where they located the pair together. They were lying on a mattress on the living room floor watching TV. Upstairs in the house police also discovered the dead bodies of 49 year old Elizabeth Edwards and her 13 year old daughter, Katie. Both had been stabbed a number of times in the neck and were found lying in bed in their respective bedrooms in their home. It was clear that both had been subjected to a brutal and sustained attack. The murder weapon, a large kitchen knife, was found in Katie's bedroom. Both youths were arrested on suspicion of murder and taken to police stations as a Murder investigation was launched.

Initially the boy refused to comment during police interviews but the girl provided a full and disturbing account of events.

She described how the Murder had been planned some time ago and was supposed to take place earlier that week but, due to circumstances, it was delayed. The boy was going to go to the house with a bag of knives and spare clothing, getting in through the bathroom window. They had agreed that he would kill Elizabeth and that she would kill Katie but, at the last moment, she decided that she didn't want to do it so the boy killed both. He attacked Elizabeth whilst she slept in her bed, stabbing her in the neck and cutting through the voicebox to prevent her from screaming, then held a pillow over her head as she struggled for her life. Once he had killed Elizabeth, he went into Katie's room and did the same. Afterwards they had a bath together (as the girl didn't like the smell of blood), had sex, watched the vampire movie 'Twilight' and ate ice-cream. Their original plan had been for both to commit suicide after the Murders but the girl changed her mind. They remained in the house with the bodies for the next 36 hours.

During her police interviews the girl appeared calm and talked about the Murders in a matter of fact way. When describing how she felt about the Murders she said "I was ok with it. The fact that it happened so quickly gave me peace of mind. It wasn't like torture or anything". At no time did she show any remorse. When the boy was made aware that the girl had provided a full account, he too explained the planning and sequence of events. When talking about the Murder of Katie he commented "I went into Katie's room, thought I stabbed her then smothered her face with a pillow too". When asked why he had killed Katie he said "Cos' she would call the police". Both youths were charged with the Murders of Elizabeth and Katie Edwards.

At subsequent court hearings both admitted Manslaughter but denied Murder. In October 2016 the boy pleaded guilty to Murder and was remanded in custody awaiting sentence. The girl however, continued to deny Murder, entering a plea of guilty to Manslaughter on the grounds of diminished responsibility. Although she accepted that she was equally responsible for the deaths, having planned them and assisted in their commission, she claimed that she could not be held responsible for her actions as she was suffering from a mental abnormality which impaired her ability to form rational judgements. The jury dismissed this claim and, less than three hours after retiring, they returned with a verdict of guilty to Murder. In November 2016 both were sentenced to life imprisonment and told that they must serve a minimum of 20 years before being considered for parole. The Judge commented "The killings were brutal in the form of executions and both victims, particularly Elizabeth Edwards, must have suffered terribly in the last minutes of their lives".

Despite being old enough to face justice the pair were considered too young for their identities to be revealed and so, at that point, Britain's youngest double-murderers remained nameless. In December 2016 the ban on naming the teenagers was lifted by the trial Judge but their identities remained secret to allow defence lawyers to appeal against the ruling.

In June 2017 the case was heard at the High Court where their sentences were reduced to 17 and a half years due to their age. At the same time the court upheld the trial Judge's view that the pair should be named. They were identified as Kim Edwards and Lucas Markham who had been in a relationship since 2015 which has since been described as toxic. Kim Edwards is the daughter of Elizabeth and the older sister of Katie. It would appear that her mother did not approve of her relationship with Markham and that she thought that her mother favoured her younger sister, Katie, over her. This seems to be the motive for the pair deciding to kill Elizabeth and Katie. There is no question that both Kim Edwards and Lucas

Markham had troubled upbringings but the premeditation, brutal violence and total lack of remorse is staggering. This case is undoubtedly one of the most shocking in recent history.

Past

Cases of teenage crime from the past are not often recorded in detail. They only came to prominence in instances in which, after capital offences were reduced in 1861, and youngsters were convicted of murder. In earlier times, the facts are hard to find, as in the following cases, which did lead to the convict in question dancing on the end of a rope.

Joseph Brown was always going to be a criminal: what we know of him makes it plain that he was always in the midst of trouble and on most occasions he was the cause of it. He was Yorkshire born, but when young he went to London and there he fell in with a rake called Hazelgrove, whom all accounts agree was 'a remarkably fine young man but of idle habits.' The two men wheedled their way into hanging around a tavern linked to suttlery, or army supplies. There was a sideline in such places of prostitution, and so the men soon learned the ways of the world in most criminal aspects of what we now think of as the Regency Underworld.

They managed to avoid the law for a while, but they indulged in such schemes as extortion by threats and then fraud. They soon realised that London was too 'hot' for them and they came north. They took to the roads and inns across Yorkshire and were smart operators for some time, working anywhere from Huddersfield to Hull. But after one arrest and a gaol term, Brown was put into one of the prison hulks. There he is reckoned to have had terrible dreams all saturated with the guilt of his wild life. But that had come too late: he had by then committed the crime that was to lead him to the gallows.

He was charged with the murder of Elizabeth Fletcher and

he pleaded not guilty. A witness stated that he was in a tavern with Brown and Hazelgrove when they were drinking with the dead woman and her sister. He said that Brown poured some unsweetened ale into a mug and gave it to Elizabeth to drink. The next morning, a Mrs Longbottom found the body, and also the sister who was in a deep sleep. When Sara awoke, she had no idea what had happened to them both. Another witness said that Brown had told him he intended to marry Elizabeth because she was worth £20. Apparently he and Hazelgrove had told everyone that they were both single. Another sister, Rebecca, told how a box with valuables in it had been stolen from the sisters and that she had seen it in Brown's room.

A druggist said that the men had come to him for laudanum, but more sensationally, he had in his possession a written confession from Brown in which he had written that he had put a large quantity of laudanum into Sarah Fletcher's beer at the public house in Ferrybridge where they were staying. He added: 'The former died early on the morning of the 22 October. We broke open her box and took out one guinea and a half. We were apprehended, heard before a magistrate, and discharged as he thought the evidence against us insufficient.'

There had also been an alleged confession of another murder, of a Selby carrier. It was all decided swiftly – Brown was guilty and must die. He was hanged along with Mary Bateman, protesting his innocence.

Chapter 13

The Coroner

Present

Coroners are independent judicial officers, appointed and paid for by local authorities, who are responsible for the investigation of violent, unnatural or sudden deaths of unknown cause. Unnatural or sudden deaths include death after accident or injury, apparent suicide or drug/alcohol overdose and sudden infant death (sometimes referred to as 'cot death'). In addition, if the deceased was not seen by a doctor during the 14 days prior to death, the death must be reported to the Coroner. Any person who is concerned about a cause of death can inform a Coroner but, in most cases, a death will be reported by a doctor or the police. During the investigation into any death referred to the Coroner, a Coroners' Officer will represent them and ensure that they are consulted and kept fully updated throughout. Coroners' Officers are often retired police officers or people with a medical or legal background. In some police areas the Coroners' Officer will attend the scene of certain deaths including Road Traffic Collisions (RTC).

Post Mortem Examination

A post-mortem examination (PM) is a medical examination carried out on a person who has died, with the aim of establishing the cause and manner of death. A post-mortem is not carried out on every person who dies, only those cases where further investigation is required, such as unknown cause of death or suspicious circumstances. If the Coroner is satisfied that the death is from natural causes then no post-mortem would be required. A post-mortem will be conducted by a Pathologist. In cases of Murder or where the death appears to have occurred as a result of suspicious circumstances, the Coroner will order that a Forensic post-mortem takes place. This is a more detailed post-mortem, sometimes referred to as a 'Home Office' post-mortem, conducted by a specially-trained Forensic Pathologist.

In a Murder case, the police Senior Investigating Officer (SIO) or their deputy will normally attend together with forensic staff and the Coroners' Officer. The findings will be explained in a written post-mortem report which is likely to be tendered in evidence in any Court proceedings. A post-mortem can only be carried out if it has been authorised by the Coroner.

The term 'autopsy' is sometimes used to describe a post-mortem but this word isn't used by police in the UK.

Inquest
An inquest is a legal investigation to establish the circum-stances surrounding a person's death including how, when and why the death occurred. In some cases an inquest will also try to establish the deceased person's identity. The investigation is held in public at a Coroner's Court in cases where a death was sudden, violent or unnatural, a death occurred in prison or police custody or the cause of death is still unknown after a post-mortem. Unlike criminal trials, inquests don't try to establish whether anyone was responsible for the death.

Evidence is given by witnesses, sometimes in front of a jury, but there is no prosecution or defence. An inquest will be opened soon after the death allowing the death to be recorded, the deceased to be identified and for the Coroner to give authorisation for a burial or cremation to take place as soon as possible. After an inquest has been opened it may be adjourned until after any other investigations have been completed. This adjournment can be for up to six months or longer in complex police investigations. In Murder cases, any criminal proceedings will be concluded before a full inquest is held meaning that a person may have been convicted or acquitted of Murder in a Criminal Court before the inquest takes place.

Verdict
At the end of an inquest the Coroner (or jury) will come to a conclusion known as the verdict. There are a number of verdicts which can be reached including accident, suicide, unlawful killing, open (where there isn't enough evidence to return a verdict) or road traffic collision. These verdicts are known as 'short form' verdicts. The Coroner has no obligation to use a 'short form' verdict but can use a 'narrative verdict' where the circumstances of the death are set out in a detailed way based upon the evidence heard. Most inquest verdicts must be decided on the civil standard of a 'balance of probabilities', in other words 'it's more likely than not' that the death of the person occurred in a particular way. Inquest verdicts of suicide or unlawful killing must be decided on the criminal standard of 'beyond reasonable doubt'.

Past
It is not hard to find records of what coroners did, even as far back as 1349, when we know from coroners' rolls that 'Inquest was taken before the coroners of the city of York concerning the death of William Yonge, slain at York at twilight...' Then, at the end of the brief report, we have the name of the coroner: 'Robert fled forthwith, and had no chattels... William was viewed and buried by Thomas of Lincoln, the coroner.'

This type of information may be found in the coroners' rolls, some published by the Selden Society, and some by the Sussex Archaeological Collections (Vol. XCV, 1957).

From 1752 to 1860 coroners had to file their inquests at the Quarter Sessions, so these will be in the Quarter Sessions records at record offices. The quickest way to locate these is through Access to Archives (A2A) as an internet search. A standard volume which has listings of holdings is *Coroners' Records in England and Wales* by J Gibson and C Rogers, and this has details of coroners' districts. Coroners' records more than seventy-five years old are usually open; and in cases from earlier times, the inquests would have been given to the judge at the assizes.

There have also been coroners' records from other jurisdictions, and these are listed in the research guide at the TNA website. These have, for example, lists of records left at the King's Bench prison between 1746 and 1839, and records from the palatinate courts. The latter were Chester, Lancaster and Durham. The Chester palatinate court was abolished in 1830, Durham in 1876, and the court of Lancaster the same year.

In the twentieth century, coroners were listed in *Whitaker's Almanac*, with this kind of information:

COUNTY OF LONDON CORONERS
> *Western District*: Edwin Smith
> Coroner's office, Battersea Coroner's Court, Sheepcote Lane,
> Battersea, S. W.

One of the most onerous and tough aspects of a coroner's work in the past was related to executions. When the body of the deceased felon was certified dead and everything finalised, the coroner had to be involved. In one Liverpool case from Victorian times, the coroner was more than a little angry at what had gone on. The hangman in question was Bartholomew Binns, and he had not at all done well.

Binns was only in the office for a year, and was sacked. Later, he assisted the more competent Tommy Scott in 1900, but in his own 'annus horribilis' as hangman he was responsible for a few botched jobs. He had helped the very professional and successful William Marwood, from Lincolnshire, who had invented the more humane 'long drop' method which involved more skilful calculations of the drop/body weight ratio. But Binns did not learn much. There were several complaints from governors and clergy about Binns's work and he was politely asked to go. He had a moment of notoriety when he was written about as the man who hanged one of the Phoenix Park murderers, O'Donnell.

But poor Dutton was to be hanged by Binns at Kirkdale. He had hanged a man for the first time just a few weeks before (Henry Powell at Wandsworth) but Duttton was only the second in line for the tyro executioner.

There was a special element of drama in the case, as two local journalists were to be present, and also Dutton had asked the chaplain to give the optional Condemned Sermon on the Sunday before the fatal hour. The sermon was given, covering three warnings that are surely totally irrelevant, if not insulting, to a condemned man: not to be drunk, not to allow a bad temper to possess you, and not to marry in haste. Unless these were likely to happen in the next world, the whole affair appears to be cruelly ironic. But in the very early hours of his last day on earth, Dutton had something to eat (cocoa, bread and butter) and took sacrament in the prison chapel.

At seven Binns arrived. For some odd reason, the governor would not allow Binns' assistant to enter Kirkdale. It was normal practice to have a hangman together with his assistant. But the prison bell began to toll at a quarter to eight and in haste, Dutton was brought to meet Binns and to be pinioned ready for the drop. Then, as the chaplain read some text concerning man's sins, the ritual walk to the scaffold began.

This final walk was in line with regulations: the chief warder led the way, followed by Dutton and two warders; then Binns was behind them, followed in line by a doctor, the under-sheriff and chaplain. So far so good. But then they reached the scaffold.

The drama came when Dutton was given the rapid final pinioning and strapping ready for the lever to be pulled; the clock for eight had not struck, and Binns walked to look at his victim, causing a rather nervous atmosphere. Dutton asked Lord Jesus to receive his soul. Then the clock struck, and the lever was pulled; Dutton dropped, but it was not a quick death.

The doctor looked down at the struggling man on the rope and said, 'This is poor work, he is not dead yet.' In a drop of almost seven and a half feet, the body spun and the man did not die for eight minutes. That was outrageously cruel by any standards. The doctor could see what the problem was: a very thick rope had been used (like a ship's hawser, the doctor said) and Dutton was very short, only five feet two inches. The result was what every hangman feared: slow strangulation rather than a snapping of the spinal column with speed and humane intention.

There was an inquest after all this farce. Mr Barker, the County Coroner attended. The prison governor, Major Leggett, made a long statement outlining the time taken for the culprit to die, and also added that nothing had been done to 'hasten the end' of the unfortunate Dutton. The doctor's evidence would make difficult reading for anyone concerned about the terrible suffering the man had experienced: only a slight separation of two bones in the vertebrae near the point of contact with the rope had happened, rather than any sharp break. In the doctor's opinion, the noose had been placed at the wrong position near the nape of the neck, rather than under the jaw or the ear. There was, it was stated, a difference of 300 pounds in weight in the drop/body ratio.

The question that must have been on everyone's lips was boldly asked by the coroner: 'Was the executioner sober?'

Major Leggett answered that he was not sure. Then this interchange took place: something that must have ensured Binns' departure from his post:

Coroner: Has the hangman left the gaol?
Leggett: Yes.
Coroner: I wish he were here.

A juryman asked the governor's opinion of the affair. Leggett said, 'I think it was inefficiently performed –clumsily. I did not like his manner of conducting the execution. He seemed, in adjusting the strap on the man, to do it in a very bungling way, which I did not like at all.'

It was one of the most disgraceful cases of a botched execution in the annals of that grim but necessarily professional task at that period. As Shakespeare said in another context, 'If it were done, 'tis good it were done well.' The coroner considered the affair to have been a disaster, referring to the fact that 'the executioner seemed to be a new hand at the work' and that he should have done what the previous man, Calcraft, had done, that is pull on the legs of any man dangling but not swiftly dying. One final irony in the Binns story is that he took part in a show featuring ex-hangmen, and that, as one writer of the time said, he 'reveals his art for the entertainment of the large crowds...' Incompetence was not to deter Mr Binns from making his year's deadly work the stuff of a media circus.

Chapter 14

A Victorian Policeman's Lot

As a postscript to the entries on cases from the past, we finish with a look at what could happen when an officer died in the line of duty in the days before all the modern provisions in support of an officer's life and responsibilities. This particular death happened at a hiring fair.

The hiring fair was a very old institution in English history, dating back over the centuries to the reign of Edward III, and later, in the Tudor period when affairs concerning masters and servants were regulated more forcefully, days were named on which labour could be hired, and the High Constable of the shire would define terms of pay and working conditions.

The annual fair then became a major event: we know from social history and from literature that the hiring fair, or mop fair as it was sometimes known, became an occasion when labour was hired for a year from Michaelmas to Michaelmas. Men and women would stand in line, set to show off their trades and skills, so that L W Cowie described, 'cowman had a tuft of cowhair, carters a piece of whipcord, shepherds a tuft of sheepswool and thatchers a fragment of women straw, while servant-girls carried a mop or wore a white apron.'

The token was taken when the individual was given work, but of course that description suggests a smooth, organised system. In fact, the fairs were occasions at which drink might flow too freely, competition might become too heated, and old jealousies and resentments might explode. No doubt the hired men and women, when the fast-penny was pressed into their hand to seal the bargain, felt in need of something to wet their whistle. All around them were the amusements of the fair, and fun was in the air. Pleasure could easily transmute into aggression.

At Alnwick in Northumberland at the March Fair in 1875, the jollification changed into a riot, and in the midst of the violence and unrest was the constable. As one account has it: ' ... the said [Sergeant] John Hately came to his death whilst in the execution of his duty in endeavouring to quiet a disturbance which took place... on the hiring day of the 6th of March.' He left a widow and eight children.

For the previous twenty years, legislation had slowly been professionalising the provincial police, and progress was uneven. But what was given least consideration was the safety of an officer. Hately was hit by a stone, flung at him from the crowd, and he died of the injuries sustained. Here was a brave man, standing out and being counted, as it were, in the force for order and reason. He paid for that bravery with his life. What had the law done to organise and streamline the force around him?

The most significant legislation came in 1856 with the County and Borough Police Act. After the report of a Select Committee on Police in 1853, it was made compulsory for county forces to be created and for some amalgamations to be effected. To supervise this, special offices were created to be called Her Majesty's Inspectors of Constabulary. The report of 1853 had stressed the vagrancy problem, as that was considered to be a major cause of crime, and in the larger rural counties we can see the implementations of this Act taking that into consideration.

In Lincolnshire, for example, the reports on the Lincolnshire Constabulary by the Chief Constable in 1857 given to the Joint Police Committee lists the strength of the force: Lindsey had seven superintendents and 43 constables; Kesteven had one superintendent and 20 constables, and Holland had one superintendent and 16 constables. The magistrates met in 1856 'convened by the Lord Lieutenant and held in the castle of Lincoln in October, 1856 for the proper taking into consideration the Act 19 and 20 Vic. Cap. 69 to render more effectual the police in county boroughs of England and Wales.'

As to the important features such as ratio of police officers to population in the counties, these varied greatly. In Norfolk, for instance, there were 196 officers in 1856, a ratio to population of 1/ 3451. In Dorset there were only twelve men at the time. Essentially, the police officer at the time of Hately's death, had no hope of assistance in times of trouble: later in the century, there were death and burial clubs of most constabularies, and superannuation came in. Some forces, such as Hull for instance, had superannuation funds as early as the 1860s, but for many, if the worst happened, it was a case of charity and humane responses to personal tragedy. Hately's force did have a superannuation fund, but with eight children that was hardly adequate. Still, as a deed of 2nd May in 1875 states, £81 was given 'as a gratuity' from the police superannuation fund 'after providing for the immediate wants of the widow and family.'

By the later Victorian years, the public were becoming so well informed and opinionated about the 'Peelers' that letters to the newspapers were common, and opinions strong, as in this letter to the *Manchester Guardian* in 1873 in response to a debate on the tendency of constables to arrest anyone supine on the streets: 'We have no wish to be hard upon the constable. Speaking generally, he is not, and cannot be expected to be, a man of discriminating mind, and he usually has a good deal of work on hand – work which, without any fault of character in himself, must tend to develop a cynical faculty. Even a policeman, however, ought to know that men and women may fall powerless to the ground from other causes than excessive drinking.' The attitude is typical of what was developing: an ambivalent attitude, sympathy mixed with negative representations.

In other words, the individual officer was a vulnerable figure. Hately tried to stop a riot. The result was that the reputation of the hiring fair for trouble and disorder was confirmed, and the community was left with a widow and eight orphans to somehow help and supervise. Documentation shows that there was, in fact, the most stunning and impressive response to the sergeant's violent death. Notices were posted across a number of parishes. The aim was to 'raise a fund for their immediate and future benefit.' Subscriptions were called for at banks and stationers' shops. The response was massive and overwhelming.

By June 21st 1875, when the trustees of the Hately Fund arranged to meet, a sum of £743-1s-4d had been raised. A list of subscribers between May 15 and May 27 that year has no less than 39 people, and they had given sums as small as one guinea, up to large amounts such as £5 from C.W Orde. By June a huge list was issued, properly in print, listing several hundred donations of sums between 2s 6d down to one shilling. His Grace the Duke of Northumberland, at Alnwick Castle, gave £25.

The records of the work undertaken on behalf of Mrs Mary Hately by the trustees shows what could be achieved, in those dangerous days before proper social welfare and support, by sheer energy and commitment, done in recognition of a deed of courage. In fact, what the trustees did was what every right-thinking person of wealth did at the time: invest in railways and in the government. Everyone was doing it, from the Rothschilds downwards. A letter from the trustees describes the matter:

'It is also declared that the said trustees shall have full power to invest the
Trust funds in government or real securities or in Railway Stock, where

The whole capital has been called up... and that all indemnity clauses under
The statute (22nd and 23 Victoria Chapter 35) to save trustees from risk, shall
Be considered as incorporated... into this deed.'

It was decided that the Trust should last '19 and a half years at least' and in the formal agreement concerning the fund's investment, there was a remarkable degree of attention given to Mary's welfare, separate from a long list of trust sums held for all the children. The deed says that all sums not apportioned for the children are 'for the benefit of the said Mary Hately for her life for her sole and separate use only and not to be subject to the debts or control of any husband she might have...'

Mary Hately was forty-years old when her husband died. She must have been astonished at the local response to the sad death of her husband of course: the result of that flying chunk of rock at the hiring fair highlights two important and fascinating mid-Victorian elements of social history: the fragile nature of every community in tough times, when hard farming work ground down the working population to seek consolation in drink and in high-jinks, and naturally, the dangerous nature of those guardians of law who faced the trouble head-on. There was solidarity when tragedy followed, and Mary Hately would have noticed that, aside from the huge sums given to her by tradesmen and professional people in her community, there was a very large sum of over £27 raised by the men at the Northumberland Constabulary, and what stands out, apart from the £7 paid by his superintendent, is the £7.12s.5d from a simple constable – P.C. Spence. We have to speculate that this man was a close friend indeed, maybe the man who grew up with him in the force.

REFERENCE GUIDE

Special Topics on Modern Policing
The Phonetic Alphabet
The Police Caution
A Brief History of Crime in Britain
The Law Courts
An A-Z of Police Terminology
An A-Z of Legal terms for Historical Fiction

SPECIAL TOPICS ON MODERN POLICING

PACE – CODES OF PRACTICE

The Police and Criminal Evidence Act (PACE) 1984 Codes of Practice regulate police powers and protect public rights. When a person is arrested and taken to a police station they are given their rights by the custody officer who authorises their detention. One of those rights is to consult a copy of the Codes of Practice which is a book outlining police powers and procedures. Copies of the Codes of Practice are available for this purpose at every police station. At time of writing there are eight Codes (A-H) which deal with the following:

Code A – The exercise by police officers of statutory powers to search a person or vehicle without first making an arrest and the need for a police officer to make a record of a stop or encounter

Code B – Police powers to search premises and to seize and retain property found on premises and persons

Code C – Requirements for the detention, treatment and questioning of suspects not related to terrorism in police custody by police officers, including the requirement to explain a person's rights whilst detained

Code D – Main methods used by the police to identify people in connection with the investigation of offences and the keeping of accurate and reliable criminal records

Code E – Audio recording of interviews with suspects in the police station

Code F – Visual recording with sound of interviews with suspects – there is no statutory requirement on police officers to visually record interviews, but the contents of this Code should be considered if an interviewing officer decides to make a visual recording with sound of an interview with a suspect

Code G – Powers of arrest under Section 24 Police and Criminal Evidence Act 1984 as amended by Section 110 of the Serious Organised Crime and Police Act 2005

Code H – Requirements for the detention, treatment and questioning of suspects related to terrorism in police custody by police officers, including the requirement to explain a person's rights whilst detained in connection with terrorism

The Codes of Practice (COP) are debated from time to time in Parliament and have been amended a number of times throughout the years. If you are going to refer to the Codes in any detail during your writing it's a good idea to carry out some internet research first to make sure that your content is accurate.

BURGLARY OR ROBBERY?

If you are writing a book which involves a crime taking place it's probably a good idea to have a basic knowledge of the offence(s) concerned because if your content is inaccurate you can be certain that a reader will pick up on it. Two of the crimes which tend to cause confusion are Burglary and Robbery, so I'll explain a little more about these offences so that you can tell the difference.

Burglary

The offence of burglary is contrary to Section 9 of the Theft Act 1968 and creates two offences, both of which require proof that the person concerned entered a building or part of a building as a trespasser, with an additional element concerning the intention or actions of the person whilst in the building. Section 9(1)(a) requires proof that the entry took place with the intention of:

- stealing
- inflicting GBH (see assaults); or
- committing unlawful damage

Section 9(1)(b) requires proof that, after the entry took place, the person

- stole or attempted to steal anything; or
- inflicted GBH on any person or attempted to do so

An offence of burglary could involve entry into a dwelling (such as a house) or a non-dwelling (such as a shop). So, if I entered a house as a trespasser (without permission) intending to steal a laptop, seriously assault a person inside or spray paint the walls, I would have committed a Section 9(1)(a) burglary. If I was invited into a shop and, whilst inside, I sneaked into the staff room and stole a purse, I would have committed a Section 9(1)(b) burglary.

There is no statutory definition of what constitutes a 'dwelling' but a tent, caravan and garden shed can all be considered as such under certain circumstances.

The maximum sentence for burglary of a dwelling is 14 years

imprisonment and for burglary of a non-dwelling is 10 years imprisonment.

In summary, burglary involves entry to a building or part of a building (such as an integral garage attached to the house) with a specific intent or committing a specified offence(s) whilst inside.

Aggravated burglary

A person has committed aggravated burglary under Section 10(1) of the Theft Act 1968 if they commit any offence of burglary (contrary to Section 9) and at the time have with them their **WIFE**. Yes, you read it correctly but it's not normally an offence to have your dearly beloved with you unless you're committing a burglary of course. **WIFE** stands for

W   **Weapon of offence**
I   **Imitation Firearm**
F   **Firearm**
E   **Explosives**

Aggravated burglary is a particularly serious offence which carries a maximum sentence of life imprisonment.

Robbery

The definition of robbery is quite complicated and requires a number of elements to be present in a particular order for the offence to be committed. A person commits robbery if they steal something and immediately before or at the time of doing so, and in order to do so, they use force on any person, or put or seek to put any person in fear of being then and there subjected to force. As you can see, force doesn't have to be used but if it is, that force or the threats must be directed at the victim and not other people for the offence of robbery to have been committed. If the theft is completed before any assault takes place then the offence of robbery cannot be proved as the force must be used 'in order to steal'.

In such a case, police may deal with the case as two separate charges, theft and assault. Robbery is contrary to Section 8(1) of the Theft Act 1968 and can only be tried on indictment (at a Crown Court). It carries a maximum sentence of life imprisonment. Examples of robbery could include a person entering a bank and threatening staff who hand over the money or a person pushing someone over and stealing their handbag. It is possible for a person to commit a burglary and a robbery at the same time, if they entered a building as a trespasser and used or intended to use force.

Where a burglary involves theft and force is used immediately before or at the time of stealing (or attempting to steal), the person may have committed an offence of robbery. In such circumstances, prosecutors would normally charge robbery rather than burglary as it is a straightforward concept easily understood by juries, it can take place inside a private dwelling or commercial property as well as outside and clearly reflects the use or threat of force.

POLICE EQUIPMENT

Long gone are the days when the 'bobby' patrolled with just a whistle and a truncheon. These days officers going out onto the streets are weighed down with a varied assortment of items for their own personal protection, the protection of others and to record evidence. The following list (overleaf) is not exhaustive but gives you an idea of some of those items.

Radio

Police radios (known as 'Airwave' radios after the company which designs them) allow officers to send and receive information. They also allow for people to speak with each other independently of the main channel. If an officer enters another borough or force area they can tune their device into the channel for that area which means that the radios are pretty universal. They have a facility for making phone calls and a small button which can be pressed if urgent help is required.

Blackberry

A number of police officers are now given personal-issue Blackberry devices. As well as providing the services which such an item includes, they are also used to record evidence which may otherwise be lost. This evidence can be copied back at the police station or sent to another officer almost immediately.

Handcuffs

Handcuffs have been used as a means of restraint for some considerable time. They used to be two metal 'rings' joined by a chain before the introduction of Kwik cuffs which are a solid unit with the two 'rings' built into a strong plastic casing. Kwik cuffs restrict movement and are easier to apply due to their design. Police officers are trained in the use of Kwik cuffs and have to undergo refresher training annually.

The application of handcuffs is considered to be 'use of force' and should be noted by the officer and brought to the attention of the custody officer upon arrival at the police station if the person is arrested. When handcuffs are applied they should be checked for tightness and double-locked.

Body armour

Also referred to by police as 'stab vests' these items are designed to offer protection to the torso area. The Metropolitan Police became the first force in Britain to issue protective vests to all front-line officers following the death of a police officer on duty in 1997. The vests are quite heavy and can prove restrictive but are now considered an everyday part of police equipment.

Baton

Replacing the wooden police truncheon, the baton has come in various shapes and sizes over the years. These include the straight side-handled baton and the solid two-foot long baton, both of which are carried around the waist area as part of the utility belt. A very popular option today is the friction-lock baton which is actually quite compact but easily increases to a length of twenty-six inches. Regular personal safety training is given in the use of the baton.

CS spray

CS spray was first approved for use by police nationally in 1996. It is now used by many police forces as a temporary incapacitant to subdue violent or aggressive people. CS was first synthesised by two scientists called Corson and Stoughton, whose initials were used to form the name of the chemical. Exposure to CS causes a burning sensation and the eyes to stream. Fresh air, clean cool water and the removal of affected clothing will help those affected. Some police forces have tried the use of alternative incapacitants such as PAVA but CS is still frequently carried by UK police officers. Initial and refresher training is provided in the use of CS spray, sometimes referred to by people as CS gas due to it's origins.

Taser

A Taser is a type of 'stun gun' which delivers an electric shock to temporarily incapacitate a suspect when fired. It fires two small, dart-like electrodes which stay connected to the main unit by conductors, allowing electric current to be delivered. The electrodes attach themselves to a person's body, rather like a hook on the end of a fishing line. Tasers were introduced in the UK in 2003 and were initially only issued to firearms officers entitled to carry guns. They are now issued to a number of patrolling officers as another alternative to protect themselves and others against violent suspects. Research has shown that Tasers are most commonly used to 'red dot' a suspect, aiming and activating the device without firing it, which enables the officer to shine a bright red dot on the suspect in the hope that this will diffuse the situation. All officers who carry Taser are specially-trained and provided with periodic refresher training. The Taser, which is classified as a non-lethal option for the police, looks like a handgun and often has a bright yellow cover. A Taser is classed as a prohibited weapon in law and, as such, it's an offence for a member of the public to possess such an item without lawful authority.

Body Worn Video
Body worn video (BWV), also known as body worn cameras, were first introduced in the UK around 2005. Following a number of trials during the next few years their use has increased. Today, they are commonly used by over 40 UK police forces. They have been found to be particularly useful in violent and Domestic Abuse situations where the evidence is captured and is often irrefutable. The cameras are worn attached to the police uniform, normally around the upper chest area, and don't permanently record. They have to be activated by the officer in appropriate circumstances. All footage recorded is subject to legal safeguards. Back at the police station the footage is uploaded to secure servers and is automatically deleted within 31 days unless it needs to be retained as evidence or for some other policing purpose. Sometimes police officers wear body worn cameras on their helmets. They are usually situated on the side of the helmet and look similar to a small Maglite type torch.

As you can see from the above list, police officers are expected to carry or wear a number of different items when out patrolling. This can prove problematic, particularly when struggling with or pursuing a suspect. It's not surprising, given the combined weight of the equipment and the uniform, that officers do tend to suffer from back problems during their careers.

* * *

THE PHONETIC ALPHABET

Some letters of the alphabet sound very similar and sometimes it can be difficult to hear exactly what people are saying, particularly in a noisy environment. For this reason, police officers use a phonetic alphabet when spelling out words or car index numbers over the radio. This prevents mistakes being made and ensures that the correct information is relayed which could prove vital in policing situations. As a writer you may wish to refer to the phonetic alphabet if your characters are passing information to others, particularly via police radio or telephone.

A-ALPHA	H-HOTEL	O-OSCAR	V-VICTOR
B-BRAVO	I-INDIA	P-PAPA	W-WHISKEY
C-CHARLIE	J-JULIET	Q-QUEBEC	X-XRAY
D-DELTA	K-KILO	R-ROMEO	Y-YANKEE
E-ECHO	L-LIMA	S-SIERRA	Z-ZULU
F-FOXTROT	M-MIKE	T-TANGO	
G-GOLF	N-NOVEMBER	U-UNIFORM	

For example, if the car index number you wished to transmit was FG66 ZLR the message would read "Foxtrot, Golf, six, six, Zulu, Lima, Romeo" and the name TAYLOR would become "Tango, Alpha, Yankee, Lima, Oscar, Romeo".

* * *

THE POLICE CAUTION

As a result of the introduction of the Criminal Justice and Public Order Act 1994, the police caution was changed to reflect the fact that people arrested were no longer able to remain silent without the potential that this course of action may prejudice their case. The caution was changed to a form of words which still apply at time of publishing as –

YOU DO NOT HAVE TO SAY ANYTHING, BUT IT MAY HARM YOUR DEFENCE IF YOU DO NOT MENTION WHEN QUESTIONED SOMETHING WHICH YOU LATER RELY ON IN COURT. ANYTHING YOU DO SAY MAY BE GIVEN IN EVIDENCE.

Simply put, you can still remain silent, but if you mention something at Court which you didn't mention when given the opportunity in a previous police interview, the Court may draw it's own conclusions as to why you didn't mention it then.

A caution should be given upon arrest, for example "I'm arresting you for criminal damage. You do not have to say" etc...... If the person is too violent or otherwise incapable of understanding the caution then it need not be given at that time but the fact that it hasn't been given and the reason why should be drawn to the attention of the custody officer. The caution should also be given at the start of recorded police interviews, including when a new set of tapes/DVD's are used.

When a person is charged with an offence or informed that they may be prosecuted, a slightly different wording is used with "when questioned" being replaced by "now". The caution on charging is –

YOU DO NOT HAVE TO SAY ANYTHING, BUT IT MAY HARM YOUR DEFENCE IF YOU DO NOT MENTION NOW SOMETHING WHICH YOU LATER RELY ON IN COURT. ANYTHING YOU DO SAY MAY BE GIVEN IN EVIDENCE.

* * *

MURDER INVESTIGATION TEAM STRUCTURE

A Murder Investigation Team (MIT), sometimes referred to as a Major Investigation Team, will vary in size and structure depending on the force(s). Having said that, I think it is useful for writers to have an idea of the ranks involved in the investigative process.

The following list is in order of seniority and includes the acronym for each rank.

Detective Superintendent – Det/Supt
Detective Chief Inspector – DCI
Detective Inspector – DI
Detective Sergeant – DS
Detective Constable – DC
HOLMES team (see 'The Murder Investigation')

There will generally only be one, or maybe two, Detective Superintendents but the numbers will increase as you move through the ranks, particularly in relation to Detective Sergeants and Detective Constables. It's important to point out that a lot of really valuable work is carried out by support staff who are not police officers but are employed by the force or region concerned. Their roles are likely to include HOLMES support, exhibits officers and forensic staff. There is every chance that an MIT will be investigating more than one Murder at the same time, although they are likely to be at different stages of the criminal justice process.

POLICE EPAULETTES

CONSTABLE

SERGEANT (SGT)

INSPECTOR

CHIEF INSPECTOR

SUPERINTENDENT

CHIEF SUPERINTENDENT

ASSISTANT CHIEF
CONSTABLE

DEPUTY CHIEF
CONSTABLE

CHIEF CONSTABLE
(CC)

DEPUTY ASSISTANT
COMMISSIONER

ASSISTANT
COMMISSIONER

DEPUTY
COMMISSIONER

COMMISSIONER

WHAT RANK DO POLICE EPAULETTES DENOTE?

The epaulettes worn by a uniformed police officer, one on each shoulder, identify the rank of that officer. There are some differences, particularly with the Metropolitan Police in London, which I will explain as we go through the ranks. Being aware of the rank insignia may help if you are a writer who wants to mention the epaulettes or describe them during a particular scene. For others, I think it's useful to know the difference although it's made a little easier these days as some officers have their name and rank printed on the front of their tunic or jumper.

Police Constable (PC)   If you are a police constable in most forces your epaulettes will display a number which is referred to as your collar number. The number may be anything from one single number to a combination of five numbers. In the example shown (police epaulettes) the officer is PC 24234. The epaulette may well also show the officer's surname. In the Metropolitan Police the epaulette will also contain the borough code. For example, an officer based in the borough of Brent would display the letters QK (Kilburn) although they may actually be based at another police station in the borough. When I left police training school at Hendon and was posted to Wembley police station in September 1982 my collar number was 727 and station code QD, both of which were displayed on my epaulettes. Had I been posted there now, my number would be accompanied by the letters QK instead.

Police Sergeant (PS or SGT)   The rank of Sergeant is denoted by three stripes. In the example shown the collar number of the Sergeant is 20300. It's fairly unusual for the collar number of a Sergeant to have more than three numbers but in larger areas this can happen. Your collar number stays with you even if you are promoted to other ranks but is rarely used above the rank of Sergeant. So if PC Jayne Faulkner joined as PC 133 and was promoted to Sergeant, she would become Sergeant 133 Faulkner. If she was subsequently promoted to the rank of Inspector she would retain the collar number but would be referred to simply as Inspector Faulkner and so on through the ranks. As with Constables, Metropolitan Police Sergeants will display their borough code as well as their collar number on their epaulettes. The shortened term 'Sarge' is often used by colleagues, particularly Constables.

Inspector   The rank of Inspector lies between Sergeant and Chief Inspector in the rank structure. An Inspector will display two 'Order of the Bath' stars, often referred to as 'pips',on their epaulettes. The rank is quite often Operational and likely to be in charge of a team or unit/department. They are sometimes referred to as 'Sir', 'Ma'am' or 'Guv' (short for Guv'nor).

Chief Inspector   The rank of Chief Inspector lies between Inspector and Superintendent. A Chief Inspector will display three 'Order of the Bath' stars ('pips') on their epaulettes. Chief Inspector was one of the ranks proposed for abolition in the 1994 Sheehy Report which was set up to examine the rank structure and conditions of service. The rank, however, survived the 'chop' and is still used today. There is normally a Chief Inspector (Operations) who will be in charge of day-to-day policing within a geographical area. The Head of Crime (CID) at a police station is usually a Detective Chief Inspector (DCI) who is a Senior Detective of Chief Inspector rank in charge of CID staff and responsible for the investigation of the most serious crimes.

Superintendent   The rank of Superintendent lies between Chief Inspector and Chief Superintendent. A Superintendent will

161

display a single crown on their epaulettes. From an Operational perspective the rank of Superintendent holds a number of responsibilities as the Authorising Officer for requests under the Police and Criminal Evidence Act (PACE) and the Regulation Of Investigatory Powers Act (RIPA) amongst others. As with the rank of Chief Inspector, there are Detective Superintendents who work in plain-clothes and often carry out the role of Senior Investigating Officer (SIO) in Murder investigations. The epaulettes on the shoulders of a Superintendent will display a single crown with red inset.

Chief Superintendent   A Chief Superintendent in a provincial force may be referred to as a Divisional or Borough Commander as they have overall responsibility for everything that happens in a specific geographical policing area. At a force HQ they may be in charge of a large Department or Unit such as Road Traffic Policing or Local Policing. Their epaulettes will display a Crown and a single 'Order of the Bath' star.

The remaining ranks are often referred to as the 'Chief Officer Group' and, in provincial forces consist of Assistant Chief Constable (ACC), Deputy Chief Constable (DCC) and Chief Constable (CC).

Assistant Chief Constable (ACC)   The epaulettes worn by an ACC are crossed tipstaves in a bayleaf wreath (see police epaulettes).

Deputy Chief Constable (DCC)   The epaulettes worn by a DCC are crossed tipstaves in a bayleaf wreath and a single 'Order of the Bath' star.

Chief Constable (CC)   The Chief Constable, the most senior officer in provincial forces, wears epaulettes displaying crossed tipstaves in a bayleaf wreath and a single crown with red inset.

The Metropolitan Police Service (MPS) uses the standard British police rank structure up to Chief Superintendent, but uniquely has five ranks above that level instead of the standard three, namely Commander, Deputy Assistant Commissioner (DAC), Assistant Commissioner (AC), Deputy Commissioner (D/Comm) and Commissioner.

Commander   This rank isn't used in provincial forces as the Chief Superintendent carries out the equivalent role. The epaulettes worn by a Commander display crossed tipstaves in a bayleaf wreath (the same as an ACC in a provincial force).

Deputy Assistant Commissioner (DAC)   The epaulettes worn by a DAC are crossed tipstaves in a bayleaf wreath and a single 'Order of the Bath' star.

Assistant Commissioner (AC)   The epaulettes worn by an AC are crossed tipstaves in a bayleaf wreath and a single crown with blue inset.

Deputy Commissioner (D/Comm)   The epaulettes worn by a D/Comm are crossed tipstaves in a bayleaf wreath, a single Crown with blue inset and two 'Order of the Bath' stars.

Commissioner (Comm)   The Commissioner of the Metropolitan Police Service wears epaulettes which display crossed tipstaves in a bayleaf wreath, a single crown with blue inset and a single 'Order of the Bath' star.

* * *

USEFUL ACRONYMS

A

ABC – Assume nothing, Believe nobody, Check everything
ABH – Assault occasioning Actual Bodily Harm
ACC – Assistant Chief Constable
AFO – Authorised Firearms Officer
ANPR – Automatic Number Plate Recognition
ARV – Armed Response Vehicle
ASNT – Area searched no trace

B

BPA – Blood Pattern Analysis
BTP – British Transport Police
BWV – Body Worn Video

C

CAIT – Child Abuse Investigation Team
CC – Chief Constable
CCTV – Closed Circuit Television
CHIS – Covert Human Intelligence Source (Informant)
CID – Criminal Investigation Department
COP – Codes of Practice
CPS – Crown Prosecution Service
CSI – Crime Scene Investigator
CSM – Crime Scene Manager
CSP – Communications Service Provider

D

DC – Detective Constable
DCC – Deputy Chief Constable
DCI – Detective Chief Inspector

DI – Detective Inspector
DNA – Deoxyribonucleic acid
DS – Detective Sergeant
D/SIO – Deputy Senior Investigating Officer
D/Supt – Detective Superintendent

E
EO – Exhibits Officer
EMSOU – East Midlands Special Operations Unit

F
FDR – Firearms Discharge Residue
FLO – Family Liaison Officer
FMT – Forensic Management Team
FOI – Freedom of Information (Act)
FPN – Fixed Penalty Notice

G
GBH – Grievous Bodily Harm
GSR – Gunshot Residue

H
H2H – House to House Enquiries
HMC – Her Majesty's Coroner
HMIC – Her Majesty's Inspectorate of Constabulary
HMRC – Her Majesty's Revenue and Customs
HOLMES 2 – Home Office Large Major Enquiry System (version 2)
HSE – Health and Safety Executive

I
IPCC – Independent Police Complaints Commission
ISP – Internet Service Provider

L
LOE – Line of enquiry

M
MDT – Mobile Data Terminal
MIR – Major Incident Room
MISPER – Missing Person
MIT – Murder Investigation Team (or Major Investigation Team)
MO – Modus Operandi
MPS – Metropolitan Police Service

N
NCA – National Crime Agency
NDNADB – National DNA Database
NFA – No Further Action (or No Fixed Abode)
NPT – Neighbourhood Policing Team

O
OIC – Officer in charge (or Officer in the case)
OM – Office Manager

P
PACE – Police and Criminal Evidence (Act 1984)
PC – Police Constable (or politically correct)
PCC – Police and Crime Commissioner
PCMH – Plea and Case Management Hearing
PCSO – Police Community Support Officer
PDR – Personal Development Review
PM – Post Mortem
PNB – Pocket notebook
PNC – Police National Computer
PNLD – Police National Learning Database
POLACC – Police Accident (RTC)

POLSA – Police Search Advisor
PPE – Personal Protective Equipment
PPO – Prolific and Priority Offender
PYO – Persistent Young Offender
PS – Police Sergeant

Q
QC – Queens Counsel

R
RIPA – Regulation of Investigatory Powers Act 2000 (pronounced 'reaper')
ROTI – Record of Taped Interview
RTC – Road Traffic Collision
RVP – Rendezvous Point
RWOC – Released without charge

S
SB – Special Branch
SIO – Senior Investigating Officer
SMT – Senior Management Team
SOCO – Scenes of Crime Officer
SPOC – Single point of contact

T
TIC – Taken into Consideration
TIE – Trace/Interview/Eliminate
TST – Take statement
TWOC – Taken without the owner's consent (refers to a vehicle)

U
UWSU – Underwater search unit

V

VIPER – Video Identification Parade by Electronic Recording
ViSOR – Violent and Sex Offender Register
VPS – Victim Personal Statement
VS – Victim Support

W

WOFD – Warrant of further detention

Y

YOT – Youth Offending Team

* * *

LEVELS OF ASSAULT

The following is a brief guide to the different levels of assault from minor to the most serious, including the legislation and type of injury.

Common Assault

Common assault is contrary to Section 39 Criminal Justice Act 1988 and is committed when a person either assaults another person or commits a battery. An assault is committed when a person intentionally or recklessly causes another to apprehend the immediate infliction of unlawful force. A battery is committed when a person intentionally and recklessly applies unlawful force to another. As you can see, you don't necessarily have to injure someone to have committed common assault, the mere apprehension of force can sometimes be enough. Where no injury or an injury which is not considered serious occurs, the appropriate charge would be common assault. The offence carries a maximum penalty of six months imprisonment.

Assault occasioning Actual Bodily Harm (ABH)

ABH is contrary to Section 47 Offences against the Person Act 1861 and reflects injuries sustained which are considered to be serious when compared to Common Assault. Examples may include a requirement for stitches or a hospital procedure under anaesthetic.

Psychological harm can sometimes amount to ABH. The offence can be tried at Magistrates or Crown Court and carries a maximum penalty on indictment (at Crown Court) of five years imprisonment and/or an unlimited fine. The factors in law that distinguish between a charge of Common Assault and ABH are the degree of injury sustained and the sentencing powers available to the court.

Unlawful wounding/inflicting grievous bodily harm (GBH)

This offence is contrary to Section 20 Offences Against the Person Act 1861 and is committed when a person unlawfully and maliciously either wounds another person or inflicts grievous bodily harm upon another person. Wounding means the breaking of the whole of the outer skin, or the inner skin within the cheek or lip. The definition of wounding may encompass injuries that are relatively minor, such as a small cut or laceration but these type of injuries should more appropriately be charged as Common Assault or possibly ABH.

An offence contrary to Section 20 should be reserved for those wounds considered to be really serious. Grievous bodily harm (GBH) means really serious bodily harm and may include injury resulting in permanent disability, fractured skull, broken jaw or a substantial loss of blood to name but a few. Cases involving the reckless transmission of sexual infection will usually be charged under Section 20. It is an either way offence which carries a maximum penalty of five years imprisonment and/or unlimited fine (Crown Court) and six months imprisonment and/or a fine not exceeding the statutory maximum (Magistrates Court).

Wounding/causing grievous bodily harm (GBH) with intent

This offence is committed when a person unlawfully and maliciously, with intent to do some grievous bodily harm, or with intent to resist or prevent the lawful apprehension or detainer of any other person, either wounds another person or causes grievous bodily harm to another person. The definitions of 'wounding' and 'grievous bodily harm' are the same as the Section 20 offence. The distinction between Section 18 and Section 20 offences is one of intent.

Factors which may indicate specific intent include a repeated or planned attack, deliberate selection of a weapon or adaptation of an article (such as breaking a glass before an attack), making prior threats or targeting a victim's head. The part of Section 18 which refers to 'the lawful apprehension..... etc' often relates to more serious assaults upon police officers, where the evidence of an intention to prevent arrest is clear, but the evidence of an intent to cause grievous bodily harm may be in doubt. Section 18 is an indictable only offence (triable only at Crown Court) which carries a maximum penalty of life imprisonment.

Attempted Murder

The offence of attempted Murder is committed when a person does an act which is more than merely preparatory to the commission of an offence of Murder, and at the time the person has the intention to kill. Unlike Murder, which requires an intention to kill or cause grievous bodily harm, attempted Murder requires evidence of an intention to kill only. This makes it a difficult offence to prove as evidence of intent can be challenging. Evidence of calculated planning, threats or admissions may assist in proving the intention to kill. On occasions, an alternative charge such as Section 18 or making Threats to Kill may be more appropriate depending on the circumstances. Attempted Murder (as with all offences which are attempted as opposed to the substantive offence) is contrary to Section 1(1) Criminal Attempts Act 1981. It is an indictable only offence which carries a maximum penalty of life imprisonment.

* * *

A BRIEF HISTORY OF CRIME IN BRITAIN FROM C. 1600

THE SEVENTEENTH CENTURY

In the years between the death of Queen Elizabeth I in 1603 and the accession of Queen Anne in 1702 the story of crime in England is crowded with high profile treason trials, violent rebellions and above all, the execution of King Charles I in 1649. That judicial killing opens up the debate about who was 'criminal' in that terrible event. It was a brutal, vicious century with a Civil War in the middle years in which brother fought brother on the battlefield and which saw the horrendous persecutions of witches in many areas of the land.

But the famous and infamous were not the only victims of the repressive criminal law: in the year that King Charles was beheaded, 23 men and one woman were hanged at Tyburn (which was where Marble Arch now stands) for burglary and robbery. It took eight carts to carry the felons to their date with the rope, and the event was the largest number of criminals ever hanged in one session in Britain. The hangings were excuses for heavy drinking and violence in the London mob.

REPRESSION AND SAVAGERY

It is in the seventeenth century that the beginnings of the proliferation of capital crimes began, and these were applied to several areas of life. In the Game Laws of 1684, for instance, the taking of game by anyone except the owner of the land was forbidden. A series of statutes established this. Only people who owned a freehold estate worth £100 a year, or a leasehold of £150 a year were allowed to take game. Poaching had always been looked upon, in rural communities, as a 'social crime' – meaning that there was a certain degree of tolerance in that often the killing of rabbits or birds might hold off starvation for a poor man's family. The thinking behind these tough laws may be seen in the 1671 Coventry Act, which made it a criminal offence to loiter with intent to maim. Sir John Coventry had been attacked and had his nose slit in London, and that prompted the legislation (of course).

In terms of political life, serious offences were punished by hanging, drawing and quartering. In October, 1660, two unfortunates, John Cooke and Hugh Peters, suffered this fate: 'When Mr Cook was cut down and brought to be quartered, one they called Colonel Turner called that he might see it.... The hangman came to him smeared in blood.' He had had the unenviable task of cutting the bodies of the men in quarters while they still breathed.

The 'Bloody Assizes' of 1685 typify this savage reprisal for treason and rebellion: after the Monmouth rebellion in June of that year, in which the Duke of Monmouth had landed with an army at Lyme in Dorset, gathered a large force and proclaimed himself king, there was a brutal reprisal waiting him after his defeat. The so-called Bloody Assizes sentenced over 300 people to death. One of the victims was seventy –year-old Lady Alice Lyle who was beheaded for treason at Winchester, convicted for harbouring traitors.

Opposing the sovereigns was always courageous and often suicidal. The great parliamentarian, John Hampden, opposed Charles I's demands for ship money and was imprisoned in

1627, for fighting the notion of a 'forced loan.' The great judge Sir Richard Hutton also refused to accept the legality of the Ship Money extortion by the King, but he escaped any punishment.

EVERYDAY LAW

But for most people in Britain at this time, the common offences of daily life were dealt with in quarter sessions before magistrates, and at church or manorial courts. The records for these are primarily in Latin in this period – until 1733. But the records are not necessarily all in the county archives. Many have been printed and translated. For instance, the Yorkshire Archaeological Society printed the quarter sessions for the West Riding in parts of this century, and these give a valuable insight into the process of law.

In 1637, for instance, Sir Francis Wortley and other dignitaries sat in judgement at Doncaster on a variety of accused persons. Katherine Booth had broken into a house and stolen a chest of goods; one man had stolen a bible and another had robbed someone of a petticoat and a 'peck of oatmeal.' At the end of the session, we had this situation:

'They were led to the bar by the sheriff and asked what they could say for themselves, why they should not have judgement of death according to the Law for the felonies aforesaid whereof they were convicted. They severally said that they were clerks and prayed for the benefit of clergy...'

This was the one way to escape hanging up until the nineteenth century. If a person could recite the 'neck verse' – the opening of the 51st psalm, they would not hang, but have their thumb branded instead. The benefit of clergy could only be given once.

But there was always the communal, public retribution for what might be called 'moral crimes.' In 1619 there was a case in the Court of Star Chamber in which William and Margaret Cripple of Burton-on-Trent prosecuted residents there: they had been attacked by a mob for 'sexual incontinency.' Not only were they dragged through the streets, they were then put in the stocks and people 'pissed on their heads.'

The *court leets* (from Anglo-Saxon *'laeth'* – a county) and manorial courts give a similar picture: a large amount of criminal business passed through these institutions and the majority are such matters as drunkenness, public nuisances, payment of dues, licences to retail goods and maintaining parish responsibilities.

HIGHWAYMEN

The word 'highwayman' now suggests a glamorous 'gentleman of the road' but in reality these men were nasty, unprincipled villains who preyed on the defenceless. In the classic 'true crime' works of The Newgate Calendar and in the sessions accounts of the Old Bailey, for instance, the name of Claude Duval is prominent. He was a footman to the wealthy turned robber; Duval even robbed the master of horse of King Charles II in his reign of terror on the open road. He was finally caught in a drunken state in Chandos Street, London and hanged at Tyburn. He was just twenty-seven years old

Captain James Hind, born in Chipping Norton in 1619, was another highway robber – the typical 'gentleman highwayman' of popular tales and ballads. He was supposed to rob only Roundheads, and some say he even robbed Oliver Cromwell; he was a celebrated Royalist and at one time, before robbing people, he said, 'I neither fear you nor any king-killing villain alive. I now have as much power over you as you had lately over the King.' He was executed for treason in 1652

AN AGE OF WITCH-FINDING

The seventeenth century was undoubtedly the era of witch prosecutions. In August, 1682 the Bideford witches were hanged at Heavitree gallows in Exeter, and then Alice Molland in 1684 – the latter being the last known execution of a witch in England: in 1736 witchcraft was no longer a capital offence. But the century began with witch trials. In 1619 there was the case of the Belvoir Witches: two 'goodwives' called Margaret and Phillipa Flower were accused by locals of witchcraft, supposedly guilty of manipulating the children of the Earl of Rutland. They were tried and hanged at Lincoln. The most famous case was that of the Lancashire Witches in 1612. A man called John Law gave evidence that he had been bewitched:

'He deposeth and saith that about eighteenth of March last past... he met with Alizon Device, who was very earnest for pinnes, but he would give her none; whereupon she seemed to be very angry, and when he was past her he fell down lame in great extremity...'

By the end of the century, thankfully this kind of accusation and trial was declining. Sir John Holt, who was Lord Chief Justice in 1689, dismissed every witchcraft case that came before him. The last conviction was in 1712, and the woman in question, Jane Wenham, was pardoned.

The Neck Verse:
Have mercy upon me, o God, according to thy loving kindness: according to the multitude of Thy tender mercies blot out my transgressions.'

An old verse explains the origins:
'If a clerk had been taken /for stealing of bacon
For burglary, murder or rape/ if he could but rehearse
(well prompt) his neck verse/ he never could fail to escape.'

Where to find Records

Old Bailey Sessions Papers: These cover the years 1674 to 1913 and are searchable online. In addition to the trial records, there are accounts by 'ordinaries' (gaolers) from Newgate between 1679 and 1772.

Records are many and varied; manorial court leets will be at county record offices. But there are indexes and these prove very useful, such as the *Index of Cases in the Records of the Court of Arches at 1660–1913* by Jane Houston (1972).

The Borthwick Institute at has similar indexes for the Diocese of York. See www.york.ac.uk/inst/bihr

Court of King's Bench (known as the Upper Bench 1649–1660) The index at KB10 is the place to start.

Assize records: Assize court records for 1559–1971 are accessed after finding out where a trial took place, using the criminal registers at HO140. From 1613 the series is at ASSI 45

Check also in the new edition of *Criminal Ancestors* by David T Hawkings History Press

Finding defendants in the regions: look at INDI/6678–6679

Criminal law and major influential events

1612   Trials of the Witches

1637–38   John Hampden opposes the King's 'Ship Money'

1642–1651 The Civil Wars

1649   Execution of Charles I

1680s–1690s   widespread riots: 1693 Food riots in; 1695 election riots at Oxford; 1697 anti-enclosure riots at Epworth in Lincolnshire.

1671   The Coventry Act

1684   Game Laws

1685   Monmouth Rebellion and the 'Bloody Assizes.'

1699   Shoplifting Act – Stealing of goods valued at five shillings and over was a capital crime.

Some Latin Abbreviations in assize records

Remember that assize records are in Latin before 1733. Even after that date, these abbreviations were used:

Ca null – for *catalla nulla* no good to forfeit (a felony meant that the criminal forfeited all possessions). 'catalla' is the root of the word 'chattels'

Cog – for *cognovit indictamentum* confessed to the indictment (charge)

Cul – for *culpabilis* guilty

Ign – for *ignoramus* 'we do not know' meaning there is no charge known.

Non cul nec re – for *non culpabilis nec retraxit* not guilty, and did not flee.

se – for *ponit se super patriam* puts himself before the country (not guilty plea)

Sus – for *suspendatur* for *let him be hanged*

TIMELINE
THE LONG EIGHTEENTH CENTURY (1700-1820)

When we think of the popular images of crime in the 'long' eighteenth century (c.1700-1837), the aspects of the period that come to mind are probably Dick Turpin the highwayman, smugglers and horrible hangings at Tyburn. These kinds of images stem partly from popular culture – mainly film and novels – but also from countless illustrations in books, magazines and documentaries depicting the sheer vicious lawlessness of that century.

But in fact the most dominant criminal events of the years were arguably the Jacobite insurrections of 1715 and 1745; the riots and disorder which occurred for all kinds of reasons; offences against the Game Laws, transportation, the birth of professional police, and sedition. Although there was a high level of homicide and crimes against the person in that period, and a series of repressive Murder Acts, what takes the limelight for crime history is the political narrative.

If we look at some of the major legislation of the time, we find a hugely influential statute in 1715, The Riot Act; then the 1718 Transportation Act, which gave courts the power to transport some felons to the American colonies; the Black Act of 1723 which added a large number of offences to the established 'Bloody Code' discussed in the last Chronicle; and finally the various acts against sedition and radicalism in the Regency years, all aimed at preventing the open or secret dissemination of radical political ideas during and after the French Revolution of 1789.

VIOLENCE AND FEAR

The period is marked at every level of crime as one of horrendous repression and punishment. The British citizen was under threat from robbers and muggers at all times in the towns and of course in London, but nocturnal fears were severe: after all, a man and his household were only protected by the 'watch and ward' officers who were generally ineffective. At the end of this period, we have Sir Robert Peel's Police Act of 1829, and much earlier there were the Bow Street magistrates and 'Runners' in London, but for the country in general, there were perils everywhere.

In 1728, for instance, John Byrom had a meeting with a highwayman. He wrote a letter to his wife describing this: ' ... about half a mile or less of Epping, a highwayman in a red rug upon a black horse came out of the bushes up to the coach, and presenting pistol, first at the coachman and then at the corporation within, with a volley of oaths demanded our money...' Shots were fired and the passengers parted with cash and silver. But the robberies went on daily: copies of *The Gentleman's Magazine* and *The Annual Register* are peppered with reports of nasty and brutal attacks, dreadful murders and brutal hangings.

The number of capital crimes gradually increased throughout this period, until by the 1820s there were over two hundred such offences. Judges on the assize circuits found a procession of culprits standing before them –often very young – who could technically be hanged for what we would think of as small thefts. For a 'grand larceny' the sentence was death, so courts and the Bench often humanely changed the value of stolen goods so that they would be related to simple larceny.

A typical crime of this time, when the country was still predominantly rural, is this from Lincolnshire in 1760, when Mary Baker prosecuted a shepherd of Willoughton for assault: he was in court for 'violently beating and abusing her with his foot and for striking her with his fist, and punching her down and striking her head against a wall...'

RIOT AND DISORDER

But it was also a time when there was trouble in the streets, in the country, and in the new mills. In 1769 attacks on mills were included in the offences subject to the Riot Act, and later in this period, political radicalism brought extreme measures. In 1799 and 1800 the Combination Act outlawed meetings in streets of more than six people; after the Luddite troubles of 1812, when machine-wreckers (named after a fabled figure called Ned Ludd) set about destroying mills in Yorkshire, a new offence of administering an illegal oath was created, so that more felons could be hanged or sent to Van Dieman's Land (Tasmania).

Some riots were not merely in response to the price of corn; the Gordon Riots of 1780 in London, lasted for six days, after Lord George Gordon presented a petition to parliament against Catholic rights. People were killed and in the end 135 people stood trial. Riots were linked to sedition, and in 1792 there was a proclamation against seditious publications, and even the great statesman Thomas Paine was tried (*in absentia*) and convicted of sedition.

Another aspect of this was mutiny. The Napoleonic Wars led to numerous side-effects, and mutiny was one of these: in 1797 after a dangerous mutiny at the Nore men were tried and hanged, and in 1819 the assembly of people for political reasons received its most brutal response from the authorities in these years when the Peterloo Massacre occurred in Manchester: here, the famous speaker Henry 'Orator' Hunt addressed an immense crowd, gathered peaceably, but the yeomanry intervened and in that bloody encounter, eleven people were killed and many more wounded.

But riots could break out for all kinds of reasons: there were food riots in Cornwall in 1727; anti-enclosure riots in the Forest of Dean in 1735, and election riots in several places in 1734.

Crowds gathered to destroy turnpikes in Bristol in 1749 and in 1751 two women suspected of being witches were murdered by a crowd in Tring.

One report in the press from 1755 gives some idea of the trouble that was often experienced:

'May, Selby, Yorks. The bellman made proclamation for the inhabitants to bring their hatchets and axes at 12 o'clock that night to cut down the turnpike erected by Act of Parliament. Accordingly, the great gate with five rails was totally destroyed by some riotous persons...'

TYBURN 'THEATRE'

The abiding image of the criminal justice system in the Georgian years is one of trials at the Old Bailey and hangings at Newgate or Tyburn, accompanied by huge crowds. Of course, there is some truth in this, but we have to recall that many were sentenced to die but also many were reprieved. Between 1814 and 1834 for instance, almost five thousand people were sentenced to hang for burglary, but only 233 hanged. But nevertheless, the hangman was busy. After the Murder Act of 1752, a felon was to be hanged within just 48 hours of sentencing. Until 1760, a 'triple tree' was used at Tyburn, a wooden frame with three sides, so that several people could be hanged at once; this was replaced by a portable gallows in that year. Hangings at Tyburn (now Marble Arch) ended in 1783, and from December of that year executions took place at Newgate. The so-called 'new drop' there was the scene of a multiple hanging in 1783, when nine men and a woman were on the scaffold.

Until 1784, a wife murdering a husband would be burned at the stake rather than hanged, as her crime was petty treason, not murder. In that year Mary Bailey was the last to suffer that horrible fate although it was common practice for the hangman, for a small bribe, to strangle the women before she was tied to the stake. For treason, a person could be hanged, drawn and quartered until 1820, when the famous Cato Street conspirators suffered that fate.

TRANSPORTATION AND PRISONS

After the loss of the American colonies, transportation was to Australia, beginning in 1787. Between 1815 and 1829, around 12,000 convicts were transported to Australia. The process involved a period in a specific colony, and then work on probation teams, so that for instance, convicts in Tasmania would at times be allocated to gaols in Richmond and work in teams to do public works, such as bridge-building.

Prisons in this period were seriously dangerous places to be. The assize system meant that prisoners on remand awaiting trial had to languish in disease-ridden cells until the judges arrived on the circuit to clear the gaols. Local gaols and houses of correction were, however, the subject of a study and survey by the great prison reformer John Howard. His book, *The State of the Prisons* (1777) was the first step in the movement towards making prisons more humane and open to some notions of rehabilitation and reform rather than mere punishment and hard work in a 'silent system.'

The eighteenth century gaol, was however, a mix of factory, punishment block and going concern – in the sense that wealthier inmates could still have communication with the community outside, buying food and drink and having visitors. Debtors lived alongside hardened criminals: John Wesley's father, Samuel, was a debtor in Lincoln gaol.

POLICE

This period saw the gradual emergence of the professional police. The brothers Henry and John Fielding had developed a reasonably successful London police force in the mid century, though its scope was very limited. Then in 1800 there was a police office established at Wapping, and in 1829 the Metropolitan Police Act, forming a paid, full-time force which operated within a radius of about seven miles of London. Provincial forces were to come later.

CRIMINAL LAW AND MAJOR INFLUENTIAL EVENTS

1715   The Riot Act

1718   Transportation Act

1745   The Jacobite Insurrection 'Bonny Prince Charlie

1753   'The Bow Street Constable' established

1780   The Gordon Riots

1789   The French revolution

1799–1800   Combination Acts

1812   Luddite Attacks

1819   the Peterloo Massacre in Manchester

1829   Metropolitan Police Act

THE VICTORIAN AGE (1837–1901)

When Queen Victoria ascended the throne in 1837 there had been significant developments in the criminal justice system, largely thanks to Sir Robert Peel. It would not be stretching the facts too much to say that there had been a revolution in crime and punishment in the ten years before she became queen. Peel had established the first truly professional police force in 1829, and his Gaol Acts had gone some way to providing regulation and inspection in regional gaols and houses of correction.

The last years of the Regency experienced the widespread fear of political and social change impacting on popular feeling and radicalism had brought massive and often terrifying disorder. But in spite of the riots, sedition and arson of the tough first years of the 1830s, there had been important developments, mainly the abolition of a large number of capital offences. Although the retribution of the courts against criminals was still swift and savage, there were signs that more humane attitudes were coming through. By 1837 only sixteen crimes had capital sentences.

By the end of the century, white collar crime had increased markedly, and serious crime against the person was less prominent, though Britain was still a society with a massive drink problem, and violence was never far away, particularly in the new towns, where long hours of hard work and deprivation combined with drunkenness to create an underclass of so-called 'habitual criminals' who crowded the police courts and magistrates' courts.

A Nation Divided

One notable feature of crime in the first half of Victoria's reign was the acceleration of the class divisions: the rich and poor were sharply aware of their differences. In Manchester in the 1840s for instance, as the novelist Elizabeth Gaskell describes in *North and South* the villas of the new rich, the masters of industry, were in one area of the city, strictly separate from the urban ghetto in which the mill workers lived in basement slums, struggling with all the problems poverty, poor public health and low wages bring.

In the 1840s, the writers were so aware of what came to be called 'The Two Englands' that it comes as no surprise that the criminal courts were busy. Theft and assault come often from desperation – men stealing to feed the family or women entering the sex trade in order to earn some extra cash.

The Reform Act of 1832 had been a huge disappointment

to many of the lower middle class, as so many features of the corrupt and divisive political structures of the land had left them without the vote and other rights. Trade unions were illegal and men were transported or imprisoned for working towards establishing unions. By 1851, the artisan class were beginning to creep into some kind of recognition in a corporate sense, with the creation of the Amalgamated Society of Engineers. But for the working man and woman, most of the Victorian period was one of very long working hours, poor pay and limited social support. The workhouse was a constant threat and was seen as little better than a prison.

The Police Reforms

Peel's Metropolitan Police were on the streets by 1829 and by the 1850s, regional forces were being created. There was resistance and suspicion from the start. People thought that a general and professional force would create a police state and they were seen as quasi-military, being compared to the repressive regime in France. After the establishment of the detective force in 1842, these fears were reinforced for many. But the fact is that the new police gradually learned and adapted, so that by the last decades of the century they had formed specialists to deal with such matters as anarchists, Irish Fenians and large-scale fraud. The C.I.D. was created in 1874, and by the end of the century the top police officers were involved in early measures towards national security.

The 1839 County Police Act gave boroughs the option of starting a constabulary, if the justices wanted to levy a rate for that purpose, and in 1856 the County and Borough Police Act made it compulsory for all counties in England and Wales to establish police forces. In the year of Victoria's accession, the first black police officer was appointed – John Kent, who joined the Carlisle police force.

Tough Punishment

The prison system and the criminal courts still maintained a central ideology of harsh repression and a very narrow, regulatory practice in terms of allowing more of the human element into the justice system. For instance, there was no probation service until 1907, though the police court missionaries did their best to keep offenders out of a recidivist life.

The first model prison was constructed at Millbank. A separate system for men and women was established. A study of the prison plans, published in parliamentary papers, for this period shows the very specific and purpose-built accommodation for different classes and sexes. By 1877 the prisons were effectively nationalised and many old local houses of correction were phased out.

Transportation continued until 1853 to Tasmania (Van Dieman's Land) and in the same year the Penal Servitude Act made the idea of punishment itself, the removal of individual freedom, the core of the penal system. By the 1860s, the application of a ticket of leave process, whereby convicts could be released early for good behaviour, led to epidemics of assaults, notably the garrotting reign of terror on 1863–5 in which gangs preyed on the rich in city streets. The response was, naturally, a call for tougher punishments and more use of the whip and birch. In 1867 transportation ended completely.

By 1861 the number of capital offences was reduced to just four: murder, arson in a royal dockyard, high treason and piracy. In that year the last execution for attempted murder took place when Martin Doyle was hanged in Chester. But public hangings continued until 1868, and up to that time the hanging of a felon was still a public spectacle on a massive scale. In popular culture, murder and hanging were placed in all kinds of narratives and entertainments. Charles Dickens reported that pictures of murderers were in the print shops, and he wrote that 'high prices were offered for murderer's clothes at Newgate.'

Hangings in a 'Civilised' Society

When we consider the surface features of the Victorian world – polite social events, dances, protocol and good manners – it is easy to forget how barbaric were the acts done in the name of civilisation. It may have been a Christian society, but after the 1857 Indian Mutiny, for instance, some of the leaders of the rebellion were 'Fired at cannon' – meaning that they were strapped across the barrel of a cannon and then obliterated.

The same attitudes lay behind the public hangings. In 1840 the murder of Lord William Russell was one of the most notorious Victorian cases: this was because he had been killed by a servant. Until 1829, this offence was classified as Petty Treason, and the killer would have been burned at the stake, not hanged. In this case, the killer, Francois Courvoisier, was hanged. At his trial, crowds pushed and shoved to find a seat at the Old Bailey; the judge presiding was short of room and the name of Courvoisier was on everyone's lips in the taverns and coffee-houses.

At the hanging there were 40,000 spectators. The novelist, William Thackeray was in the crowd, and he wrote afterwards:

' I came away from Snow Hill that morning with a disgust for murder, but it was for the murder I saw done.... So salutary has the impression of the butchery been upon me that I can see Mr. Ketch at this moment, with an easy air, taking the rope from his pocket...'

The hangman was William Calcraft, a celebrity at the time. He had to let the body hang for an hour before he could cut it down. The body was then buried within the walls of Newgate.

But just a month after, Courvoisier was seen in waxwork effigy at Madame Tussaud's.

Courts and Trials

There was a massive amount of legislation throughout the Victorian years affecting the criminal courts. As the century wore on, the police courts took on most of the everyday work, as there was such a high level of petty crime that the magistrates could not cope. But for more serious crime, the assizes and the Old Bailey were the arenas where serious crime would be affected by various developments. In the matter of defences for instances, both insanity and provocation were extremely hard to prove. The 1843 McNaghten Rules were the main guidance for barristers and judges: Daniel McNaghten at that time tried to murder Sir Robert Peel but was judged to be insane. He was 'labouring under such defect of reason, from disease of the mind, as not to know the nature and the quality of the act he/she was doing.'

For provocation and insanity, there were hundreds of homicide cases in which the killer (usually a husband) tried to claim either 'temporary insanity' because of drunkenness, or provocation because the wife or woman in question was inconstant.

Imprisonment for debts under £20 was abolished in 1844, and in 1861, imprisonment for debt ended completely.

But amazingly, it was not until the 1890s that the accused could speak in court, and also there was no general court of criminal appeal until 1907. The only chance of a rethink about a criminal court sentence before the end of the century would have been the 'Crown cases Reserved' in which a judge would press the matter in a select group of learned colleagues.

Industrial Relations and Commercial Crime

With the Industrial Revolution and the widespread shift of labour to the new urban conurbations, and the large-scale immigration of workers needed for the new industries, crime came not only with the social divisions and the 'haves and have-nots' but through industrial strife. In terms of industrial problems, the illegality of unions led to constant trouble when 'black-leg' labour was imported. The 1859 Molestation of Workmen Act tried to do something about this, but in 1866, the 'Sheffield Outrages' typified the lamentable results of union problems: non-union cutlery workers were attacked by their fellow workmen. In the following year the Master and Servant Act put some limitations on the mechanism for prosecuting strikers for breach of contract, but members could still face the law if they were thought to be 'aggravated cases.'

But trouble was always there, ready to erupt. Typical of this was the nine-week strike of cotton weavers in Lancashire in1878 in which there were confrontations in Preston and Blackburn, and then the celebrated London dockers' strike of 1889 in which the dockers won six pence an hour. In 1893 two people were killed at Featherstone when soldiers and strikers clashed at Acton Hall colliery.

There was an increase in white-collar crime in the second half of the century, and fraud, forgery and deception were often in the news and reported from the courts. Typical of this was what became the first 'true crime' story on film, when a clerk called Thomas Goudie forged cheques while working with the Bank of Liverpool. He was threatened by a racetrack gang to do this, but was found out and arrested, being given a sentence of ten years but died in gaol after serving six years. Dramatic scenes from Goudie's story were filmed by local film-makers, Mitchell and Kenyon (see *The Lost World of Mitchell and Kenyon*, BBC DVD).

In the City of London, naturally, such crimes proliferated, and always did. But recent research has unearthed a number of little-known sources of material on forgery from the Bank of England, for instance. A cursory trawl through the London magistrates' courts and the Guildhall, Old Bailey sessions papers and assizes will show the escalation of fraudulent offences in these years.

The Queen's reign began with trouble in the streets, social divisions and violent domestic crime, and ended with the dominance of counterfeiters, forgers and con-men. The high-profile murders were still there, but the 'crimes of the brain' were stealing the headlines from the muggers and thieves.

Timeline of Important Legislation

1829	The Metropolitan Police Act. This created a police force with full professional organisation
1839–1842	Chartist demonstrations and troubles: spies used by the Government
1843	The McNaghten Rules established for insanity pleas.
1856	County and Borough Police Act: all counties were forced to set up constabularies
1861	Capital offences reduced to just four Imprisonment for debt abolished
1867	The end of transportation
1868	Public hangings abolished. The last public hanging (in) takes place: Michael Barrett at Newgate
1873	A single High Court is created, replacing seven existing courts
1877	The Prison Act nationalises the prisons
1894	The 'Borstal' scheme first planned

The twentieth century is surely remembered in the history of crimes for arguably the most sickening and extreme of all offences: the war crimes of the Nazis and the Holocaust. But that statement would be rivalled by the genocides in Russia, Viet Nam and elsewhere. If we have to keep the focus on Britain, then certain landmark moments steal the light of historical enquiry. The century began with the street battles against anarchists and ended with some large-scale 'white collar' frauds and new dimensions of mass and serial murder. In contrast, in 1907 the Court of Criminal Appeal made appeals possible for almost anyone, the case brought by lawyers. But in between, the spin-off crime of two world wars and massive urban development give us the spine of the criminal narrative of the last century.

Edwardian Horrors

The years between c.1900 and 1920 saw some astonishing developments in crime-fighting, such as the use of fingerprinting and specialist police squads. The Great War years also saw the first great achievements of the fledgling MI5 in the war against spies on the domestic front. But what steals the headlines is murder. Perhaps the most notorious at the time was that of the murder of Cora Crippen by her husband, Dr Hawley Crippen. Recent work in mitochondrial DNA has cast doubt on exactly whose body lies in the cellar of 39, Hilltop Crescent, but at the time Crippen was sentenced with her murder, after the first arrest brought about by the use of the 'wireless' as Crippen and his mistress Ethel le Neve were spotted on board the SS Montrose by the alert captain. Crippen was hanged at Pentonville in November, 1910 and Ethel emigrated to Australia.

But there were other fears in the streets as well as the terror of murder; there were anarchists about in London, and in the famous Siege of Sidney Street in 1911 some members of a gang of Latvian political refugees who had been involved in the Houndsditch murders of 1909 in which a child and a police officer had been shot dead and seventeen other people injured. At number 11, Exchange Buildings a gang led by George Garstein killed two police sergeants and a constable. Winston Churchill himself (the Home Secretary) joined the troops and detectives who finally trapped the killers, and the building was destroyed, along with the gang, in a fire.

Everyday Killings and Law Reform
After the Great War, the records show an increase in domestic murder: the usual event was the strangling or throat-slitting of the female victim, often by her husband or lover. The war had left thousands of men mentally scarred, and what was called neurasthenia or 'shell shock' was often treated simply with rest rather than direct therapy. Large numbers of ex-servicemen were destined for the scaffold for murder in this kind of situation, like John Crossland, who had fought at Mons where he was wounded; his marriage failed on being demobbed and eventually he battered to death his wife Ellen in Blackburn in May, 1919.

But as murder was still a large-scale social problem and the hangman was kept busy until 1964 in England, there were important reforms in criminal law as the century went on. In 1922, for instance, infanticide was made a version of manslaughter rather than murder, and in 1938 the Infanticide Act dealt with the medical factors, as there was more understanding on post-natal psychosis, and although there were some executions of women – notably Ethel Major at Hull in 1934 and Ruth Ellis in 1955 – capital punishment reforms were gradually carried through.

The Homicide Act of 1957 made clear some guidelines on diminished responsibility. The line of thought was that if a person was suffering from such abnormality of mind when the homicide was committed that his or her judgement was impaired, then the conviction would be for manslaughter.

Yet, amazingly, the Witchcraft Act was not abolished until 1951, and this statute had been used in the prosecution of Helen Duncan in March 1944, after this psychic medium claimed to know about the sinking of HMS Barham before the news was released by the government. An apparition of a sailor appeared at her séance and had the ship's name on his hat when he reputedly said, 'Sorry, sweetheart, my ship sank in the Mediterranean.. I've crossed over to the other side.' Duncan served a spell in gaol for that 'breach of national security' and was the last woman tried under the Witchcraft Act in England.

Another very significant date in this context was 1961 when the Suicide Act abrogated the act as a criminal offence; but complicity in a suicide carried a prison term of fourteen years, and so some notable cases of suicide pacts meant that serious crimes were committed.

The last hangings in this country took place in 1964 when Peter Allen and Gwynne Evans were hanged in April, 1964, on the same day, one in Manchester and one in Liverpool. Then in 1965 the Murder (Abolition of Death Penalty) Act was passed, ending capital punishment for murder.

Gangs, Rackets and Spivs

The 1920s and the years of the second world war saw a notable increase in gangs and in black market rackets. The influence of Hollywood gangster movies may have been a factor in this, and there was glamour attached to stars of the underworld such as Al Capone and Dillinger. But there was nothing glamorous about the fights and killings between the London and provincial gangs who ran racetrack protection rackets and fought over their 'patch' with guns and knives.

The Sabini gang was started by Charles 'Darby' Sabini, a

middleweight boxer who had dressed like a tramp and lived in a hovel, and he has been described by writer Dick Kirby as someone who 'dressed scruffily in hat and scarf and was painfully uneducated.... With his mouthful of gold teeth, he liked to portray himself as a simple peasant like Robin Hood....' Joe was one of his brothers, along with George, Fred and Harryboy. They were involved in protection rackets and often fell foul of the law. In some ways this established the pattern of later organisations such as the infamous Krays, Ronald and Reginald, who controlled the London underworld in the 1960s.

There was gang rivalry with the Krays too, of course: their main threat being the Richardson gang. In 1965 a full gang war began after a Richardson member called Cornell pushed too far with insults about Ronnie Kray. Ronnie shot Cornell dead, before several witnesses, but no-one wanted to tell the tale. Reggie followed suit, killing Jack 'The Hat' McVitie after luring him to a party.

But on a more everyday level, the middle years of the century saw all kinds of variations on theft and robbery, particularly after the second world war, because gangs were formed who had weapons left over from the war. The 1950s saw a flood of armed robberies, many on small shops and clubs or factories. There were also the spivs: the word spiv had been in use for decades before the 1940s, but that was the decade in which it became something in general use. A book called *The Other Half: The Autobiography of a Spiv* by John Worby was published in 1937 and that had an impact. The spiv was often only working for small amounts but was also a 'wide boy' –someone well aware of the criminal fraternity and open to offers and opportunities. In that way the word also began to be used of a fashion and an attitude to life.

The wartime black market was a massive influence on all the rackets and underworld scams of course, a typical example being the appropriation of parachute material to be made into ladies' underwear. As there was wartime rationing, then naturally the criminal class found ways of providing goods and materials in short supply – for a price. Forgery was a part of this too, with such items as ration books and coupons being forged.

Of course, the Great Train Robbery of 1963 in some ways towers above all of this: Bruce Reynolds and his gang of professional thieves who based themselves at a farm near a railtrack and succeeded in breaking into a Royal Mail carriage and in 24 minutes stole over two and a half million pounds. This was split seventeen ways and each man had around £150,000.

The late twentieth century saw the increase in both numbers and intensity of the serial and mass killers, and lessons were learned by police after the notorious case of the Yorkshire Ripper who terrorised women in Yorkshire in between 1975 and 1981, killing at least nine victims. From that case came a number of prominent criminological advances, including mapping and the use of profiling more extensively.

In 1987 one of the first horrendous mass killings of modern times took place at Hungerford in Berkshire, when Michael Ryan shot and killed 16 people and wounded another fourteen. Some label this a 'spree' killing, and like a serial killer, the spree or mass killer is an increasingly common phenomenon today.

The DNA Revolution

In 1984 Professor Alec Jeffreys at Leicester University discovered a way of studying and monitoring DNA sequences and so it became possible to individuate samples from crimes, locating the presence of the criminal with great certainty. Over the next twenty years DNA evidence became an accepted part of court evidence as well as of police detective work. Within the last year there have been four high-profile arrests with reference to crimes committed thirty years ago, made possible by more advances in DNA sampling.

The century began with the first conviction made possible by fingerprinting (in 1905) and ended with several arrests done with DNA science behind the police work.

Timeline

1905	The first convictions given on fingerprint evidence
1907	The court of criminal appeal established
1910	The arrest of Dr Crippen after the use of wireless to catch him
1910–1911	The Houndsditch Murders and the Siege of Sidney Street
1922 and 1938	Infanticide legislation shifting it from the murder category
1961	Suicide no longer a criminal offence
1963	The Great Train Robbery
1964	The last hangings in Britain
1971	Crown Courts introduced
1975–1981	The reign of terror of the Yorkshire Ripper
1987	The Hungerford Massacre
1984	DNA Sampling established

Where to Find Records

The Old Bailey Sessions Papers online: full accounts of trials 1674–1913

Assize court indictments These were in Latin until 1733. Start with criminal registers at TNA HO 27, then consult TNA Assizes: Key to Criminal Trails 1559–1971

Judges reports at TNA start at 1783. See HO 47 for 1783–1830.

Transportation: TNA series T1 and in T53 for America, and HO 11 for Australia (1787–1867)

Prison: County Record Offices will have quarter sessions material and calendars of prisoners.

Police: see Stephen Wade *Tracing Your Police Ancestors* (Pen and Sword 2009)
Comprehensive Reference for all areas: David T. Hawkings, *Criminal Ancestors* (Sutton, 2009)

* * *

THE LAW COURTS IN HISTORY

1 ASSIZE COURTS

The story of the assize courts is a reflection of how the criminal law gradually developed and found a system which would have parity across the land. The courts represent the boldest step by which central legal power began to cover the King's domains, using the local and the national elements together. In each shire, the sheriff, who had been there since very early times, gathered the jury and the other machinery of law, ready for the visit of the assize judges, because that is what assizes were – courts done in transit – giving the assize towns distinguished visitors and a high level of ritual and importance for a few days each year.

Originally, the law courts followed the King, and his own court was the *Curia Regis*. Then in Magna Carta (1215) there was this sentence: 'Common pleas shall not follow our Court but shall be held in some certain place.' The result was that Westminster was made that 'place' but then the notion of having the top judges moving around to deal with criminal and civil cases became a workable option, with economic and logistical benefits of course, as persons accused would be retained and then tried mostly in their own counties or provinces.

Since early Medieval times, there had been assizes – literally 'sittings together' – to try causes and to gather officials in the English regions to compile enquiries and inventories into local possessions and actions. These were 'eyres' of assize, but they were not courts. The assize courts came when travelling justices went out into the counties to try cases: the Assize of Clarendon in 1166 and the Council of Northampton in 1196 decreed that the country should be split into six areas in which the judges of the High Court would sit. These became known as circuits.

In Edward I's reign an act was passed to create court hearings in the local place of jury trial, before a summons for the jury to go to Westminster. The people involved were to come to London unless the trial had happened before: in Latin *nisi prius* (unless before). What developed over the centuries was that serious offences, crimes needing an *indictment*, had to be tried before a jury. The less serious offences, summary ones, could be tried by a magistrate. In addition to that, the terms *felony and misdemeanour* also existed until they were abolished in 1967: a felony was a crime in which guilt would mean a forfeiture of possessions and land, so the offender's children would lose their inheritance. A misdemeanour was a less serious crime.

Business and Organisation
The justices of assize had a number of powers. First, they had

a commission of *oyer and terminer* (to listen and to act) on serious cases such as treason, murder, and any crime which was labelled a felony. They also had to try all people who had been charged and who had been languishing in gaol since their arrest, and they tried cases *nisi prius.*

The assize circuits became established as the Home, Midland, Norfolk, Oxford, Eastern, Western and Northern, and the records for these run from 1558 to either 1864 or 1876 when assizes were reorganised, or to 1971, when the assizes were abolished and crown courts created. From the beginning, the assize circuits covered all counties except Cheshire, Durham, Lancashire and Middlesex, the first three being referred to as the Palatinate Courts. In 1876, some courts moved from one circuit to another.

The result of all this means that a criminal ancestor who committed a crime in Leeds, for instance, after 1876, would be tried in Leeds rather than in York, the former seat of an assize for the West Riding.

The family historian needs to access the location of the court and trial as a first step. A useful source for checking on which assizes were on the circuit at any time between the late eighteenth century and the end of the nineteenth is to look at *The Gentleman's Magazine*, which listed assizes and names of judges presiding at each one. This journal appeared annually. The assizes were held twice a year, from the thirteenth century until they ended in 1971, and these sessions were referred to as Spring and Winter. A third session could be held at times if the gaols were full – as in times of popular revolt and riots, or activities by gangs.

Civil and Criminal

The assizes were divided into two areas: for civil cases, referred to as 'crown' – and criminal cases. Two judges would be on the road, each with a responsibility for one of the two areas of law. In the law reports in *The Times*, these are clearly marked, in capitals. For instance, for the Winter Assizes in York in December, 1844, we have:

WINTER ASSIZES NORTHERN CIRCUIT
YORK, DECEMBER 5. (Before Mr Justice Coleridge)

The newspapers tend to use the terms, 'Crown side' and criminal side.'

The Records and Where they Are

Records for these courts began to be more systematically kept after 1559. There are gaps, such as the years 1482–1559 in listings – calendars of assizes. Most records before 1733 are in Latin so there is another obstacle to progress there. However, for most family historians, the period of most interest is going to be Georgian through to the last years of assizes, post World War Two. The documents relating to the assizes include:

Indictments: these are statements expressing exactly what the offence in question is. They include the plea, verdict and sentence. The indictment also gives more information on the accused, including the parish in which they lived or where they were when arrested.

Calendars of prisoners: These give the prisoner's name, the crime, also age, occupation, level of literacy, given place of residence (not reliable) and the date on which they were gaoled. They were printed before the assize took place, and therefore there may have been other prisoners who appeared but were not listed, so the press reports become even more important in research. They usually also give the name of the committing magistrate.

Calendars of sentences: These were printed after the assize, so they have details of the sentences. A typical entry is this from the Lincoln assizes in 1848:

Ann Smith, aged 18, charged with having, on the 3rd of May at Bourn in the parts of Kesteven, wilfully and feloniously set fire to a wheat stack, the property of John Gentle 18 months Imprisonment

Gaol Delivery calendars: These documents give the names of the convicted prisoners, along with brief details of their crime: printed after the assize.

Depositions: When these are available, they are of special interest, because they are a sworn statement of testimony by a witness. They have details of residence, age and occupation of the witness. The document binds the person to appear in court and a fine was imposed for non-appearance. A deposition of 1799 for instance, states that the fine was one shilling – a considerable amount of money at that time.

For early records, materials are in TNA at JUST 1 –JUST 4 and there are indictments for these earlier times in the King's Bench records at KB9, and some letters from assize judges at SP1. Then, from 1559, if the researcher knows the name of the prisoner and where the trial took place, the next step is to find the assize records at the County Record Office. At TNA there are sheriff's assize vouchers, but only for 1714–1832, so if there are no assize records locally for those years, then the vouchers will help. They are concerned with costs incurred for moving, watching and feeding prisoners.

The stages of enquiry are:
➤ First, check the probable dates and place of the offence.
➤ Look in *The Times Digital Archive* for a court report, searching with the criminal's name or the assize location.

> At the record office where the assizes records are held, look at the calendar of prisoners.
> Search for any other documents relating to the trial.

Special Jurisdictions

The assize for London, from 1834, was the Old Bailey, and that court covered Middlesex and parts of Essex as well as London. The Old Bailey Sessions Papers are online for the dates up to 1913 and may be searched free, and with a full text of the proceedings (www.oldbaileyonline.org). For London and Middlesex before 1834 sessions of oyer and terminer and gaol delivery were held before the Lord Mayor and so these records are with materials from the Corporation of London.

For Wales, after the 1543 Act of Union, assize business was handled at the courts of Great Sessions. These records are at the National Library of Wales, Aberystwyth; they were abolished in 1830 and a Welsh circuit created, followed by a split after 1876 into North and South Wales, and these are at Aberystwyth also. (See www.llgc.org.uk)

The records for palatinate courts of Chester, Durham and Lancaster are all now held at TNA.

Finally, the TNA have a comprehensive listing of assize records for all counties, giving dates and reference numbers; these are found by searching for Assizes: Key for Criminal Trials 1559–1971. That is essential, because you may see at a glance which records are available for certain years, and which records have been lost.

As usual with searches for the black sheep of the family, there are always obstacles and false trails, but at least with assize records, we are talking about serious crime (at least what were considered serious at the time). Felonies were usually well reported, but it is as well to remember that between c.1720 and 1830 there was a gradual increase in capital offences, all felonies, and so assize courts then were trying crimes that we would now think far from serious, such as stealing cloth or taking an oath.

Other Support Material
Books

Amanda Bevan *Tracing Your Ancestors in the National Archives* (TNA, 2006)

David T Hawkings *Criminal Ancestors: a guide to historical criminal records in England and Wales and* (Sutton, 2009)

Ruth Paley and Simon Fowler *Family Skeletons* (TNA, 2005)

Stephen Wade *Tracing Your Criminal Ancestors* (Pen and Sword, 2009)

Web Sites
ww.ancestry.co.uk. Ancestry have recently added to their sources court records from the nineteenth century, so that for a subscription, more criminal records may be accessed from home rather than having to visit record offices.

www.blacksheepancestors.com This is a site with listings of all criminals mentioned in newspapers from the nineteenth century to the mid twentieth century. For a small fee, the text of the cutting can be ordered

www.nationalarchives.gov.uk The TNA site provides short and informative guides to aspects of assizes and also provides the list of dates and locations of assize records

www.oldbaileyonline.org
This free site provides transcripts of trials at the old Bailey (properly the Central Criminal Court) between 1674 and 1913

2 QUARTER SESSIONS

The Quarter Sessions courts were always the workhorse of the criminal justice system throughout British history. They began in 1351, and they handled every kind of offence and local tribulation that came their way. They were the domain of the justices of the peace (magistrates) and met, as the name suggests, four times a year. Before the justices came concerns relating to drunkenness, pub brawls, arguments over land, nuisances on the highway, problems with beggars, licensing of beer houses, provision of constables, maintenance of bridges and other affairs, the topics changing as the years passed and society had new laws and fresh social problems. All the justices of the county generally sat on the bench at Quarter Sessions.

DEVELOPMENT

Matters were running smoothly through the years until an Act of 1831 which stipulated specific dates for the courts, so as not to interfere with the Assizes (which dealt with felonies, more serious crime). This statute said: ' ... Quarter Sessions for the peace by law ought to be held... in the first week after the 11th of October, in the first week after the 28th of December, in the first week after the 31st of March, and in the first week after the 24th of June.' From the early nineteenth century, details of the sessions were given in almanacs, sometimes locally but always in the *British Almanac,* published by the Society for the Diffusion of Useful Knowledge. This publication listed all the quarter sessions for the coming year, with dates and venues.

It was in the Tudor period that the justices really found their workload accelerating: a succession of legislative measures to deal with the increasing problems of vagrants, wanderers from other parishes and disabled soldiers, and also of affairs relating to apprentices and workmen, street crime and the regulation of all local matters pertaining to the social order. The magistrates were first created as a fresh form of the previous 'Keeper of the Peace' and it is no accident that they appeared and were more clearly defined at a time of massive social crisis. The Black Death of 1348 and the horrendous years of famine previous to that, along with other epidemics and social revolt, made the year of 1361 one of the most significant in British legal history. It was followed by an Act which set up Quarter Sessions the next year. The immediate context was one of the widespread threat of violence and roving gangs across the land.

Quarter Sessions dealt with capital offences until the 1660s and from that time there were also an increasing number of petty sessions, hearings often dealing with many of the matters the Quarter Sessions normally handled. The everyday offences before the magistrates were misdemeanours, crimes that could be tried without a jury. Of course, they were the place where the first appearance of a person arrested for a felony would appear too, the cases being handed on to the Assize hearing that came up next on the calendar.

In the nineteenth century, many local offences were dealt with by police courts, which were yet another form of petty session, but the quarter sessions went on, the centre of the great law machine in the heart of the social upheavals of the Industrial Revolution, when massive threats of riot and disorder were everywhere in the first three decades, in which Luddites, 'Captain Swing' rural crime and the Chartist movement added to the burden of the justices.

A Novelist on the Bench
In his book, *A Farmer's Year* (1899) we have accounts of the novelist's work as a justice in Norfolk , where he was an important landowner, and he reflects, for instance, on some petty crimes from June 1898: after hearing a case of egg-stealing, in which a man described as a marine dealer was

accused of sending a box of 251 partridge eggs to another dealer, the man was fined a shilling an egg or two months in gaol. Haggard's thoughts on poaching gave us an insight into some of the main issues magistrates dealt with. He notes: '... I have on several occasions seen poaching cases dismissed when the evidence would have been thought sufficient to ensure conviction. it is extraordinary what an amount of false sentiment is wasted in certain quarters upon poachers, who, for the most part, are very cowardly villains...'

On the other hand, in his note for April 20 in the same year, there is a case of lunacy. He writes, in his capacity as the magistrate appointed to be in action in cases under the Lunacy Acts, 'About breakfast time on Sunday morning I was requested by an overseer to attend in a neighbouring village to satisfy myself by personal examination as to the madness of a certain pauper lunatic...' He did indeed, and then he signed the orders needed for her removal to an asylum. It was a sad occasion and a huge responsibility for him He adds, 'It seems that it was not considered advisable that the patient should remain longer out of proper control, so, as she could not be removed without a magistrate's order, I was followed to the church.'

No End of Business

The justices had a massive amount of responsibility before them and they had to deal with several issues related to non-judicial duties as well as the criminal cases needing due process of law.

If we look at how trials at Quarter Sessions were conducted, there was generally a sequence of actions and topics. This organisation reflected the varied business of the court. First there would be *presentments* applied to all the waiting accused persons. These are statements of the alleged offences, so in turn these would appear to be charged. If the offence was a misdemeanour, this would be typical of what happened:

First, the Accused
John Holmes of Keighley, blacksmith, for assaulting there on 13th March and maltreating John Greene, clerk. Witn. Ja. Ibbetson... (Puts himself not guilty at Skipton 18 July 1638)

His case had progressed to the Quarter Sessions from a hearing at petty sessions.

Then Appeals and Supervisions
This could include assessments of property, highway maintenance fines, repairs of bridges, issues relating to parish constables, financial accounts of various people in office, appeals against assessments, and until the Municipal Corporations Act of 1835, other business would include supervising boards of health, poor law unions and town councils. The non-judicial duties retained after that were mainly of licensing premises, arbitrating in master and servant disputes, supervising county rates, the sale of coals, bread and flour regulations and ensuring that friendly societies and trade unions (in the latter case with adaptations as such unions became legal).

Finally, Orders – all Matters of a parish or civil nature
This may be most clearly seen at times of peril and threat towards the authorities, for instance during the Luddite violence around 1811–1812 or the Chartists agitations of the 1830s and 1840s. Equally, in the Tudor period and through to the 1834 Poor Law reforms, there would be issues such as vagrancy and social responsibility at this point.

West Riding Sessions, 1637
The 1637 sessions record a long list of crimes, and most were felonies, and so one possible punishment was death. Reading the account today, there is a deep sense of foreboding in the wording; sixteen men and two women were 'Put for good or ill

upon the country, whereupon a jury was called.' We can imagine them all lined up before the twelve good men and true, waiting for their fate. The report goes on:

'... they were led to the bar by the sheriff and asked what they could say for themselves why they should not have judgement of death according to the law for the felonies aforesaid whereof they were convicted. They severally said that they were clerks and prayed for benefit of clergy to be granted them.'

What happened next was going on along the length and breadth of the land. The 'Benefit of Clergy' ruling meant that if a felon could read what was called the 'neck verse' –which they could claim on only one occasion, then they would be branded rather than hanged. The neck verse was the opening of the 51st psalm: 'Have mercy upon me, O God, according to Thy loving kindness: according to the multitude of Thy tender mercies blot out my transgressions.'

The neck verse was originally intended to give clergy an exemption from the criminal law process. An old verse explains:

'If a clerk had been taken
For stealing of bacon,
For burglary, murder or rape.
If he could but rehearse
(well prompt) his neck verse,
He never could fail to escape.'

But the unhappy line of men and women in 1637, although they had learned the words well, had further pain to come. By a statute of Henry VII they had to be branded: each was burned in his left hand, according to the Statute.' The old Statute said: 'every person so convicted of murder, be marked with an M upon the brawn of the left thumb, and if he be convicted for any other felony the same person to be marked with a T in the same place upon the thumb, and these marks to be made by a gaoler openly in court before the judge.' There were screams of agony that day in the courtroom.

RECORDS
County archives
The records for Quarter Sessions are mostly at County record Offices and the materials there will often be in a bundle of papers and documents related to a case. The above example includes: an appeal document, a statement of police charges, letters from the solicitor, statements from the brewery and a recognisance for a court appearance.

In a wider sense, the records will often have a calendar of prisoners, with full information of those charged and the sentence given; summonses and recognisances, legal papers relating to the case. Until 1733, Latin was the language of legal matters and there may well be Latin texts in the records in Quarter Sessions. But the good news is that, because so much of the material was from ordinary people, their statements were taken down verbatim, and so often the records have very direct, often slangy and dialectal vocabulary. The most commonly found records are:

Depositions: these were the statements given by the accused and by witnesses; these were given to the magistrate.

Indictment Book: This was the formal record of what the charge against the accused was, naturally it was expressed in a highly formalised vocabulary.

Recognisance: This was a statement which bound the writer or speaker to appear in court, and they were sworn to pay a specified sum should they not attend.

Sessions Roll/Order Book: This was the proper and official record of the trial. From the Regency, it is noticeable that pro forma papers were used, and so the process of research becomes easier in some ways.

Newspapers

If the ancestor was a criminal, or was tried and acquitted, but the exact dates of the offence and charge are not known, then the local and regional newspapers (and sometimes the national ones) are a good place to start. *The Times Digital Archive* provides reports from all kinds of courts, from 1785, including Quarter Sessions. But for the regions, the *Nineteenth Century British Newspapers* resource, again online, is very useful. These newspapers usually gave quite full details of court events, although for Quarter Sessions, often there is no more than a list of names and crimes, along with prison sentences or other results.

CONTACTS

Quarter sessions from pre-eighteenth century records are included in publications by county record societies and other organisations:

The Selden Society

School of Law,
Queen Mary,
Mile End Road,
London E1 4NS
w. www.selden-society.qmw.ac.uk

The Surtees Society

Faculty Office,
Elvet Riverside Block 2
New Elvet,
Durham DH1 3JT
www.surteessociety.org
t. 0191-3342908

The National Archives
Ruskin Avenue, Kew, Richmond TW9 4DU
w. www.nationalarchives.go.uk
e. enquiries@nationalarchives.gov.uk
t. 02083925200

FURTHER READING
Criminal Ancestors
David T Hawkings, 2009, The History Press, 2009
ISBN 978-0-7509-5057-2

Family Skeletons
Ruth Paley and Simon Fowler, 2005, The National Archives.
ISBN 9781903365546

Tracing Your Criminal Ancestors
Stephen Wade, 2009, Pen and Sword Books
ISBN 9781848840577

* * *

AN A–Z OF LEGAL TERMS IN HISTORICAL CRIME
The history of crime and law in Britain reflects all the major elements of social and political change; what better way to understand the repercussions of important and radical forces acting on a nation or on a community than a look at the cases before the courts? There is the legal language to overcome, of course, and the layperson tends to think that law reports are written with a basis of thinking summed up in the words: why use a sentence when three chapters will do? But leaving legal vocabulary aside, the point is that the records of everyday law,

civil and criminal, makes for exciting, humorous and sometimes totally bizarre reading.

Pottering around my local antiques centre recently, I came across a box of old wills. Some of those documents were from three centuries ago, and were probably all about chattels and land, who inherited them and who gave them. I say probably because not only were the documents composed of very long sentences, they also had words which seemed to have been formed from a wayward mix of dead Latin and something else that the lawyers made up from a game of fridge magnet scrabble.

I imagined the relatives sitting around the lawyer as he read out a will. Half an hour would pass, and then there would be a long silence followed by, 'Could you read that again please... in English?'

It has always been difficult to avoid being involved in the law in some way. Even Shakespeare had to appear in court, at the Court of Requests, to testify that someone owed someone else some money. That was fortunate for the scholars in one way, but possibly not, because in the time he had to stand in court, after waiting to take his place, he could have written part four of *Henry IV* or a sequel to *Hamlet*.

The vocabulary of the law has always been intractable and baffling. As far back as Anglo-Saxon times, the early laws produced by kings in Kent and Mercia were teeming with bizarre terms such as *frankpledge, tithingman* and *ingfanthief*. We can imagine King Offa plotting to devise the most surreal and hard-to-pronounce Germanic words, just to confuse the rabble he had to deal with.

Lawmakers started to dream up bizarre rules such as compensation for offences: if an offence was committed on a holy day, for instance, the fine was twice as high. If a man's ear was cut off in a fight, the fine was twelve shillings; if a front tooth was knocked out, then the attacker had to pay just six shillings.

All this helps us to understand why Shakespeare produced the immortal line from Julius Caesar: 'Let's kill all the lawyers.' They were in as much danger as the poets when the mob were in a foul mood.

Social history has its own difficulties when we wish to read and understand events and stories from the past in which the process of law has been involved. A dictionary of law is not enough to explain to the layman what exactly happened or what was meant by the legal language employed.

In the business of researching crime stories from the centuries of British history in which criminal justice systems came and went, and in which definitions of what was criminal shifted constantly, I came to see that readers of narrative history needed some help to find their way through the labyrinths of legal vocabulary.

A famous judge once said that, as he made his way to court that morning, he saw twenty-five crimes committed. These included everything from dangerous driving to infringement of by-laws. Of course, he could do nothing about it unless he had been in the mood to make dozens of citizens' arrests.

But in years gone by, a man could find himself battered and bewildered as much by the explanation of the crime he had committed as by the arrest and detention. Governments have a way of legislating to achieve their ends, come what may. In the worst years of the Luddite machine-smashing around 1812–1814, the Home Secretary needed an offence that would make it easy to stick a capital charge on the trouble makers. They had done lots of nasty things but an offence was needed that would make sure they would swing on the gallows at York. In haste, the offence of taking an illegal oath was created. They had got their men.

Hopefully, my guide and dictionary will provide explanation

along with some entertaining tales from the past. My stories perhaps confirm the wise words of Cicero: 'it is ignorance of the law rather than knowledge of it that leads to litigation.

My aim here is to provide explanations along with the stories, but the narrative interest comes first. In my career as a true crime writer I have had to learn to understand legal process, the whole knotty business in criminal justice in which records are either in jargon or in Latin, so I have some idea what it is like to plough through tortuous sentences and levels of pomposity beyond belief. The main element of entertainment I offer here are the tales of hapless individuals through the centuries, wanting to sue someone, avoid a fine or inherit granddad's stash. My stories are sometimes of criminals but also of innocent victims, the common people caught up in social change and in the jaws of rapacious businessmen.

Yes, let me come clean here. I have no degree in law: I'm writing simply as a writer and historian who has had to struggle through masses of legal documents from past years, and so learn by mistakes and false paths. A typical example is my research for a famous murder case in Lincolnshire, in which the killer was tried at a court in Lincoln – the assizes. But one local report on the cases referred to the court being *nisi picus.* As everyone knows from television crime dramas, law is packed with Latin vocabulary, and here was an example for me. I reached for my copy of *Lawyers' Latin* by John Gray, and found no such words. Then, by a process of good luck and persistence, I discovered that the journalist had got it wrong; he meant *nisi prius.* This means 'unless before' and means that a case will be tried at the court in London unless the assize date falls before that date. It is a writ to the sheriff to gather jurors for such a trial. Now, to a layman, that was quite a challenge, and such matters face us every day, even as general readers, as the Law Reports in *The Times* illustrate every day.

With all this in mind, my little guide should be at your elbow or within reach of your seat at the desk when tackling crime and law from past times.

A

Act of God

Legally, an Act of God is applied to something that could not have been foreseen or guarded against. This story is a crazy example of that, and it saved a man from the gallows.

It reads like such a simple, uncomplicated statement of a killing: 'York Assizes: Abraham Bairstan, aged 60, was put to the bar, charged with the wilful murder of Sarah Bairstan his wife, in the parish of Bradford.' In the busy, overworked courts of the regency, dealing with new and often puzzling crimes from the labouring classes in the fast-growing towns, it was maybe just another 'domestic' that went too far. But this is far from the truth, and the Bairstan case gives us an insight into the plight of those unfortunate people at the time who were victims of ignorance as well as of illness. In this instance it was an awful, anguished mental illness that played a major part in this murder.

When the turnkey brought Bairstan into the court he commented that he had not heard the prisoner say a word since he was brought to York and locked up. This was nothing new to the man's family. Mr. Baron Hullock, presiding, was shocked but also full of that natural curiosity of someone who just does not understand something. He pressed the gaoler to explain. He asked if the man in the dock understood the spoken word, and the answer was no. He also ascertained that Bairstan appeared to have no response to any sound whatsoever, nor any movement.

It makes painful reading in the court report to note that the prisoner was a 'dull and heavy looking man who... cast a vacant glance around the court.' The reporter in 1824 noted that the man 'appeared totally insensible of the nature of the proceedings.'

Poor Hullock had a real challenge to try to communicate with the man, trying his best to make the prisoner make any sound at all, asking several questions but receiving no answer. When he asked 'Do you hear what I say to you?' Bairstan simply stared at the officer next to him.

It was obviously going to be one of those trials at which many people were thinking that this silence was the best ruse if a man wanted to avoid the rope. The judge had to instruct the jury about potential fraud and the possibility that this was a tough and amoral killer with a canny wit and impressive acting skills. In legal jargon, the point was, was the man standing there fraudulently, wilfully and obstinately, or 'by the act and providence of God?' It was going to be a hard task, one might think, but not so: enter his sons and a close friend. They told a very sad story, and an astounding one, given that Bairstan managed to marry and raise a family.

His friend stated that he had known the prisoner for over fifty years, and that he was sure that ten years had passed since Bairstan had fallen silent. He explained that his two sons had been looking after the old man in that time. His key statement was that 'while he was sane, his wife and he had lived together very comfortably.' The man, Jeremiah Hailey, added that his friend had been capable of merely saying yes or no, and that the last time he had heard the man speak was when he had asked him if he knew his friend Jeremiah. 'He said aye, but I think he did not know me.'

Bairstan's two sons confirmed that their father had been silent in that ten-year period, only excepting one or two words. Henry said that since being locked up, his father had been pressed to speak and had answered something sounding like.

'Be quiet... be quiet'. The other son, Joseph, confirmed that his father had been 'out of his mind' for ten years.'

There had been enough in him to marry and earn a living, but we must see with hindsight and more relevant knowledge, that Abraham Bairstan had been struck by a paralysis, perhaps combined with a depressive mental illness. In 1824, the most meaningful explanation was to put it down to God's will, so the jury found that the prisoner stood mute 'by the visitation of God.'

Or, if one is pressed to say that it had all been a wonderfully impressive family performance, then would not this be the sure way to keep the old man from the noose? On the other hand, he was destined to be shut away for ever in awful conditions, being criminally insane. The truth will perhaps never now be known.

B
Bad Character
The Vagrancy Act of 1824 defined a vagrant as being one of these categories of person:

(a) idle and disorderly
(b) rogue and vagabond
(c) an incorrigible rogue.

In common parlance, officers of the law were in the habit of referring to some of these types as 'bad characters' and simple though that Act appears to be, a case in Grimsby illustrates the problem with it.

In English criminal law, a person standing charged with an offence has to be tried on the grounds of that specific offence, and nothing else beyond that. Courts in the past have often run into trouble and made mistakes because of contravening that rule. In the case of a known criminal in Grimsby a mistake was made.

In October, 1955, Mr Fitzwalter Buller found himself acting for a group of people whose property had been under threat from a 'vagrant' named Fuller. It was going to be a simple matter to show that the man had been up to no good on some premises, as the recorder at the quarter sessions in Grimsby had been given a long list of the man's previous convictions. That was a step that the aggrieved parties may have regretted because the case went to the court of appeal.

It was a case of a record of a known 'bad character' being given in court to prejudice a decision. Fuller had been asked why he had not accepted work, as he had not appeared in court at an earlier time. Then, on the night in question, he had been found in a place where he was almost certainly going to commit an offence.

The drifter was a man who had caused a series of confrontations with the local police and he was often under observation; it was known that he was the type who could easily shift from minor offences to other, more serious ones, and when he was caught and charged on this particular occasion, that thinking lay behind the police actions. But it was in the court that things went wrong for everyone concerned, and all because of a too enthusiastic court officer.

Fuller had been given a three month prison sentence for that offence, under the old Vagrancy Act of 1824, so there was a feeling of certainty that he was out to do a burglary or even worse. But, as the appeal court noted, to haul him up in court and then place the list of convictions in front of the judge was malpractice. The judge at appeal said, 'The merest glance at the report by anyone accustomed to that class of document, as every recorder would be, would show him that he was dealing with what might be called 'an old hand.' The mere sight of the document, it was said, would show that the appellant was a man with a long list of previous convictions.

The outcome was that if there was an appeal against a conviction, then no details of previous convictions should be made visible. The man had gone to prison on what in legal terms is called an 'unsafe' judgement. Clearly, this all became a matter of prejudice, and that was not difficult to show before the High Court Judge, Mr Justice Ormerod.

Here was a case of a 'bad character' who nevertheless found himself languishing in gaol because he had received a 'punishment' for things allegedly done well before the latest appearance in court. Maybe his defence in court – that he had been on the property when he was arrested looking for work – did not really convince the magistrate, but he was badly handled, and that was the bottom line.

The fateful list, given to the Recorder, could not have been put in front of a jury, and so a basic principle of law had been breached. The basis of the debate was in the operation of the so-called 'Sus laws' and these were common causes of discontent at the time. The famous detective Jack Slipper, on the streets at the same time as the Grimsby event, has this to say about these laws which enabled officers to stop anyone 'on suspicion': 'As I became more experienced I had a number of good arrests, thanks to the Section Four of the 1824 Vagrancy Act which allows a police officer to arrest someone he suspects of being about to commit an arrestable offence. That doesn't mean you can pick up someone just because you thought he might be a criminal...'

In other words, the Grimsby affair happened largely because the officers concerned knew the man in question. He was not 'just someone.'

Barratry
This is nothing to do with the construction of new estates and small detached houses. This offence was concerned with

troublemakers. Common barratry was the offence of frequently inciting and stirring up suits and quarrels between Her Majesty's subjects. This was abolished by the Criminal Law Act of 1967. Many barrators in criminal history had interesting experiences, frequently with reference to prison life. The most frequent occurrences tend to refer to barratry on board ship – 'any wilful or fraudulent act committed by the master of a ship... causing damage to the ship or cargo...'

The famous Judge Jeffreys tried two brothers called Williamson for barratry and he had them both put in the pillory. Jeffreys' opinion of the offence was 'an offence committed by scurrilous attorneys in trumping up cases and encouraging hopeless litigation.'

C
Conjugal Rights
This was repealed by the Matrimonial Causes Act of 1973. But for so long this was the kind of case that dragged on and created hell. It was a suit by a husband to compel a wife to live with him, or by a wife to compel a husband to take her back.

Most cases in the massive legal records relating to this are of course dull and predictable, but there are always cases to raise a smile, such as the case of Conolly v Conolly. These two Americans married in 1831, and Mr Conolly was a clergyman in the Episcopal Church of America. That seems quite straightforward, but then they both succumbed to the allure of the Catholic Church in that age of dogma and swerving faith. They not only decided to live apart, so he could follow the path of celibacy: they went to the Pope himself to have a separation granted, and Gregory XVI obliged. They then went to total extremes. Not only did the husband become a priest, but the wife became a nun, and so keen was she on her new life that she founded a religious order in Derby.

Mr Conolly, clearly a man who vacillated and doubted, following his passions and the cooling off, wished to return to the Protestant fold. The old life had to include his wife, and she was fond of her new habit, so a suit was instigated for the Reverend's conjugal rights. The judge was evidently defeated by this complexity and demolished the business on the grounds that the separation at Rome had not been 'sufficiently set forth.'

Another odd tale concerns the Earl of Stair, Mr Dalrymple. He eloped with a young woman called Miss Gordon, but things turned sour for him and the marriage became a burden; he rejected her but she sued for conjugal rights. Stair was living with his new sweetheart and so his solution to the problem was to engage a lothario to court Miss Gordon, and arrange for an embarrassing situation to be come across. If that succeeded, the good earl was to pay the man a large amount of cash.

What happened then was that Mrs Dalrymple sued for a divorce and had one granted, before any embarrassing situation could be arranged. The lover sent by Earl Stair then turned cool and rebuffed her, with the result that she lost her wits and was placed in an asylum. Twenty seven years later she regained her sanity, but her commission was superseded – the action was finally cancelled. What happened to the lothario is a mystery.

D
Doli Capax
This means 'capable of crime' – this indicates that in a case, a child between the ages of eight and fourteen has sufficient understanding to discern between good and evil, and so know that his or her action in a circumstance would be criminal. In years gone by, many liked to explain the 'spare the rod, spoil the child' remedy.

In January, 1889, a minor episode of shoplifting in Doncaster reached the national newspapers and caused a lengthy debate.

That may have been unusual for a Doncaster story, but the subject was certainly nothing new. The general public had been well informed about 'rings' of child thieves most famously by Charles Dickens in *Oliver Twist* back in 1838 and after that year there had been a constant fear of child criminals. The main statutory measures against the problem had been the establishment of the reformatories in the 1850s. That had been one way of dealing with juvenile crime – take the little villains away from home and work them into submission!

These tough measures had not really addressed the heart of the problem. If we accept that in the history of crime drink and poverty have always been causal factors, then that was central to the Victorians, and they had those problems in the absolute extreme. The massive demographic shift of labour into the new towns after the Enclosure Acts (accelerated after 1801) and the proliferation of the factories and mills had created a general need of child labour, and education had been slow to develop as a remedial measure – something to make childhood happy and hopefully imaginative. But it has to be said that the universal influence of beer shops and the habit of drinking gin at all times was a formative tendency in making poverty a massive social issue.

The result was that the late Victorian years had new debates about children and the law. One of the commonest features of this was the context of what we now try to deal with in issuing the ASBO: children left out to roam, create trouble and fend for themselves.

This was the case in Doncaster at this time, and the story that reached the dignified pages of *The Times* was one featuring two children: a brother and sister called Margaret and Daniel Fell. They went on a stealing spree in Doncaster one day and stole £2 from a confectioner in Hall Gate called Miss Brooks. That was quite a lot of money, but matters were more serious when it was found that they had raided several other shops, averaging a few pounds in cash from each one.

The boy was ten and the girl seven; they had been taught to steal by a mysterious child called Harker, and of her there is nothing else known but her name. Margaret and Daniel took their booty and met another child, then all three decided to have a day out in Lincoln. There, they appear to have spent their takings, and not stolen anything; they went for a number of rides on the trams, and it was while on one of these that a driver became suspicious of them and called the police.

At the Doncaster Police Court, the children faced their punishment. The Chief Constable, Isaac Gregory, recounted the events of the day of the spree, and he said that their parents 'Had a good deal of trouble with these children.' He told a familiar story: that the children were never supervised and the parents never had an idea where they were; he said they were 'allowed to go prowling about at night.' It is surely unusual that the Chief Constable was there to speak. It is hardly a job for the senior police officer. Perhaps that tells us that this case was merely one of many similar ones and that juvenile crime was reaching mammoth proportions.

That appears to be the case when we consider the response to this crime. But what caused the heated response was the punishment. In Doncaster, the magistrate ordered Daniel Fell to receive 'six strokes from the birch rod' whereas Margaret received no punishment and was too young to be sent to a reformatory. The only additional action taken was that the parents (who bothered to turn up) were admonished and told to take better care of their children in future. A correspondent to *The Times* picked up the story and wrote:

'The reason why the real thief was dismissed scot-free and her less guilty brother whipped was of course, not the one given by the magistrates... Had the girl been the child of one of the magistrates, there probably was not one of them who, when he got home, would not have given her a child's whipping.'

The author of the letter was the Earl of Meath, and he was really making a point about the reformatories and the age at which young offenders could be sent to one of those institutions. From 1854 the ruling had been that only girls under the age of sixteen could be sent to a reformatory. For children such as Daniel and Margaret, the punishment was whipping and a caution. In earlier times, public humiliation had been the punishment, with the use of stocks and pillory, but in these supposedly more enlightened times, a beating was considered to be a civilised measure. As early as 1816 there had been a Parliamentary Committee to investigate juvenile crime, but little was done; children could still be sent to prisons along with adults of course, and this continued until the year following this hearing in Doncaster. Just thirteen years after these Doncaster children were in court – in 1902 – the first Borstal was established.

But the issue of fair punishment was still there at the time. The Earl of Meath was answered by 'a Board Master' anonymously. He argued that, 'I must join issue with him in his suggested remedy – viz., the substitution of the birch for the cane.' The schoolmaster was worried about the repercussions, saying of the birch, 'That instrument has hitherto been looked upon only as an adjunct to police courts, and its introduction into schools would, I fear, stir up popular clamour.'

J
Judges and Juries

Some of the law's most curious tales have come from the records of the assize courts. In the Georgian and Victorian years, the judges had such extreme power, and they were often notably eccentric and whimsical, that their cases generated stories which are bizarre and sometimes puzzling.

Take for instance the events of December, 1857, when Mr Justice Crompton presided. Before him was a poaching case but there was a shortage of jurors. The jury foreman, Sir C H J Anderson of Lea, said he was the presenter in a poaching case committed by four men on his own estate. He naturally applied to be excused duty and had arranged for another man to step in. Justice Crompton said, 'I cannot see how I can substitute one grand juryman for another after the charge has been delivered... I have never known such a thing before.' His Honour was aware that having the knight and plaintiff on his jury could be seen to be a problem, saying he wanted to avoid any impression from the lower classes that would reflect badly on the administration of justice. What was he to do? The only solution was to drop the whole affair and discharge the alleged poachers.

Then there was the strange behaviour of Mr Justice Maule, a notable character on the bench, who in 1852 complained that there was no fresh air in his court and ordered all the windows to be opened. But there was no response, so he had a fit of temper and threatened to have the windows broken if his wishes were not immediately obeyed. He passed a stout stick to a member of the jury to be used to smash the windows if he was not obeyed.

The man who could open all the windows was incredibly slow, so Mr Justice Maule wasted no time in ordering all the windows to be smashed. *The Times* reported on what happened:

'The smashing of the glass, as it came tumbling on the heads of the people below, and peals of laughter which were in consequence elicited from the bar and the whole court, produced a scene which will be remembered by those who witnessed the occurrence. His Lordship, evidently wincing under the ridicule which his eccentric behaviour had excited, intimated, in not the most calm and dignified manner, and at the same time

looking down upon the bar, that those gentlemen who wished to
indulge in such indecorous behaviour had better go and indulge
themselves out of the court...'

At length, the court resumed its normal business and there was no problem with the hot air.

In 1821 there had been a riot at Stamford and a certain Mr Williams was indicted for breaking windows at the home of a Mr Hunt. Although the defence lawyer argued that there had been no riot, the judge disagreed, saying that no man on his oath could say that the events had not been a riot. The jury withdrew and after two hours, eleven of the jury could agree but one man held out. Might the eleven men be discharged? The judge said that was impossible.

The jury then spent another five hours and there was no change. The resolute juryman told the court that he could not 'reconcile it to his conscience' that Mr Williams had riotously demolished the said windows. The judge would not let him withdraw. The man said, 'I would sooner eat mortar from the ceiling than give in.' With that state of affairs, the jury would have had to go with the judge to Nottingham , so they thought long and hard and finally handed in a note to the judge at the lodgings by the castle saying that they agreed for the defendant. No mortar had to be eaten that night.

M
Malfeasance
This is the doing of any act which, although the said act might not be unlawful – is to be understood in contrast to *nonfeasance,* which is the not doing of an act a person lawfully has to do. Then we have *misfeasance,* which is the wrongful doing of an action that should be lawfully done. Got that? In the mid Victorian years, in the Court of Chancery, the case of Connor v

Connor. Mr Connor left some property worth £8,000. His next of kin was given the power to act on that by a church court. But a woman came forward, claiming to be the dead man's widow 'by virtue of a Scotch marriage.' She brought a suit to force the production of a marriage certificate which was in the husband's papers, to prove her status.

The Vice-Chancellor intervened to put an injunction on the administrator, to prevent any actions being taken with the property of the dead man. Messrs parker and prior for the application to discharge the order, said that no interference must take place with the property *'in the absence of any malfeasance.'*

Quite dull, perhaps, but this was not the case of the poachers before the judge in 1854. A writer to the Times pointed out that these poachers had trespassed and tried to steal. They had claimed that they were on the land simply to go fishing. But as the writer pointed out:' they went to carry out their *malfeasance* by force, if necessary, of the deadliest kind... men do not go with guns to kill fish...' That is a much more interesting use of the term – the poachers going fishing was in itself unlawful, but they were charged with murder, and so they were guilty of *nonfeasance* in terms of their trespass for fishing, but also *misfeasance* perhaps, as they were not able to fish. Got that?

N

Necessaries

Traditionally, these items are the essential requisites for a child. These included drink, apparel, meat, drink and physic. By the Sale of Goods Act of 1893, these were 'goods suitable to the conditions of life for such an infant, and to his actual requirements...' This may not seem so significant in law, but before that, a wife could pledge her husband's credit if she had to when 'necessaries' were urgent. This was abolished as recently as 1970.

Clearly, this business was an issue for the audience watching The Importance of Being Earnest when it was first performed at the St James' Theatre in 1895 because Algy was found in a handbag at a railway station, abandoned by a feckless romantic novelist. There were no necessaries in the bag at all, we understand.

Neifty

This is defined as 'the condition of being a serf.' Back in the twelfth and thirteenth centuries, the unfree members of society had a bad time. In fact, a powerful lord could imprison a man by licence of neifty. He was totally a possession of the Lord, who was his only heir. Another word, *sequela*, was used to describe the fruit of his loins, and the same word was used of pigs and cattle. That was the lot of the *neif*. The word *knave* relates to this.

Newgate

It would be fitting to use Dante's words here 'abandon all hope ye who enter here.' It was also known as 'The Whit' after Dick Whittington, one time Lord Mayor of course. It was an ancient place, called by some the prototype of Hell' and the 'bottomless pit of violence.' But if a prisoner happened to have some money with him, this 'rhino' could buy some comfort. In fact he could order anything he liked. The turnkeys lived by what they could force or cajole from their victims, a custom called 'garnish.'

Yet the place was hardly completely secure. The celebrated robber jack Sheppard broke out of the place in 1724 even though he had been handcuffed, manacled and chained to the floor. Daniel Malden got out of the condemned cell and scuttled away through a sewer.

These adventures and the woeful tales of those who were to die at the end of the hangman's rope were in great demand, and the 'ordinaries' or keepers of the gaol made a handsome profit from selling these stories on broadsheets.

Of all the Newgate tales, the hangings are the most sensational. The condemned had to walk through Birdcage walk to their doom, an alleyway under which bodies of former felons were interred. Waiting for the unfortunates outside by the scaffold were crowds of voyeurs. In 1807 thirty people were crushed during an execution 'show.'

Nominal Damages

This refers to a trifling amount of money in a case in which, although the action is maintainable, the plaintiff has not really had any extreme damage done against him or her. One of the most famous examples is that of James McNeill Whistler, the artist, who sued the critic John Ruskin for libel. Ruskin had led a smear campaign against the Impressionist school of painter, and after looking at Whistler's painting 'Nocturne in Black and Gold' he wrote that he had 'never expected to hear a coxcomb ask two hundred guineas for flinging a pot of paint in the public's face.'

Whistler was asked in court if he really was asking such a huge sum for the work of just two days, and he answered 'No, it was for the knowledge gained through a lifetime.' The judge awarded one farthing damages and Whistler had to pay his costs of £500.

But this has its negative side too, as in a case at the Old Bailey in 1990 when two youths were cleared of stealing two cans of lager worth £1.80 and the costs of the suit totalled £131,000.

Nonage (or nonagium)

This referred to the ninth part of a person's movable possessions which used to be paid to the clergy on that person's death, but more often it was the 'absence of full age' so this was used to get young blades and fools out of various dilemmas in the past.

In 1834, for instance, there was an action to recover the sum of £8 supplied to Lord Louth who was in debt to a tobacconist. The plaintiff was James Bacon. But Louth was a young noble man who was away in Italy in 1834, and the alleged offence had been committed in 1828. As the brief for Mr Bacon said, 'Why had the tradesman waited five years?' The point was that the law said a person was liable to pay debts contracted during his minority. A witness was called to support the *nonage* of Louth at the time. All the fuss was over a meerschaum pipe.

Non Sequitur

'It does not follow'. This would apply perfectly to the barristers who indulged in tedious speeches and who annoyed the court by their eccentricities. One of the most odd examples was the strange behaviour of Mr Justice Maule, a notable character on the bench, who in 1852 complained that there was no fresh air in his court and ordered all the windows to be opened. But there was no response, so he had a fit of temper and threatened to have the windows broken if his wishes were not immediately obeyed. He passed a stout stick to a member of the jury to be used to smash the windows if he was not obeyed.

The man who could open all the windows was incredibly slow, so Mr Justice Maule wasted no time in ordering all the windows to be smashed. *The Times* reported on what happened:

'The smashing of the glass, as it came tumbling on the heads of the people below, and peals of laughter which were in consequence elicited from the bar and the whole court, produced a scene which will be remembered by those who witnessed the occurrence. His Lordship, evidently wincing under the ridicule which his eccentric behaviour had excited, intimated, in not

the most calm and dignified manner, and at the same time looking down upon the bar, that those gentlemen who wished to indulge in such indecorous behaviour had better go and indulge themselves out of the court...'

At length, the court resumed its normal business and there was no problem with the hot air.

Notice to Treat

Clearly, this must mean that a certain person is to take another out shopping, or arrange for a wild party in celebration of the lucky one. In fact, it relates to compulsory land purchase. It is a notice given by an Act of 1845, to the poor victim whose land is about to be grabbed.

In the middle years of the nineteenth century, when the railway boom was in full swing, rail companies were serving notices to treat almost every week. But they met their match in 86 year-old Mrs Lipscomb in 1857. The company wanted to build over her land, which was at Liss in Hampshire, and in 1853 the firm agreed to pay the old lady £100 per acre, and they wanted to build on three acres. When they finally served the notice to treat in1856 the land stated there was more than the three acres.

Mrs Lipscomb went to court and she claimed money and damages, and also the right to take back her land. She won: the company's notice to treat was taken as an abandonment of the first agreement. The wine flowed freely that night at the Lipscomb's residence. The judge said that 'the company should not be embarrassed by the possibility of the trustees insisting on the agreement of 1853...'

O

Obscenity

The Obscene Publications Acts of 1959 and 1964 defined

'obscene' as a product that would 'deprave or corrupt persons who are likely to read, see or hear the matter contained in it...'

Donald McGill was the artist who produced the famous 'saucy postcards' once found at all English seaside resorts. The humour of his cards was one of the treats of being on holiday and thousands of his cards were sent home by people who were relishing their time in the sun or in the pub. A typical card was one showing a scene in a bedroom in which a busty and scantily-clad blonde says to her lover, 'Blimey, here's my husband – can you come back tonight?' The man, looking suitably flushed and disturbed, is the stereotype milkman, and he replies, 'What in my own ruddy time – are you kidding missus!'

But in the 1950s, McGill and his publishers were in trouble. The images and jokes were running into problems with the obscene publications legislation. He had experienced trouble before then, but not very often. McGill once said, with this trouble in mind, 'During the whole period of my career the authorities have made no complaints about the post cards drawn by me, with the following exceptions: in or about 1906 I recollect that an order was made for the destruction of a very large number of cards in the North of England; in or about 1920 proceedings were taken against the retailers of cards but no order was made.'

It comes as a shock to read about the problems in 1954, because McGill has the status of being recognised and complimented by no less a literary figure than George Orwell, who wrote an essay, *The Art of Donald McGill* in 1941, and in a letter to Anthony Powell in 1947 was well aware of the likelihood of offence caused by the cards when he said, 'Thanks so much for your postcard which I think was rather lucky to get here – at any rate I think the crofter who brings the post the last seven miles might have suppressed it if he had seen it.' He was living on the Isle of Jura, and he feared that the community there were too austere and morally righteous to accept the kind of ribald humour on a McGill card.

After the return to government of the Conservatives in 1951 there was a moral reaction to the slippage in 'standards' of morality in the arts as it was perceived at the time. In the five years following that date there were 167,000 books censored. It was only a matter of time before attention turned to the saucy postcard. At the time there were 'watch committees' at seaside resorts, and Cleethorpes was no exception. It was a regular occurrence to have complaints voiced against such things as the postcards, and many people considered them to be lewd rather than harmless fun. It was inevitable that there would be police raids on premises where cards might be in stock, and actions began to be taken in Grimsby. Police raids resulted in the arrest and prosecution of both publishers and artists.

The Grimsby County Petty Sessional Division court issued writs on behalf of the Director of Public prosecutions against merchants who produced the McGill cards. The wording of the summons was 'unlawfully published an obscene postcard named Donald McGill Comics no. 811'. The Cleethorpes Chamber of Trade was worried too: in 1953 the Honorary Secretary wrote to Messrs D. Constance Ltd in London to find out about the circulation and distribution of the cards, because as the secretary wrote, 'seventeen shops in the town were raided by the police.' He added that 'Quantities of comic cards were taken away, so no doubt proceedings will follow to the annoyance to everyone of the traders concerned.' He wanted to know if the cards in Cleethorpes were typical of the merchandise going elsewhere. Obviously, if there were a set range of cards going to every town, then there would be a massive number of raids and potential prosecutions.

This legal action stemmed from the 1857 Obscene Publications Act: the outcome locally was a prominent trial in Lincoln on 15 July, 1954. McGill's own defence was that in most of the images he had 'no intention of double meaning and in fact in some cases, a 'double meaning' was pointed out to me...' He was found guilty and had to pay £50 in a fine and £25 in costs. Obviously, large amounts of cards were destroyed; many of the smaller postcard producers were ruined.

The onslaught against publishers and shopkeepers was relentless: in Brighton in July 1953 magistrates ordered the destruction of 113 out of 175 varieties of postcards. One of the defendants spoke up on behalf of the general grievances felt by seaside traders when he said, 'You are a kind of arts council on this matter. When the Obscene Publications Act of 1857 was passed, England was worrying about Napoleon and standards of morality were lower than today (he needed a history lesson). One merchant conceded that the cards were sometimes 'a little near the knuckle' but the most that could be said in criticism was that there was an innuendo in the image and the text.

At that time, people in Cleethorpes had been more worried by recent floods and extremely bad weather, but the affair certainly disturbed the normal equanimity of the Cleethorpes traders. As for George Orwell, he had his own defence of McGill: 'The comic post cards are one expression of his point of view, a humble one, less important than the music halls, but still worthy of attention. In a society which is still basically Christian they naturally concentrate on sex jokes..,. Their whole meaning and virtue is there unredeemed lowness. They stand for the worm's eye view of life...'

In other words, as with all humour of the baser kind, they remind us of the absurdity of moral strictness to the extent of denying communication about such topics as sex. But that view was too advanced for the austere world of 1950s Britain. With hindsight, it would be easy to see this case as a storm in a tea-cup – something rather more eccentric than important. But in fact the reasoning behind the bans was the significant factor. Here was a case in which a harmless and titivating ingredient of the English seaside experience was removed for the sake of 'decency' and of course today we are able to judge that in terms which seem unreal and distorted, because our modern political correctness has no room for what was then merely considered by most people to be 'saucy' in a way like the *Carry On* films.

But the McGill case turned out to be little more than yet another instance of what Lord Macaulay called, sarcastically, a 'fit of morality': 'We know of no spectacle so ridiculous as the British public in one of its periodical fits of morality.' Naturally, at the time it brought out yet again the debate about what is art and what is smut. Only six years after this fiasco Britain would have to cope with the attempt to understand the *Lady Chatterley's Lover* trial. Like the McGill case, it would seem to many to be little more than victimisation on the part of the 'jobsworth' attitude. Nevertheless, it is difficult today to bring to mind the kind of apprehensions felt by ordinary people, running their small business, in such a strange moral climate.

Oyez and Terminer
In the days of the assizes, courts held across the land in the shires and presided over by traveling justices, the duties of the judges included the business of 'hearing and ending' cases and of 'gaol delivery' – concluding the cases involving the poor devils who had languished behind bars in the months before the court of the assize was finally held. Some of the sorting out of cases waiting decisions were horrendous, including death sentences of course. But there was a lighter side, as for instance in the Castle Journal report of a case at Carlisle in 1828:
The prisoner pleaded not guilty. The counsel for the prosecution

*being out Of court, the judge called upon the witnesses, and was
in the act of examining the first one, when Mr Peter Hodgson of
Whitehaven, the attorney for the Prosecution, came into court,
and stopping the business, addressed his Lordship:*

*"My Lord, Mr Coltman, the counsel for the case, is at present
engaged in Another court.".*

JUDGE   Well, I can't help that.

HODGSON   (after a pause) My Lord, shall I bring him here?

JUDGE   Don't interrupt me. Go and do your business.

*(Mr Hodgson's precipitate retreat occasioned a titter through-
out the court).*

Petty Treason (also called petit treason)

This is a lower order of treason, the aim to kill or do harm to a
sovereign, and in past times it could be committed by a servant
killing his or her master; by a wife killing her husband, or by
a churchman killing his superior, someone to whom he owed
obedience. The clearest way to grasp the horrific consequences
of such acts is to recall a case from the Georgian period.

Over the centuries, York Castle has witnessed some terrible
scenes of human suffering, but few can equal the story of
Elizabeth Broadingham. The narrative vaguely echoes the
actions of Lady Macbeth ('lacking the 'milk of human kindness')
except that the setting and the motives are the lowest and most
despicable imaginable.

John Broadingham, her husband, was not exactly a pillar
of the community. He was locked away in York dungeons for
robbery when Elizabeth began her affair with Thomas Aikney, a
man younger than she. It was a case of extreme passion, 'while
the cat's away', and she liked the pleasures of loving and sex
with the other man so much that she moved in with him.

A man coming out of prison after all kinds of deprivations
expects some comfort and loyalty from his family. John

Broadingham found none of this: he merely found that his wife had left the home. Elizabeth appears to have wanted more than simply living with Aikney as his partner; she wanted to be free of the marriage with John, and to remove the husband from the scene altogether was her aim.

She began to work on Aikney with a view to leading him into the murder of John. The younger man at first resisted these pleas and wiles, but after some time he began to be influenced. It is recounted, though not definitely known, that Elizabeth made sure that Aikney had plenty of alcohol in him and tempted him in all the ways she could invent, as she allured him into a murderous pact. He finally went along with the plan.

Elizabeth must have been a very influential speaker and something of an actress; not only had she inveigled her way into Aikney's life, she now played the part of good wife, returning to John and apparently wanting to return to the marital harmony they once had. John took her back. But only a week or so after moving back home, she was talking to Thomas Aikney about their plan, and sorting out the details of where and when it would be done. The lover still vainly tried to resist, but she was relentless. Poor Thomas thought that the best move was to run away and avoid the confrontation, to make a new start elsewhere.

Things came to a head on the night of 8 February, 1776 when Elizabeth woke her husband as there was a loud noise downstairs; John staggered down to investigate and made his way to the door where Aikney was pounding on the wood. As John Broadingham opened up, Aikney knifed him in the chest and then, as the frenzied attack continued, he stabbed the man in the thigh and the leg. With the knife stuck in his belly, John managed to walk out into the street where he was seen by neighbours.

So badly was the husband hurt that he had almost been

eviscerated in the assault; he was clutching his stomach and his guts were exposed. The report at the time states that he was 'supporting his bowels.'

John Broadingham died the day after the attack. It took only a short time for neighbours and the magistrate to find Aikney and then the whole story was revealed. Elizabeth and Thomas confessed and he was hanged at York on 20th March. In this tale lies the incredible difference between punishment for murder and petty treason; Aikney's body, as was the custom, was cut down and then transported to Leeds Infirmary for use in dissection work with medical education. But Elizabeth had committed petty treason. Her fate was to be burnt at the stake. The only humane act in these cases was that the executioner normally strangled the woman before the fire was set alight, and he did so for Elizabeth. She was burnt and some ghoulish witnesses collected her ashes as souvenirs.

Mercy never entered into the matter when a woman was considered for the death penalty in the late eighteenth century and in the early nineteenth century. The great journalist of the period, J W Robertson Scott, has a memory of a woman on a scaffold at this time: ' ... *it was an old woman, a mere old wrinkled, wretched bundle. She was said to have killed a bastard. She cried, "You cannot hang me!" But they did.*'

Burning for petty treason, as explained in the introduction, was abolished in 1790: too late for Elizabeth Broadingham.

R

Recognisance
Document recording that a statement made before a court or a magistrate, which binds the writer to fulfil an obligation with regard to a charge made. This little pro-forma would have been the brief statement of an accusation in most cases.

S

Sentence of death recorded

This was a record of a verdict, noted even if the death was not effected; it was for records only, but is a strong reflection of the system when hanging was common. The list of sentenced felons would be put before a committee basically, and decisions made.

Sheriff

The term derives from the term 'shire reeve' in the medieval period, and goes back to pre-Norman times. In the earlier centuries, it was a position entailing considerable everyday powers and responsibilities, but in 1887 The Sheriffs' Act, which is still in force, established that the position lasted for one year, and was in the hands of the monarch. The most expressive signification of the office today is surely the remarkable dress. This includes a white and yellow 18-carat gold chain, a black velvet coat, sword and cocked hat. The most striking, and very dashing feature is the lace jabot worn around the neck.

In early times, the sheriff was appointed by the sovereign, but with advice from a permanent council. But there was more to it, as one writer on county sheriffs explains: 'The sheriffdom might be the inheritance of a private family. Normally, the sheriff received a commission from the crown, the king's choice being guided by the advice of one or more of his great officers...'

There is a very long list of sheriffs of course, and this has always been kept and updated by the Controller of Her Majesty's Stationery Office.

Slander

Defamatory language used of one to another, not in written form.

T

Treason

This was defined by the Treason Act of 1351: 'When a man compasses or imagines the death of our Lord the King, of our Lady his Queen or of their eldest son or heir' and also, 'If a man do levy war against our King in his land.'

Y

Year and a Day Ruling

In the definition of murder in the classic legal documentation backing up statute law, the stipulation is that a person had to die, after being attacked with murderous intent or with intent to cause grievous bodily harm, within a year and a day of the attack. This was an ancient ruling in common law, and the scope and applications of the law were always unclear. Lord Dormand commented as the move for its repeal was in progress: 'It certainly applies to murder, manslaughter, and aiding and abetting suicide...'

This lasted until 1996. In previous periods, it made a lot of sense to have a period in which to ascertain motives if there was some complexity involved. But in recent times, with medical knowledge advancing so markedly, the maintenance of life in hospital by life-support machines left the ruling open to abuse and problems of interpretation.

The case of *Ann Todd* in Cottingham is an example of this being applied, though the case is unsolved. In 1901, in Cottingham, Hull, Ms Todd went to her door and was viciously attacked. She survived, but with very severe injuries. Then, on 1 February 1901, while staying with a relative in Anlaby Road, she died. The attack took place on 25 February, 1900.

A Select Bibliography

Classics
De Quincey, Thomas   *On Murder* (Oxford, 2009) First published 1827
Jesse, F. Tennyson   *Murder and its Motives* (Harrap, 1924)
Roughead, William   *Classic Crimes* (New York Review Books, 2000)

General and Reference:
Cyriax, Oliver   *The Penguin Encyclopaedia of Crime* (Penguin, 1996)
Donaldson, William   *Rogues, Villains and Eccentrics* (Phoenix, 2002)
Hawkings, David   *Criminal Ancestors* (Sutton, 2008)
Woodley, Mick   *Osborn's Concise Law Dictionary* (Thomson, 2007)

Writing Skills and research
O'Byrne, Michael   *The Crime Writer's Guide to Police Practice and Procedure* (Hale, 2009)
Turner, Barry   *The Writer's Handbook Guide to Crime Writing* (Macmillan, 2003)
Wade, Stephen   *Writing True Crime* (Straightforward Publishing, 2006)
Wilson, Keith D.   *Cause of Death* (Writers' Digest, 1992)
Wynn, Douglas   *The Crime Writer's Handbook* (Allison and Busby, 2003)

History
Bourke, Joanna   *Rape: A History from 1860 to the Present* (Virago, 2007)
Godfrey, Barry, and Lawrence, Paul   *Crime and Justice 1750–1950* (Willan, 2005)
Hibbert, Christopher   *The Roots of Evil* (Sutton, 2003)
Sharpe, James   *Dick Turpin: the Myth of the English Highwayman* (Profile, 2004)
Wilson, David   *A History of British Serial Killing* (Sphere, 2009)

Prison/Convicts
Halliday, Stephen   *Newgate: London's Prototype of Hell* (Sutton, 2006)
Hughes, Robert   *The Fatal Shore* (Vintage, 2003)
James, Erwin   *A Life Inside* (Atlantic Books, 2003)
Morris, Norval and Rothman, David J.   *The Oxford History of the Prison* (OUP, 1998)

Thompson, Ronnie *Screwed* (Headline, 2008)

Biography (literary)
Busby, Sian *The Cruel Mother* (Short Books, 2004)
Morton, James *The First Detective* (Ebury Press, 2004)
Rees, Sian *The Floating Brothel* (Headline, 2001)
Smith, David James *Supper with the Crippens* (Orion, 2005)

Psychology and Forensics
Beavan, Colin *Fingerprints* (Fourth estate, 2003)
Guy, William *Victorian CSI* (History Press, 2009)
Lane, Brian The *Encyclopaedia of Forensic Science* (Headline, 1992)
McDermid, Val *Forensics: The Anatomy of Crime* (Profile Books, 2015)
Putwain, David and Sammons Aidan *Psychology and Crime* (Routledge, 2002)
Stout, Martha *The Sociopath Next Door* (Broadway, 2004)
Vronsky, Peter *Serial Killers: The Method and Madness of Monsters* (Berkley, 2004)
White, P. C. *Crime Scene to Court* (Royal Society for Chemistry, 2004)

Documentary
Fletcher, Connie *What Cops Know* (Pocket Books, 1992)
Graef, Roger *Talking Blues* (Fontana, 1990)

Police
Emsley, Clive *The English Police* (Pearson, 1991)
Moss, Alan, and Skinner, Keith *The Scotland Yard Files* (National Archives, 2006)
Nown, Graham *Watching the Detectives* (Grafton, 1991)

Regional and Case Books:
See the websites of: The History Press, Amberley, Carlton, Carnegie and Wharncliffe.

Acknowledgements
Particular sources used for police law are:
Cook, Tony and Tattersall, Andy, *Blackstone's Senior Investigating Officer's Handbook* (OUP, 2008)
The website: www.cps.gov.uk

APPENDIX 1

KEY LEGISLATION INTRODUCED SINCE 2017

Offensive Weapons Act 2019

The Offensive Weapons Act 2019 (OWA) received Royal Assent on 16th May 2019. Changes to legislation brought about by the OWA mean that from 14th July 2021 it is now an offence to possess certain items, even in private. These items include knuckledusters, telescopic truncheons, flick knives, 'zombie' knives, gravity knives, push daggers and throwing stars. The Act will also seek to make it harder for young people to buy dangerous weapons, both at the point of sale and delivery. From 6th April 2022, further legal obligations have been placed on retailers and delivery couriers to prevent knives, corrosives and other offensive weapons from being sold or delivered to those under the age of 18. The OWA also places new responsibilities on retailers and delivery companies during online sales and delivery of knives/corrosives to ensure that age verification procedures are followed, that the packaging is clearly marked as to the contents and that it is personally handed/delivered to a person aged 18 or over. In addition, the new restrictions make it a criminal offence to possess a corrosive substance in a public place, with those found guilty facing up to four years imprisonment. The sale of corrosive substances to anyone under 18 is now also prohibited.

The Act is divided into eight parts with two additional schedules and covers subjects such as the possession, sale and delivery of knives and corrosive substances, knife crime prevention orders and the prohibition of certain firearms.

Part 1 – Corrosive products and substances

The number of assaults involving the use of corrosive substances has doubled during the last few years and it's a crime which often results in life-changing injury, both physically and emotionally. This part of the OWA deals with specific offences and penalties.

Section 1(1) states that a person commits an offence if they sell a corrosive product to a person who is under the age of 18

Section 1(2) provides a defence for a person charged in England, Wales, or Northern Ireland with an offence under subsection (1) to prove that they took all reasonable precautions and exercised all due diligence to avoid the commission of the offence.

In Scotland, the defence applies if it can be shown that the accused believed the person to whom the corrosive product was sold was aged 18 or over AND either the accused had taken reasonable steps to establish age or that no reasonable person could have suspected from their appearance that the purchaser was under 18. Documents which may be considered as proof of age include a passport, a photocard driving licence or any other document prescribed by Scottish Ministers.

Section 1(7) states that a person guilty of an offence under subsection (1) is liable –

(a) on summary (Magistrates) conviction in England and Wales, to imprisonment for a term not exceeding 51 weeks, to a fine or to both;

(b) on summary conviction in Scotland or Northern Ireland, to imprisonment for a term not exceeding 6 months, to a fine not exceeding level 5 on the standard scale or to both.

The term 'corrosive product' means –

(a) a substance listed in the first column of Schedule 1 , or

(b) a product which contains a substance listed in the first column of that Schedule in a concentration higher than the limit set out for that substance in the second column of that Schedule.

SCHEDULE 1 (Corrosive products)

Name of substance and Chemical Abstracts Registry number (CAS RN)	Concentration limit (weight in weight)
Ammonium hydroxide (CAS RN 1336-21-6)	10% w/w
Formic acid (CAS RN 64-18-6)	10% w/w
Hydrochloric acid (CAS RN 7647-01-0)	10% w/w
Hydrofluoric acid (CAS RN 7664-39-3)	0% w/w
Nitric acid (CAS RN 7697-37-2)	3% w/w
Phosphoric acid (CAS RN 7664-38-2)	70% w/w
Sodium hydroxide (CAS RN 1310-73-2)	12% w/w
Sodium hypochlorite (CAS RN 7681-52-9)	10% w/w
Sulfuric acid (CAS RN 7664-93-9)	15% w/w

Section 3 relates to the delivery of corrosive products where the seller and buyer are not in each others' presence at the time of the sale and states – (2) the seller commits an offence if, for the purposes of supplying the corrosive product to the buyer, the seller delivers the product, or arranges for its delivery to residential premises or a locker (3).

Section 4 confirms that it is an offence to deliver a corrosive product to someone who is under 18, when the seller and buyer are not in each other's presence at the time of the sale and the seller is outside the UK at that time.

Sections 6-12 of the OWA 2019 relate to the possession of corrosive substances, the penalties on conviction and search powers.

Section 6(1) states that a person commits an offence if they have a corrosive substance with them in a public place. A 'corrosive substance' is defined as a substance which is capable of burning human skin by corrosion.

(7) A person guilty of an offence under subsection (1) is liable – (a-b) on summary conviction in England,Wales and Scotland, to imprisonment for a term not exceeding 12 months, to a fine or to both; (c) on summary conviction in Northern Ireland, to imprisonment for a term not exceeding 6 months, to a fine not exceeding the statutory maximum or to both; (d) on conviction on indictment (Crown or Higher Court), to imprisonment for a term not exceeding 4 years, to a fine or to both.

Sections 10-12 outline police powers to search for corrosive substances in England, Wales, Scotland and Northern Ireland. In relation to England and Wales, the current power authorising a constable to stop and search persons, vehicles etc (*Section 1 Police and Criminal Evidence Act 1984*) has been amended to include an offence of having a corrosive substance in a public place (Section 6 OWA 2019) and the equivalent legislation in Northern Ireland (*Article 3 Police and Criminal Evidence (Northern Ireland) Order 1989* likewise.

CASE STUDY
A man has been charged after reportedly blinding another man with bleach during a fight. Andrew Maloney appeared in court after the disturbance which took place in a kebab shop on Lydd High Street in Kent. Police were called to the fight which took place in the early hours

of the morning in April 2022. A police spokesman confirmed that a man in his 20's had suffered pain and temporary loss of vision following the incident. Maloney was charged with attempting to cause grievous bodily harm, affray, possession of a corrosive substance in a public place, making threats with an offensive weapon and criminal damage to a police car. He was remanded in custody and later sentenced to 16 months imprisonment.

Part 2 – Knife Crime Prevention Orders

Knife Crime Prevention Orders (KCPO's) are civil orders designed to, with the approval of the Court, provide the police with a tool to help steer young people and others away from knife crime and from routinely carrying knives in public. The intention is that KCPO's will be preventative rather than punitive and that their use, where appropriate, will help to prevent knife crime. The relevant authorities who can apply for a KCPO will be the police and the Crown Prosecution Service (CPS). There are different occasions when a KCPO may be made.

KCPO made on conviction
A KCPO may be made by any court dealing with the defendant (Crown Court, Magistrates Court, or Youth Court).

Section 19 of the OWA sets out the conditions that must be met for the court to make a KCPO on conviction –
- Firstly, the court must be satisfied, on the balance of probabilities (the civil standard of proof) that the defendant has committed an offence. This offence must be a 'relevant offence' that is, an offence involving violence (or the threat of violence) or where a bladed article was used or carried by the defendant or any other person in the commission of the offence. The conviction to which the KCPO is related must post-date the coming into force for the relevant provisions in Part 2 of the OWA.
- Secondly, an application must have been made by the prosecution. The court may not make an order of its own volition. The application would normally be supported by evidence from the police.
- Thirdly, the court is required to consider that it is necessary to make the order to protect the public generally, or particular persons (including the defendant) from the risk of physical or psychological harm involving a bladed article, or to prevent the defendant from committing an offence involving a bladed article.

KCPO made other than on conviction

The courts have the power to make KCPO's in cases other than on conviction. A KCPO may be made in relation to any person who is over the age of 12.

Section 14 of the OWA sets out the conditions that must be met for the court to make a KCPO other than on conviction –

- Firstly, the court must be satisfied that an application has been made in accordance with section 15 OWA 2019. The application is made by complaint.
- Secondly, the court must be satisfied, on the balance of probabilities (the civil standard of proof), that the person has on at least two occasions in the relevant period, had a bladed article with them in a public place, on school premises or on further education premises without good reason or lawful authority. (A bladed article is an article to which *Section 139 Criminal Justice Act 1988* applies and the 'relevant period' means a period of two years preceding the date on which the order is made).
- Thirdly, it is a requirement for the court to consider it necessary to make the order to protect the public generally, or particular persons (including the defendant) from the risk of physical or psychological harm involving a bladed article or to prevent the defendant from committing an offence involving a bladed article.

Prohibitions

Section 21(4) OWA 2019 sets out a list of possible prohibitions that can be imposed on a defendant by a KCPO. The Act also lists possible effects of prohibitions, such as:

- an exclusion zone
- non-association with other individuals
- non-participation in particular activities
- being in a particular place between particular times on any given day or days
- preventing the defendant from using or having particular articles with them
- using the internet to facilitate or encourage crime involving bladed articles

This list of prohibitions is non-exhaustive and the court may decide to include other prohibitions on a case-by-case basis.

Duration of a KCPO
Generally, a KCPO or interim KCPO will take effect on the day it is made. In relation to a defendant who is in custody, who is subject to a custodial sentence or who is on licence, the order will take effect once they are released or no longer on licence. A KCPO must specify its duration and must last for a fixed period of at least 6 months but no more than 2 years. Orders issued to anyone under 18 should be regularly reviewed in consultation with the relevant Youth Offending Team and social care (where appropriate).

Notification requirements
Any person who is subject to a KCPO or an interim KCPO must notify the police, within three days, of their name(s) and address. They must also notify the police, within three days, of any subsequent changes to this information, specifically, the use of a new name, a change to their home address or an address at which they will live for one month or more. Notification is to be given in person by attending a police station in the area they live or by giving an oral notification to a police officer or another authorised person.
A person subject to a KCPO commits an offence if they, without reasonable excuse, fail to comply with the notification requirements of if they notify to the police any information which they know to be false (Section 25(1) OWA).
A person guilty of an offence under subsection (1) is liable –
(a) on summary conviction, to imprisonment for a term not exceeding 12 months, to a fine or to both;
(b) on indictment, to imprisonment for a term not exceeding 2 years, to a fine or to both.
It is also an offence for a person to breach a KCPO without reasonable excuse (Section 29). The penalties on conviction are the same as with Section 25.

CASE STUDY
A man has been jailed for 6 months and issued with a knife crime prevention order after pleading guilty to possession of a knife and other offences in Walthamstow, London. Stephen Smith, no fixed address, punched the owner of a vehicle which he had broken into and was subsequently found to be in possession of a Stanley knife when arrested. Smith was sentenced to 24 weeks in custody and fined £300 in relation to

a number of offences. He was also given a knife crime prevention order, which aims to prevent crime and protect the public from knife-related offences. The order means that Smith should not be in possession of a knife unless for the immediate purpose of eating or preparing a meal. The order will come into force once Smith is released from prison.

Part 3 – Sale and delivery of knives etc
Sections 34–42 OWA relate to the sale and delivery of bladed articles to persons under 18 and to residential premises along with the statutory defences for such offences.

Part 4 – Possession etc of certain offensive weapons
Sections 43–49 OWA relate to the definition of a "flick knife" along with the prohibition and surrender of certain knives and weapons.

Part 5 – Threatening with offensive weapons
Section 50 OAW provides some amendments to *Section 1A of the Prevention of Crime Act 1953* (the offence of threatening with an offensive weapon in public).

Section 51 OAW amends *Section 139AA of the Criminal Justice Act 1988* (the offence of threatening with an article with a blade or point or with an offensive weapon) with the following subsection 1(A) –

1(A) – A person is guilty of an offence if that person –

(a) has an article to which this section applies with them on further education premises,

(b) unlawfully and intentionally threatens another person (A) with the article, and

(c) does so in such a way that a reasonable person (B) who was exposed to the same threat as 'A' would think that there was an immediate risk of physical harm to 'B'

An article includes a bladed article contrary to *Section 139 (Criminal Justice Act 1988)* or an offensive weapon within the meaning of *Section 1 of the Prevention of Crime Act 1953*.

Section 52 OAW introduces an offence of threatening with an offensive weapon etc in a private place –

(1) A person (A) commits an offence if –

(a) while 'A' is in a private place, 'A' unlawfully and intentionally threatens another person 'B' with an article or substance to which this subsection applies, and

(b) 'A' does so in such a way that there is an immediate risk of serious physical harm to 'B'.

An article has the same meaning as with Section 51 and also includes a corrosive substance.

Section 53 authorises a constable, who suspects that an offence under Section 52 relating to corrosive substances is being or has been committed on school or further education premises, to enter and search the premises and any person on them for a corrosive substance.

Part 6 – Firearms

Sections 54–63 OWA relate to the prohibition, surrender, payments in respect of, and conditions applying to certain firearms covered by the *Firearms Act 1968*.

Part 7 – Enforcement of offences relating to sale etc of offensive weapons

Section 64 OWA lists the legislation which can be enforced by the local weights and measures authority.

Part 8 – Supplementary

Sections 66–71 OWA provide further guidance in relation to the legislation.

That's a comprehensive summary of the Offensive Weapons Act 2019. If you would like to look at the Act in its entirety, then please visit the following link which will allow you to view every Section https://www.legislation.gov.uk/ukpga/2019/17/contents/enacted

Coronavirus Act 2020

The Coronavirus Act came into force on 25th March 2020, as a reaction to the COVID 19 pandemic. Its stated aim was to introduce new powers to protect public health, increase NHS capacity, strengthen social care and support the public. The measures in the Act were considered as temporary, proportionate to the threat and only used when strictly necessary. The legislation was time-limited for two years and could only be extended with formal Parliamentary approval. Several of the Act's provisions were revoked earlier than the two-year point whilst others were extended for a further six months beyond the two years. **As we enter 2023 it's important to note that all provisions have now expired or been revoked but are included here for reference purposes only.**

The Coronavirus Act (CA) is split into two parts with a number of appended schedules and has 102 Sections. As you can imagine, it's rather lengthy and covers public health, NHS and social care issues as well as police and court matters.

Sections 1–21 relate to the NHS, social care and the registration of deaths.

Investigatory powers

Section 22 CA allows for the appointment of temporary Judicial Commissioners to carry out functions conferred by the *Police Act 1997, the Regulation of Investigatory Powers Act 2000, the Regulation of Investigatory Powers (Scotland) Act 2000 and the Investigatory Powers Act 2016.* Any such appointments must be due to a shortage of persons able to carry out the functions of the role, as a result of the effects of coronavirus. A temporary Commissioner may be appointed for one or more terms not exceeding six months each and not exceeding 12 months in total.

Section 23CA authorises the Secretary of State to alter time limits in relation to urgent warrants granted under the *Investigatory Powers Act 2016,* specifically –

(a) the period within which a Judicial Commissioner must decide whether to approve a decision to issue an urgent warrant;

(b) the period at the end of which an urgent warrant ceases to have effect;

(c) the period during which an urgent warrant may be renewed;

(d) the period within which a Judicial Commissioner or other appropriate person must decide whether to approve any decision to make an urgent modification of a warrant.

A modification may not increase the length of a period so that it ends after the 12th working day after the day on which the warrant was issued, or, as the case may be, the modification was made.

Fingerprints and DNA profiles

Section 24 CA authorises the Secretary of State to extend the period of retention of fingerprints and DNA profiles for up to six months when they may otherwise have been destroyed. This extension could only be granted due to the impact of coronavirus and if retention was in the interests of national security. The section relates to samples taken under the *Police and Criminal Evidence Act 1984* and specific Terrorism legislation.

The power may be exercised on more than one occasion, but not so as to extend the period for which any fingerprints or DNA profile may be retained by more than 12 months in total. If the Secretary of State has not exercised the power before the end of the period of 3 months beginning with the day on which this Act was passed, this section ceased to have effect.

Sections 25–29 CA relate to the supply of food during the pandemic.

Sections 30–52 relate to a variety of health and social care issues affected by COVID.

Sections 53–57 CA and Schedules 23–27 deal with the expansion of the use of video and audio technology in courts and tribunals.

Sections 59–70 address the postponement of elections across the UK whilst the remainder of the Coronavirus Act covers financial issues and Parliamentary guidance.

Although the Coronavirus Act was introduced as a temporary measure during the pandemic, there is a lot of detail contained in the legislation which you may wish to look at for research purposes. The following link will provide access to the whole Act and associated Schedules: https://www.legislation.gov.uk/ukpga/2020/7/contents/enacted

Covert Human Intelligence Sources (Criminal Conduct) Act 2021

A Covert Human Intelligence Source (often referred to as simply a 'CHIS') is the modern-day term for a person who used to be known as an 'informant'. A CHIS will seek to covertly gather information from another person(s) without that person knowing why or what they intend to do with that information. The police (amongst others) can register a person as a CHIS and task them to try to find out information to assist in the prevention and detection of crime. It's vitally important that the true identity of any CHIS and details of their covert activity is protected for their own safety. The police officer/staff who registers the CHIS is known as the 'handler' and will meet with them and task them as and when appropriate. The police can apply to reward CHIS, financially or in other ways, should they provide information which results in a positive outcome (such as the arrest/conviction of other people, recovery of drugs/stolen property etc).

In 2018, CHIS operations led the National Crime Agency (NCA) to disrupt over 30 threats to life, arrest numerous serious organised criminals, seize over 3000kg of Class A drugs, safeguard over 200 people, and take nearly 60 firearms and 4000 rounds of ammunition off the street. In the last year, the Metropolitan Police have made 3500 arrests, recovered over 500 weapons and over £2.5 million in cash, as a direct result of CHIS operations. CHIS are also crucial in preventing and safeguarding victims from many serious crimes including terrorism, drugs and firearms offences and child sexual exploitation.

Participation in criminal conduct is an essential and inescapable feature of CHIS use, to enable them to appear credible and gain the trust of those under investigation. This enables them to work their way into the heart of groups seeking to cause us harm, gathering information and intelligence which other investigative measures may never detect.

The Covert Human Intelligence Sources (Criminal Conduct) Act 2021 makes provision to authorise CHIS to participate in conduct which would otherwise constitute a criminal offence. The Act provides a clear legal basis for a longstanding tactic, vital for national security and crime prevention/detection.

The provisions of the Act include:

- Inserting a Section 29B into the *Regulation of Investigatory Powers Act (RIPA) 2000* that creates a Criminal Conduct Authorisation (CCA) which allows undercover law enforcement agents or covert sources to break the law in the interests of national security, to prevent or detect crime or disorder or in the interests of the economic well-being of the UK. Applications must be proportionate, only used to prevent more serious crimes from being committed and when there is no other practicable legal path by which the same outcome could be achieved.
- Inserting a Section 29C into *RIPA* that introduces safeguards in cases where the covert source is under the age of 18. The additional require-ments prior to the issue of a Juvenile Criminal Conduct Authorisation (JCCA) include the completion of a specific risk assessment, special arrangements for meetings and steps to safeguard the minor.
- Inserting a Section 29D into *RIPA* that implements safeguards where the covert source is a vulnerable adult.
- Listing the bodies capable of using undercover agents and CCA's. These include any police force, National Crime Agency, Serious Fraud Office, any of the intelligence agencies and HMRC amongst others.

Further details of this Act, if required, can be found via the following link: Covert Human Intelligence Sources (Criminal Conduct) Act 2021 https:// www.legislation.gov.uk/ukpga/2021/4/contents/enacted

Domestic Abuse Act 2021

The Domestic Abuse Act 2021(DAA) has been introduced to provide improved protection for victims of domestic abuse and the strengthening of measures to tackle perpetrators. The Act is split into 7 parts and contains over 90 sections.

Key provisions include –

- a new wide-ranging statutory definition of domestic abuse, which includes emotional abuse, coercive or controlling behaviour and economic abuse
- recognition that an abuser can exert controlling or coercive behaviour towards a victim, even if the parties don't live together
- increasing access to special measures in courts to help prevent intimidation, such as the use of screens and giving evidence via video link
- non-fatal strangulation is to become a specific criminal offence, carrying a sentence of up to 5 years imprisonment
- introduction of Domestic Abuse Protection Notices (DAPN) and Domestic Abuse Protection Orders (DAPO) aimed at preventing perpetrators from contacting victims
- Domestic Violence Disclosure Scheme, also known as 'Clare's Law', allowing individuals to contact police to ask if they, or someone they know, is in a relationship with someone who could pose an abuse risk towards them, now recognised by statute

Section 1 of the Domestic Abuse Act 2021 defines 'domestic abuse' as follows –

Behaviour of a person ('A') towards another person ('B') if –

(a) 'A' and 'B' are each aged 16 or over and are personally connected to each other, and

(b) the behaviour is abusive.

Behaviour is 'abusive' if it consists of any of the following –

(a) physical or sexual abuse;

(b) violent or threatening behaviour;

(c) controlling or coercive behaviour

(d) economic abuse

(e) psychological, emotional or other abuse;

and it does not matter whether the behaviour consists of a single incident or a course of conduct.

'Economic abuse' is defined as any behaviour that has a substantial adverse effect on the ability of 'B' to –

(a) acquire, use or maintain money or other property, or

(b) obtain goods or services.

For the purposes of this Act, the behaviour of 'A' may be considered as behaviour towards 'B' despite the fact that it consists of conduct directed at another person (for example, a child of 'B').

Any reference in this Act to a victim of domestic abuse includes a reference to a child (a person under 18) who –

(a) sees or hears, or experiences the effects of the abuse, and

(b) is related to 'A' or 'B'.

Part 2 – Domestic Abuse Commissioner

Part 2 of the Act addresses the appointment of a Domestic Abuse Commissioner as an independent voice to speak on behalf of victims and survivors. The Commissioner will use their statutory powers set out in the Act, to raise public awareness and hold both agencies and government to account in tackling domestic abuse. You can find out more about the role at: https://domesticabusecommissioner.uk/

Part 3 of the Act covers Domestic Abuse Protection Notices and Orders

Domestic Abuse Protection Notice

Section 22 DAA states that –

(1) A senior police officer (of at least the rank of Inspector) may give a domestic abuse protection notice to a person (P) if conditions A and B are met.

(2) A domestic abuse protection notice is a notice prohibiting 'P' from being abusive towards a person aged 16 or over to whom 'P' is personally connected.

(3) Condition A is that the senior police officer has reasonable grounds for believing that 'P' has been abusive towards a person aged 16 or over to whom 'P' is personally connected.

(4) Condition B is that the senior police officer has reasonable grounds for believing that it is necessary to give the notice to protect that person from domestic abuse, or the risk of domestic abuse, carried out by 'P'.

(5) It does not matter whether the abusive behaviour referred to in subsection (3) took place in England and Wales or elsewhere.

(6) A domestic abuse protection notice may not be given to a person who is under the age of 18.

Section 23 states –

(1) A domestic abuse protection notice may provide that the person to whom a notice was given (P)

(a) may not contact the person for whose protection the notice is given;

(b) may not come within a specified distance of any premises in England or Wales in which that person lives.

(2) If 'P' lives in premises in England or Wales in which the person for whose protection the notice is given also lives, the notice may also contain provision –

(a) prohibiting 'P' from evicting or excluding that person from the premises;

(b) prohibiting 'P' from entering the premises;

(c) requiring 'P' to leave the premises.

A domestic abuse protection notice must be in writing and served on 'P' personally by a constable.

It must also state –

(a) the grounds on which it has been given,

(b) that a constable may arrest 'P' without warrant if the constable has reasonable grounds for believing that 'P' is in breach of the notice,

(c) that an application for a domestic abuse protection order will be heard by a magistrates' court within 48 hours of the time of giving the notice and a notice of the hearing will be given to 'P',

(d) that the notice continues in effect until that application has been determined or withdrawn,

(e) the provision that a magistrates' court may include in a domestic abuse protection order.

If a constable has reasonable grounds for believing that a person is in breach of a domestic abuse protection notice, the constable may arrest the person without warrant (Section 26(1)).

Domestic Abuse Protection Order

A domestic abuse protection order is an order which, for the purpose of preventing a person (P) from being abusive towards a person aged 16 or over to whom 'P' is personally connected –

(a) prohibits 'P' from doing things described in the order, or

(b) requires 'P' to do things described in the order.

A court may make a domestic abuse protection order against a person (P) on an application made to it by –

(a) the person for whose protection the order is sought;

(b) the appropriate chief officer of police;

(c) a person specified in regulations made by the Secretary of State;

(d) any other person with the leave of the court to which the application is to be made.

An application for an order must be made to the family court unless the application is made by a chief officer of police, in which case it must be made by complaint to a magistrates' court.

Where a person (P) has been given a domestic abuse protection notice (Section 22), a chief officer of police is required to apply for a domestic abuse protection order against 'P'. This application must be heard by the magistrates' court not later than 48 hours after the notice was given to 'P'. Other than by way of an application, the court may decide to make a domestic abuse protection order in a case they have been dealing with, should the circumstances warrant this course of action.

Section 32 DAA states that –

(1) The court may make a domestic abuse protection order against a person (P) if conditions 'A' and 'B' are met.

(2) Condition A is that the court is satisfied on the balance of probabilities that 'P' has been abusive towards a person aged 16 or over to whom 'P' is personally connected.

(3) Condition B is that the order is necessary and proportionate to protect that person from domestic abuse, or the risk of domestic abuse, carried out by 'P'.

(4) It does not matter –

(a) whether the abusive behaviour took place in England and Wales or elsewhere, or

(b) whether it took place before or after the coming into force of this section.

(5) A domestic abuse protection order may not be made against a person under the age of 18.

Section 35 sets out the provisions that may be made by an order which mirror those listed for a domestic abuse protection notice (see Section 23). A domestic abuse protection order takes effect on the day on which it is made and lasts –

(a) for a specified period

(b) until the occurrence of a specified event, or

(c) until further order.

Breach of order

Section 39 DAA states –

(1) A person who is subject to a domestic abuse protection order commits an offence if without reasonable excuse the person fails to comply with any requirement imposed by the order.

(5) A person guilty of an offence under this section is liable –

(a) on summary conviction to imprisonment for a term not exceeding 12 months, to a fine or to both;

(b) on conviction on indictment, to imprisonment for a term not exceeding 5 years, to a fine or to both.

A constable has the power to arrest without warrant any person reasonably suspected of breaching a domestic abuse protection order (*Section 24 Police and Criminal Evidence Act 1984*).

Notification requirements and offences

Where a person is subject to a domestic abuse protection order they must, within three days beginning on the day the order is made, notify the police their name(s) and home address. If the person in question changes their name or home address, or ceases to have any home address they must also notify police within three days of the change (Section 41).

A notification can be given by attending a police station in the appropriate police area and giving an oral notification to a police officer or any person authorised for the purpose by the officer in charge of the station.

Section 43 DAA states –

(1) A person (P) commits an offence if 'P' –

(a) fails, without reasonable excuse, to comply with a requirement imposed by or under section 41, or

(b) notifies the police, in purported compliance with such a requirement, of any information which 'P' knows to be false.

(3) The penalty for breaching notification requirements is the same as that for breaching a protection order (see Section 39).

(4) A person commits an offence under subsection 1(a) on the day on which the person first fails, without reasonable excuse, to comply with a requirement imposed by or under section 41.

(5) The person continues to commit the offence throughout any period during which the failure continues.

(6) But the person may not be prosecuted more than once in respect of the same failure.

CASE STUDY

Officers were called to a domestic incident in Spalding, Lincolnshire where a 50-year-old man had reportedly been assaulting his partner over the course of a number of days. The alleged victim disclosed that physical violence had taken place but that no injuries had been caused. She did not wish to make a formal complaint of assault. The officers attending decided that it was proportionate and necessary to impose a Domestic Abuse Protection Notice to protect the alleged victim from the potential for further domestic abuse and so that support could be sought. Two days later, Lincoln Magistrates' Court heard an application for a Domestic Abuse Protection Order and, on the balance of probabilities, granted the order to protect the partner for an initial period of 28 days, despite the alleged perpetrator not attending court for the hearing. The following day, the man breached the order and was sentenced to 30 days in custody. Domestic Abuse Protection Orders/Notices are sometimes referred to as Domestic Violence Protection Orders/Notices.

Part 4 of the Act outlines local authority support.

Part 5 of the Act outlines the protection for victims and witnesses during legal proceedings.

Special measures

Section 62 DAA deals specifically with 'special measures' (screens, video links and other appropriate safeguards) in criminal proceedings for offences involving domestic abuse. The relevant legislation (*Chapter 1of Part 2 of the Youth Justice and Criminal Evidence Act 1999*) which allows special measures directions in cases of vulnerable and intimidated witnesses has been amended to include a new sub-section of 'any other offence where it is alleged that the behaviour of the accused amounted to domestic abuse within the meaning of Section 1 of the Domestic Abuse Act 2021'.

Sections 63–64 allow for special measures directions during family and civil proceedings respectively.

Sections 65–66 outline the circumstances where the cross-examination in person of a victim or other witness is prohibited in family and civil proceedings respectively.

Part 6 of the Act involves some offences involving abusive or violent behaviour.

Section 68 DAA amends the offence of controlling or coercive behaviour in an intimate or family relationship (*Section 76 of the Serious Crime Act 2015*) with explanations of the terms 'personally connected' and 'parental relationship'.

Section 69 provides amendments to the offence of disclosing private sexual photographs and films with intent to cause distress (*Section 33 of the Criminal Justice and Courts Act 2015*).

Section 70 DAA introduces a new offence of non-fatal strangulation or suffocation which will be introduced into *Part 5 of the Serious Crime Act 2015* as Section 75A –

(1) A person (A) commits an offence if –

(a) 'A' intentionally strangles another person (B), or

(b) 'A' does any other act to 'B' that –

(i) affects 'B's ability to breathe, and

(ii) constitutes battery of 'B'.

(2) It is a defence to an offence under this section for 'A' to show that 'B' consented to the strangulation or other act.

(3) But subsection (2) does not apply if –

(a) 'B' suffers serious harm as a result of the strangulation or other act, and

(b) 'A' either –

(i) intended to cause 'B' serious harm, or

(ii) was reckless as to whether 'B' would suffer serious harm.

(4) 'A' is to be taken to have shown the fact mentioned in subsection (2) if –

(a) sufficient evidence of the fact is adduced to raise an issue with respect to it, and

(b) the contrary is not proved beyond reasonable doubt.

(5) A person guilty of an offence under this section is liable –

(a) on summary conviction, to imprisonment for a term not exceeding 12 months, to a fine or to both;

(b) on conviction on indictment, to imprisonment for a term not exceeding 5 years, to a fine or to both.

(6) in this section 'serious harm' means –

(a) grievous bodily harm (*Section 18 Offences Against the Person Act 1861*),

(b) wounding (*Section 18* as above), or

(c) actual bodily harm (*Section 47 Offences Against the Person Act 1861*).

Part 7 of the Act deals with miscellaneous issues.

You can view the whole of the Domestic Abuse Act 2021 via the following link: https://www.legislation.gov.uk/ukpga/2021/17/contents/enacted

Police, Crime, Sentencing and Courts Act 2022

The Police, Crime, Sentencing and Courts Act 2022 (PCSC) became law in April 2022. The main objective surrounding the proposal of this Act was to impose further restrictions on actions such as protests, crimes against children and further sentencing limits and guidelines. The Act has received its fair share of criticism from some quarters due to its perceived wide-ranging powers. It is a lengthy and, at times, complex piece of legislation consisting of over 200 sections which are divided into 14 separate parts. Subjects covered include public order, road traffic, cautions and custodial sentences. The following is a summary of the Act.

Part 1 – Protection of the police etc

Section 1 contains provision for the Secretary of State to prepare an annual police covenant report for parliament. This report will be about the health and well-being of members and former members of the police, the physical protection of such people and the support required by their families.

Section 2 increases the penalty for conviction on indictment in relation to an offence of common assault or battery (*Section 1 of the Assaults on Emergency Workers (Offences) Act 2018*) from 12 months to 2 years. This increase applies to convictions after 28/6/22.

CASE STUDY

A 22-year-old man has been jailed for 2 years for assaulting a police officer in Hull. Callam Jordan was requested to stop whilst riding a motorbike through Orchard Park. After failing to stop, officers pursued him and when he was caught he struck one of them in the face before fleeing. He was detained a short time later. In June 2022, at Hull Crown Court he was sentenced for the offences of driving whilst disqualified, assaulting an emergency worker and escaping lawful custody

Harper's Law

Section 3 relates to the required life sentence on conviction for the manslaughter of an emergency worker acting in the exercise of their function. There are three parts to this section depending on whether the person convicted is a youth or an adult at the time. All parts contain the following proviso –

'The court must impose a life sentence unless the court is of the opinion that there are exceptional circumstances which –

(a) relate to the offence or the offender, and

(b) justify not doing so.'

This particular section of the Act was implemented following the tragic death on duty of PC Andrew Harper in 2019 and is now often referred to simply as 'Harper's Law'.

Sections 5–7 provide amendments to the *Road Traffic Act 1988* in relation to the standard of police driving.

Part 2 – Prevention, investigation and prosecution of crime

Serious violence

Sections 8–23 (PCSC) outline the duties and powers of specified authorities to collaborate, with the aim of preventing and reducing serious violence, in particular domestic abuse, sexual offences, violence against property and threats of violence.

Offensive weapons homicide reviews

Section 24 states –

(1) Where a review partner considers that –

(a) the death of a person was, or is likely to have been, a qualifying homicide,

(b) the death occurred, or is likely to have occurred, in England and Wales,

(c) such other conditions as the Secretary of State may specify by regulations are satisfied,

(d) the review partner is one of the relevant review partners in respect of the death,

the review partner must join with the other relevant review partners in respect of the death in arranging for there to be a review under this section of the person's death.

The homicide of a person is a 'qualifying homicide' if –

(a) the person was aged 18 or over, and

(b) the death, or the events surrounding it, involved the use of an offensive weapon.

'Relevant review partners' are likely to include the chief officer of police, a local authority or a clinical commissioning group for the area where the death occurred.

Extraction of information from electronic devices

Section 37 states –

(1) An authorised person may extract information stored on an electronic device from that device if –

(a) a user of that device has voluntarily provided the device to an authorised person, and

(b) that user has agreed to the extraction of information from the device by an authorised person.

(2) The power in subsection (1) may be exercised only for the purposes of –

(a) preventing, detecting, investigating or prosecuting crime,

(b) helping to locate a missing person, or

(c) protecting a child or an at-risk adult from neglect or physical, mental or emotional harm.

To exercise the power under subsection (1) an authorised person must reasonably believe that information stored on the electronic device is relevant to a reasonable line of enquiry or purpose and that it is necessary and proportionate to achieve the purpose for which the person proposes to exercise the power.

An 'authorised person' will usually mean a police officer or member of police staff but could mean a member of another agency or body. A full list of 'authorised persons' is available at Schedule 3 of the Act.

Pre-charge bail

Section 45 and Schedule 4 of the PCSC Act includes a detailed section on the issue of pre-charge bail. The schedule is split into four parts and provides some amendments to the *Police and Criminal Evidence Act 1984, the Bail Act 1976 and the Criminal Justice Act 2003.*

Part 1 addresses the granting of pre-charge bail and now puts an emphasis on releasing those in detention on bail providing that certain pre-conditions are met. This is a move away from the position where a large number of people were released under investigation (RUI) rather than being released on bail. RUI was subject to no timescales, unlike bail, and didn't allow for any bail conditions to be placed on the detained person prior to release. This new approach should provide more protection for victims of crime and witnesses and allow the police to manage suspected offenders more effectively.

Part 2 outlines the factors to be taken into account in deciding whether to grant pre-charge bail, whether at the police station or elsewhere and provides the following guidance –

'In determining whether releasing the person on bail is necessary and proportionate in all the circumstances, the custody officer must have regard in particular to –

(a) the need to secure that the person surrenders to custody

(b) the need to prevent offending by the person

(c) the need to safeguard victims of crime and witnesses, taking into account any vulnerabilities of any alleged victim of, or alleged witness to, the offence for which the person was arrested where these vulnerabilities have been identified by the custody officer,

(d) the need to safeguard the person, taking into account any vulnerabilities of the person where these vulnerabilities have been identified by the custody officer, and

(e) the need to manage risks to the public.'

Part 3 outlines the duty of the police, where possible, to seek the views of the victim prior to the granting of bail conditions and to make sure that they are given the opportunity to comment on the suitability or otherwise of those conditions. This part also provides a definition for a vulnerable victim.

Part 4 makes amendments to the *Police and Criminal Evidence Act 1984* in relation to time limits on any period of police bail without charge. The period for which a person may be granted bail (*Section 30A PACE*) has been extended from 28 days to 3 months in police cases. Serious Fraud Office (SFO), National Crime Agency (NCA) and other listed agencies also now have extended limits on bail.

Further time limits of bail have also been extended to 9 months and 12 months in relation to standard and non-standard cases respectively. There are options to extend further with appropriate authority and necessity.

Part 5 amends *Section 47 PACE* (bail after arrest) with the following insertion –

'Where a person has been arrested under Section 46A (failing to answer police bail or suspected of breaching a bail condition) the period of 3 hours beginning with the time at which the person arrives at a police station following the arrest is not to be included as part of any period of police detention which falls to be calculated in relation to the person under this Part of this Act.'

In other words, the first 3 hours of detention are not counted as part of that person's detention clock.

Part 6 provides some guidance from the College of Policing on the subject of pre-charge bail.

Sexual offences

Section 47 PCSC Act defines a 'position of trust' with regards to the *Sexual Offences Act 2003*.

Section 48 introduces a new offence in relation to breast-feeding to add to the offence of voyeurism (*Section 67A Sexual Offences Act 2003*) as follows –

(2A) A person (A) commits an offence if –

(a) 'A' operates equipment,

(b) 'A' does so with the intention of enabling 'A' or another person (C), for a purpose mentioned in subsection (3), to observe another (B) while 'B' is breast-feeding a child, and

(c) 'A' does so –

(i) without B's consent, and

(ii) without reasonable believing that 'B' consents

(2B) A person (A) commits an offence if –

(a) 'A' records an image of another (B) while 'B' is breast-feeding a child,

(b) A' does so with the intention that 'A' or another person (C) will look at the image for a purpose mentioned in subsection (3), and

(c) 'A' does so –

(i) without B's consent, and

(ii) without reasonably believing that 'B' consents.

The purposes mentioned in subsection (3) are –

(a) obtaining sexual gratification (whether for A or C);

(b) humiliating, alarming or distressing 'B'.

It's irrelevant whether 'B' is in a public place while breast-feeding, whether breasts are exposed nor which part of B's body is intended to be observed or recorded by 'A'.

Prosecution time limit in assault domestic abuse cases

Section 49 PCSC Act increases the time limit for the prosecution of common assault or battery in domestic abuse cases to –

(a) within 2 years from the date of the offence to which the proceedings relate, and

(b) within six months from that date that the complainant has provided a witness statement or been interviewed on video.

Power to photograph, fingerprint and take samples at police station

Powers already exist under *PACE* to photograph, fingerprint and take certain samples from detained persons.

Section 52 PCSC Act adds a number of sub-sections for when a photograph can be taken from a person who is or has been detained, without their consent.

Section 53 provides the police with the power to specify a date on which a person should attend a police station to provide fingerprints and other samples, where appropriate.

Search of premises for human remains

Section 55 relates to the process by which a justice of the peace (magistrate) may issue a warrant to enter and search premises when there are reasonable grounds for believing that there is material on the premises that consists of, or may relate to the location of, relevant human remains.

'Relevant human remains' means the body or any other human remains of –

(a) a person who the constable making the application reasonably believes to have died in England and Wales but whose death has not been registered under *section 15 of the Births and Deaths Registration Act 1953.*

(b) a person whose death has been registered under that Act following an investigation under *section 1(5) of the Coroners and Justice Act 2009*, or

(c) a person in respect of whom a declaration has been made under *section 2 of the Presumption of Death Act 2013.*

Section 56 and Schedule 6 make provision for a constable to obtain access to excluded material or special procedure material that consists of, or relates to, the location of relevant human remains.

Sections 62–70 of the PCSC Act cover offences relating to hares and other game.

Part 3 – Public order

Sections 73–75 PCSC Act provides amendments to Sections 12 (imposing conditions on public processions) and 14 (imposing conditions on public assemblies) of the *Public Order Act 1986* with the following key amendments –

Sub-section (1)

'(aa) in the case of a procession (or assembly) in England and Wales, the noise generated by persons taking part may result in serious disruption to the activities of an organisation which are carried on in the vicinity of the procession (assembly),

(ab) in the case of a procession (assembly) in England and Wales –
(i) the noise generated by persons taking part may have a relevant impact on persons in the vicinity of the procession (assembly), and
(ii) that impact may be significant.
(2A) The cases in which a public procession (assembly) in England and Wales may result in serious disruption to the life of the community include, in particular, where –
(a) it may result in a significant delay to the delivery of a time-sensitive product to consumers of that product, or
(b) it may result in a prolonged disruption of access to any essential goods or any essential service, including, in particular, access to –
(i) the supply of money, food water, energy or fuel,
(ii) a system of communication,
(iii) a place of worship,
(iv) a transport facility,
(v) an educational institution, or
(vi) a service relating to health.

An additional sub-section relating to processions and assemblies, states that –
'(1A) The senior police officer may give directions imposing on the persons organising or taking part in the assembly –
(a) in the case of an assembly in England and Wales, such conditions as appear to the officer necessary to prevent the disorder, damage, disruption, impact or intimidation mentioned in subsection (1);
(b) in the case of an assembly in Scotland, such conditions as to the place at which the assembly may be (or continue to be) held, its maximum duration, or the maximum number of persons who may constitute it, as appear to the officer necessary to prevent the disorder etc'.
   Any person who fails to comply with imposed conditions is guilty of an offence.
The legislation has been amended to reflect the problems caused by protests interrupting the running of businesses etc and adversely affecting other people.

Part 4 relates to unauthorised encampments

Part 5 – Road traffic

Section 86 PCSC Act has increased the penalties on conviction for the offences of causing death by dangerous or careless driving when under the influence of drink or drugs from 14 years imprisonment to life imprisonment.

Section 87 creates a new offence of causing serious injury by careless or inconsiderate driving (*section 2C Road Traffic Act 1988*) with a maximum sentence on conviction of 2 years imprisonment on indictment.

Part 6 – Cautions

This Part makes provision for new disposals known as diversionary cautions and community cautions, both of which can be given to a person aged 18 or over in respect of an offence. Diversionary and community cautions must have one or more conditions attached to them. Conditions may include rehabilitation/reparation, unpaid work or not to engage in specified activity, amongst others. Breach of a condition may result in prosecution for the offence (in the case of a diversionary caution) or a financial penalty (community caution). There is a power of arrest without warrant if a constable has reasonable grounds for believing that the offender has failed, without reasonable excuse, to comply with any of the conditions attached to a diversionary caution.

Sections 98–121 PCSC Act provide detailed guidance in relation to these cautions.

Part 7 – Sentencing and release

Section 122 increases the maximum sentence on conviction for the offence of cruelty to a child under 16 (*section 1 Children and Young Persons Act 1933*) from 10 years to 14 years imprisonment (with effect from 28/6/22). Section 124 outlines the minimum sentences the court must impose for particular types of offences as follows –

- threatening with a weapon or bladed article = appropriate custodial sentence
- third class 'A' drug trafficking offence = a minimum term of at least 7 years
- third domestic burglary = a minimum term of at least 3 years
- repeat offence involving weapon or bladed article = appropriate custodial sentence

The above applies unless the court is of the opinion that there are exceptional circumstances which –

(a) relate to any of the offences or the offender, and

(b) justify not doing so.

These guidelines apply to any offences committed on or after the day that Section 124 came into force (28/6/22).

Section 125 documents that the starting point for the premeditated murder of a child will be a whole life order (life imprisonment).

Section 126 alters the range of sentence for those aged under 21 who are convicted of murder from a previous starting point of 12 years to anything between 8 and 27 years imprisonment, depending on the age of the offender and the circumstances.

Sections 129–131 PCSC Act confirm that detainees will serve two-thirds of their sentence prior to being considered for release. This will be applied to cases where a life sentence is imposed for an offence where the sentence is not automatically life, as well as other certain violent or sexual offences. For the majority of cases, this has been increased from serving half of any sentence courtesy of the *Release of Prisoners (Alteration of Relevant Proportion of Sentence) Order 2020.*

Assaults on those providing a public service

Section 156 provides an insertion of an additional section to the *Sentencing Act 2020* as follows –

'68A (1) This section applies where –

(a) a court is considering the seriousness of an offence listed in subsection (3),

(b) the offence is not aggravated under section 67(2).

(2) If the offence was committed against a person providing a public service, performing a public duty or providing services to the public, the court –

(a) must treat that fact as an aggravating factor, and

(b) must state in open court that the offence is so aggravated.

(3) The offences referred to in subsection (1) are –

(a) an offence of common assault or battery, except where section 1 of the *Assaults on Emergency Workers (Offences) Act 2018* applies;

(b) an offence under any of the following provisions of the *Offences Against the Person Act 1861*–

(i) *section 16* (threats to kill);

(ii) *section 18* (wounding with intent to cause grievous bodily harm);

(iii) *section 20* (malicious wounding);

(iv*) section 47* (assault occasioning actual bodily harm);

(c) an inchoate offence in relation to any of the preceding offences.
This section has effect in relation to a person who is convicted of the
offence on or after the date on which section 156 of the Police, Crime,
Sentencing and Courts Act 2022 comes into force (28/6/22).

Part 8 – Youth justice
Sections 157–161 relate to youth remand, detention and training orders
and youth rehabilitation orders.

Part 9 relates to secure children's homes and other secure accommodation

Part 10 – Management of offenders

Serious violence reduction orders
Section 165 PCSC Act amends Part 11 Chapter 1 of the *Sentencing Code*
in relation to the power to make a serious violence reduction order as
follows –
342A
(1) This section applies where –
(a) a person aged 18 or over ('the offender') is convicted of an offence
which was committed on or after the first appointed day (28/4/22), and
(b) the prosecution makes an application to the court for a serious
violence reduction order to be made in respect of the offender .
(2) Subject to subsection (6), the court may make a serious violence
reduction order in respect of the offender if –
(a) the condition in subsection (3) or (4) is met, and
(b) the condition in subsection (5) is met.
(3) The condition in this subsection is that the court is satisfied on the
balance of probabilities that –
(a) a bladed article or offensive weapon was used by the offender in the
commission of the offence, or
(b) the offender had a bladed article or offensive weapon with them
when the offence was committed.
(4) The condition in this subsection is that the court is satisfied on the
balance of probabilities that –
(a) a bladed article or offensive weapon was used by another person in
the commission of the offence and the offender knew or ought to have

known that this would be the case, or

(b) another person who committed the offence had a bladed article or offensive weapon with them when the offence was committed and the offender knew or ought to have known that this would be the case.

(5) The condition in this subsection is that the court considers it necessary to make a serious violence reduction order in respect of the offender to –

(a) protect the public in England and Wales from the risk of harm involving a bladed article or offensive weapon,

(b) protect any particular members of the public in England and Wales (including the offender) from such risk, or

(c) prevent the offender from committing an offence involving a bladed article or offensive weapon.

(6) The court may make a serious violence reduction order in respect of the offender only if it

(a) does so in addition to dealing with the offender for the offence, and

(b) does not make an order for absolute discharge in respect of the offence. An offender who is made the subject of a serious violence reduction order must, within 3 days, inform police of their name, home address and any other address where they regularly reside or stay.

342D

(1) A serious violence reduction order takes effect on the day it is made and must specify the period for which it has effect, which must be a fixed period of not less than 6 months and not more than 2 years (2).

342E

Where a serious violence reduction order is in effect, a constable may search the offender for the purpose of ascertaining whether the offender has a bladed article or an offensive weapon with them. This power, which also enables a constable to use force, if necessary, and to seize any such item found, may be exercised only while the offender is in a public place.

342G

(1) Where a serious violence reduction order is in effect, the offender commits an offence if the offender –

(a) fails without reasonable excuse to do anything the offender is required to do by the order,

(b) without reasonable excuse does anything the offender is prohibited from doing by the order,

(c) notifies to the police, in purported compliance with the order, any information which the offender knows to be false,

(d) tells a constable that they are not subject to a serious violence reduction order, or

(e) intentionally obstructs a constable in the exercise of any power conferred by section 342E.

(2) A person guilty of an offence under this section is liable –

(a) on summary conviction, to imprisonment for a term not exceeding 12 months, or a fine, or both;

(b) on conviction on indictment, to imprisonment for a term not exceeding 2 years, or a fine, or both.

Sections 168–183 PCSC Act deal with the management of sex offenders. Sections 184–189 deal with the management of terrorist offenders.

Section 184 provides a power of arrest without warrant pending a prison recall decision with the insertion of section 43B of the *Terrorism Act 2000* – 43B

(1) Subject to subsection (2), a constable may arrest without warrant a terrorist offender who has been released on licence if the constable –

(a) has reasonable grounds for suspecting that the offender has breached a condition of their licence, and

(b) reasonably considers that it is necessary, for purposes connected with protecting members of the public from a risk of terrorism, to detain the offender until a recall decision is made.

(2) A terrorist offender who is detained under this section must (unless recalled or otherwise detained under any other power) be released –

(a) if a recall decision is made not to revoke the offender's licence (and accordingly the offender is not recalled to prison), as soon as practicable after that decision is made, or

(b) if a recall decision has not been made by the end of the relevant period, at the end of that period.

Further additions at 43C and 43D provide the power to search persons and premises –

43C

(1) A constable may stop and search a terrorist offender who is within subsection (2) if the constable is satisfied that it is necessary to do so for purposes connected with protecting members of the public from a risk of terrorism.

(2) A terrorist offender is within this subsection if –
(a) the offender has been released on licence (and not recalled), and
(b) the offender's licence includes a search condition.
(3) The power in subsection (1) may be exercised in any place to which the constable lawfully has access (whether or not it is a place to which the public has access).
Further subsections provide a power to stop and search a vehicle and anything in or on it for purposes connected with protecting members of the public from a risk of terrorism.
43D
(1) A justice may issue a warrant under this section if, on the application of a senior police officer of the relevant force, the justice is satisfied that the requirements in subsection (2) are met.
(2) The requirements are –
(a) that the person specified in the application is a relevant offender who has been released on licence (and not recalled),
(b) that there are reasonable grounds for believing that the person resides, or may regularly be found, at premises (whether residential or otherwise) specified in the application,
(c) that it is necessary, for purposes connected with protecting members of the public from a risk of terrorism, for a constable to enter and search premises specified in the application, and
(d) the occupier of the premises is unlikely to consent to a constable entering or searching the premises specified in the application.
In this section 'justice' means –
(a) a justice of the peace in England and Wales,
(b) a sheriff or summary sheriff in Scotland, or
(c) a lay magistrate in Northern Ireland.

A 'senior police officer' means an officer of the rank of Superintendent or above.
Sections 190–192 provide amendments to the *Football Spectators Act 1989* in relation to banning orders and relevant offences.

Part 11 – Rehabilitation of offenders
Section 193 PCSC Act provides amendments to Section 5 of the *Rehabilitation of Offenders Act 1974* (rehabilitation periods for particular sentences) as follows –

(3) Sentences excluded from rehabilitation include –

(b) any of the following sentences, where the sentence is imposed for an offence specified in Schedule 18 to the *Sentencing Code* (serious violent, sexual and terrorism offences) or a service offence as respects which the corresponding offence is so specified –

(i) a sentence of imprisonment for a term exceeding 4 years;

(ii) a sentence of youth custody for such a term;

(iii) - (viii) a sentence of detention or corrective training for such a term under various other statutory Acts.

Part 12 deals with the subject of disregards and pardons for certain historical offences

Part 13 – Procedures in courts and tribunals

Section 198 relates to the *Courts Act 2003* and the insertion of a new section 85A which deals with remote observation and recording of proceedings by the direction of a court or tribunal.

Section 199 inserts a new section 85B which creates an offence as follows –

(1) It is an offence for a person to make, or attempt to make –

(a) an unauthorised recording, or

(b) an unauthorised transmission,

of an image or sound within subsection (2) or (3).

(2) An image or sound is within this subsection if it is an image or sound of court proceedings that is being transmitted to the place where the recording or transmission referred to in subsection (1) is made or attempted to be made.

(3) An image or sound is within this subsection if it is an image or sound of a person while that person is remotely attending court proceedings.

(4) A person is remotely attending court proceedings at any time when the person –

(a) is not in the same place as any member of the court, and

(b) is taking part, watching or listening to the proceedings by way of a transmission.

(8) A person guilty of an offence under subsection (1) is liable on summary conviction to a fine not exceeding level 3 on the standard scale.

(9) Conduct that amounts to an offence under subsection (1) is also a contempt of court.

But a person cannot, in respect of the same conduct, be both convicted of the offence and punished for the contempt.

(10) For the purposes of this section it does not matter whether a person making, or attempting to make, a recording or transmission intends the recording or transmission, or anything comprised in it, to be seen or heard by any other person.

Section 200 PCSC Act amends Section 51 of the *Criminal Justice Act 2003* in relation to the use of video and audio links in criminal proceedings as follows –

(1) The court may, by a direction, require or permit a person to take part in eligible criminal proceedings through –

(a) a live audio link, or

(b) a live video link.

(2) A direction under this section may be given in relation to a member of a jury only if the direction requires all members of the jury to take part through a live video link while present at the same place.

Subsection (3) provides a comprehensive list of what are considered to be 'eligible criminal proceedings' which includes hearings, trials and other proceedings at both magistrates and Crown Courts.

(4) The court may not give a direction under this section unless –

(a) the court is satisfied that it is in the interests of justice for the person to whom the direction relates to take part in the proceedings in accordance with the direction through the live audio link or live video link,

(b) the parties to the proceedings have been given the opportunity to make representations, and

(c) if so required by section 52(9), the relevant youth offending team has been given the opportunity to make representations.

Part 14 addresses some final provisions relating to the Act

Section 207 PCSC Act clarifies that the Act extends to England and Wales only, with the exception of some listed provisions (sections) which also extend to Scotland and Northern Ireland.

As you can see, the Police, Crime, Sentencing and Courts Act 2022 is a wide-ranging and, at times, complex piece of legislation which will embed itself into our criminal justice system as time passes. If you would like to take a look at the whole Act, including the appended Schedules, you can do so via the following link:

https://www.legislation.gov.uk/ukpga/2022/32/contents/enacted

Crown Court (Recording and Broadcasting) Order 2020

From the end of July 2022, you will now see Judges appearing on television as they deliver sentences to defendants in the Crown Court. This will become a regular occurrence as a result of a change in the law. On 28th July 2022, an Old Bailey sentencing was broadcast for the first time on TV after the law change, which now allows cameras into the Crown courts of England and Wales. The BBC and Sky News showed Her Honour Judge Sarah Munro deliver sentencing remarks in the case of Ben Oliver, who had pleaded guilty to the manslaughter of his grandfather in south London.

'This is a complex sentencing exercise', the Judge commented as she carefully set out how she had reached the decision of life imprisonment with a minimum term of 10 years and eight months. Time spent on remand was to be deducted, resulting in a term of 9 years and 63 days, the Judge told Oliver. 'Once you have served that term, you will be entitled to apply for parole. However, you will not be released by the Parole Board unless they conclude you no longer pose a risk to the public. If you are released, you will remain on licence for the rest of your life,' she said.

Under the Crown Court (Recording and Broadcasting) Order 2020, broadcasters may film High Court and senior Circuit Judges sitting in the Crown court. Broadcasters must still apply to film the sentencing remarks and the Judge will decide whether to grant the request. To protect the privacy of victims, witnesses and jurors, only the Judge must be visible in the broadcast.

Some Court of Appeal and Supreme Court cases are already 'live-streamed' and journalists can already apply to record and broadcast certain hearings in Scotland's higher courts. The Lord Chief Justice hailed the latest development as a 'very positive step' in promoting open justice. 'It's something that I was really keen should happen and I started working on it in 2017. The law was introduced in 2020 and we all hoped that we would start filming sentencing remarks in high-profile criminal cases in the summer of 2020, and were it not for Covid, that would have happened, but now it is happening. I think it's an exciting development, because it will help the public to understand how and why criminals get the sentences that they do in these very high-profile cases.'

Index